COMMERCIALISING CELEBRITY PERSONA

This book investigates the commercialisation of celebrity persona in the UK, New York and California. Interviews with 68 practitioners across the advertising, merchandising, film and video game industries provide insight on the differences in approaches across jurisdictions, as well as the similarities caused by non-legal factors. Furthermore, the book addresses the developments in technology, social media and social norms that have made collaboration attractive to maintain favour with fans.

The book considers how the extension of passing off in the UK to include persona rights impacts the dispute resolution and transactional spheres involved in the commercialisation of persona. It compares the industry landscape to that of the US where the right of publicity has been recognised since 1953 and has gone as far as to protect 'identity'. The book argues that non-legal factors significantly impact the commercialisation of persona across the jurisdictions and interact with the law to encourage permission-based behaviours. However, there remains a divergence in the dispute resolution sphere.

Anyone who is interested in the multi-million dollar business of celebrities as assets will benefit from this book.

Commercialising Celebrity Persona

Intellectual Property Law and Practice

Emma Perot

•HART•
OXFORD • LONDON • NEW YORK • NEW DELHI • SYDNEY

HART PUBLISHING

Bloomsbury Publishing Plc

Kemp House, Chawley Park, Cumnor Hill, Oxford, OX2 9PH, UK

1385 Broadway, New York, NY 10018, USA

29 Earlsfort Terrace, Dublin 2, Ireland

HART PUBLISHING, the Hart/Stag logo, BLOOMSBURY and the Diana logo are trademarks of Bloomsbury Publishing Plc

First published in Great Britain 2023

A catalogue record for this book is available from the British Library.

A catalogue record for this book is available from the Library of Congress.

ISBN: HB: 978-1-50996-609-7
ePDF: 978-1-50996-611-0
ePub: 978-1-50996-610-3

Typeset by Compuscript Ltd, Shannon

For my mom and dad for giving me a UK legal education,
and for fellow Caribbean woman Rihanna for suing TopShop
and inspiring my research.

PREFACE

This is the first book to undertake empirical research on persona protection. It is unique, as it provides a comparative approach by interviewing lawyers in London, New York and California. The advertising, merchandising, film and sports video-games industries use persona as a key component of their products. Empirical research reveals that while the law influences the permission to be sought, these industries often contract with individuals to add value to their products via collaboration, and to avoid damage to reputation that might occur if permission were not sought in accordance with social norms. While these non-legal influences were observed in the transactional sphere, the differences in legal frameworks between the United States (US) and the United Kingdom (UK) marked a divergence in the approaches to dispute resolution. This book therefore argues that while the law plays a significant role in persona commercialisation and redress against unauthorised uses, industry practices are also influenced by non-legal factors.

Emma Perot
Trinidad and Tobago
February 2023

ACKNOWLEDGEMENTS

This book was inspired by the case of *Fenty v Arcadia*, which I learnt about during my LLM at University College London (UCL). I am thankful to Dr Matt Fisher, who supervised my LLM dissertation and supported my PhD application. Thank you to King's College London (KCL) for providing me with a scholarship that allowed me to pursue this research. My supervisor at KCL, Professor Tanya Aplin, was and continues to be an excellent mentor. Thank you, Professor, for giving me structure and support, and for challenging my thoughts. Thank you also to my examiners, Professor Robert Burell and Dr Marta Ildajica, for their helpful feedback and encouragement.

I could not have got through the PhD and this book-writing process without the help of some very important people to whom I am most grateful. My parents, Sean Perot and Hazel Ross-Perot, encourage me to pursue my academic dreams, and provide a haven when things are less than ideal. Kams, my second mom, provides comfort and unconditional love. My partner, Justin Koo, has supported me throughout my academic life, from LLB onwards. Thank you for being my sounding board, for providing feedback on multiple drafts and helping to put the vicissitudes of life into perspective.

There are many friends who have uplifted me during this journey. Leenz and Freeze, my 'day 1s', thank you for making me laugh, listening to every minor detail of my life and being there for me every single day. Izzy, my little sister, our chats about every topic under the sun give me sustenance and revive me. Taz, your hospitality made my fieldwork possible; you will always be my twin soul. Shaina, my first university friend – thank you to your dad for making sure we connected. I will always cherish our Canterbury days and all the new experiences we shared, both academic and otherwise. Putney Trinis, Shivy and Brandon, thank you for the adventures: from DDI to London and Banff, our time together makes all our work worth it! Zoë, thank you for always being up for a lime, for keeping it real and for attending my PhD graduation. My afternoon tea buddies, Elisabeth and Anne, you have showered me with love since our UCL days and made my London experience unforgettable. Last but by no means least, my Somerset Philosophers, Adrienne, Ioanna, Mathilde and Ermioni: seeing you all succeed has inspired me, and I am proud to join the Hart crew! You brilliant women have empathised and provided guidance and stress relief. A special thanks to Adrienne for hosting me during summer 2019.

Finally, thank you to all the lawyers and industry experts who volunteered their time, knowledge and expertise for this book. I literally could not have done it without you, and I truly appreciate your kindness.

CONTENTS

TABLE OF CASES

Advertising Code/FTC Decisions

UK ASA

USA FTC

Cases

UK

ECtHR

USA

1

Introduction

I. The Value of Fame and the Consumption of Celebrity

Celebrities sell. They sell concert and movie tickets, airline tickets, shoes, clothing, skin care, hair products, cell phones, fast food … the list goes on. Their commercial potential is vast, and the limits continue to be stretched with developments in technology that enhance para-social relationships. 'Para-social', the term coined by American psychologists Horton and Wohl in 1956[1] when mass media was widely accessible in the developed world, describes the spectator–performer relationship.[2] With the world connected via social media, anyone can become a celebrity, and the opportunities for forming para-social relationships have increased tenfold since Horton and Wohl put forward this concept. The traditional notion of celebrity has expanded from covering talented musicians, actors and athletes[3] to include reality television stars and social-media influencers. Despite this proliferation of famous individuals, there remains a constant demand for information, photographs and videos, and for products by celebrities. Marketing literature has been saturated with studies on celebrity endorsements since the 1990s.[4] The most successful celebrities earn significant sums from their art form, but complement this by endorsing products and creating merchandising. For some, their art form involves displaying the daily activities of their lives, and the global success of the Kardashian empire makes it apparent that there is a willing consumer base, to tap into which companies pay large sums.[5]

Celebrities finesse the commercial sphere by leveraging their personas: name, voice, likeness, signature and other identifying characteristics.[6] According to the

[1] Horton, D and Wohl, R, 'Mass Communication and Para-Social Interaction' (1956) 19 *Psychiatry* 215.

[2] Anon, *Understanding Media and Culture: An Introduction to Mass Communication* (University of Minnesota Libraries Publishing 2010) ch 1.3.

[3] Athletes have been entering into endorsement deals since the beginning of the 20th century – Mcghee, T, 'The rise and rise of athlete brand endorsements' (2012) 1(1) *J of Brand Strategy* 79.

[4] Wang, S and Liu, MT, 'Celebrity endorsement in marketing from 1960 to 2021: a bibliometric review and future agenda' (2022) 11(8) *Asia Pacific Journal of Marketing and Logistics* 342.

[5] Lueck, JA, 'Friend-zone with benefits: The parasocial advertising of Kim Kardashian' (2015) 21 *J of Marketing Comm* 91.

[6] The scope of legally protected persona depends on the jurisdiction being examined. For example, New York lists certain aspects of persona that are protected under s 50 and s 51 of the New York Civil

Forbes 2022 'Highest Paid Earners' list, 'Jay-Z, Dwayne "The Rock" Johnson and Kanye West all grabbed spots among the top five with their own 9-figure sums, most of it earned not from rapping, producing or acting, but from selling champagne, tequila and sneakers.'[7] Social media star Charli D'Amelio shot to stardom in 2019 as a result of her popular dance videos on TikTok.[8] She was the highest TikTok earner in 2022, collecting $17.5 million, partly from her content, but largely from sponsored advertisements and deals with Invisalign, Morphe Cosmetics and a co-branded merchandise line with Hollister.[9] Athletes who have assumed celebrity status can earn more money from their endorsement deals than their profession.[10] LeBron James earned $36.9 million from playing basketball, but $90 million from endorsements in 2022. Roger Federer earned only $725,000 from his athletics but $85 million from endorsements. Serena Williams earned $270,000 from tennis and $35 million from her deals with Nike, Wilson, Pepsi and Gatorade to name a few.[11] The potential for earning outside of their sport, and the risk of a short-lived career as an athlete, makes it apparent why student athletes felt disadvantaged by the former rules of the National Collegiate Athletic Association, which prohibited amateurs from being paid.[12] In 2021, the rules were changed to allow students to profit from their name, image and likeness.[13]

Celebrity endorsement deals are so lucrative that Kanye West reportedly lost a substantial chunk of his net worth after he was dropped from a number of brand partnerships following antisemitic comments in October 2022.[14] Tiger Woods, once the highest-earning athlete endorser, collecting $100 million per year

Code, whereas the California common law right of publicity protects 'identity', which is subject to interpretation on a case-by-case basis.

[7] Voytko, L, 'The Highest-Paid Entertainers 2022' *Forbes* (9 February 2022) at www.forbes.com/sites/lisettevoytko/2022/02/09/the-highest-paid-entertainers-2022/?sh=603b320c331a (accessed 16 January 2023).

[8] Natividad, A, 'How Charli D'Amelio become one of the biggest social media starts in the world' *The Richest* (8 July 2022) at www.therichest.com/rich-powerful/how-charli-damelio-became-one-of-the-biggest-social-media-stars-in-the-world/ (accessed 16 January 2023).

[9] Freeman, A, 'Top-Earning TikToker-ers 2022: Charli and Dixie D'Amelio and Addison Rae Expand Fame – And Paydays' *Forbes* (7 January 2022) at www.forbes.com/sites/abrambrown/2022/01/07/top-earning-tiktokers-charli-dixie-damelio-addison-rae-bella-poarch-josh-richards/?sh=7c88a8963afa (accessed 16 January 2023).

[10] Badenhausen, K, 'The World's Highest-Paid Athletes 2022: LeBron scores $127 million' *Sportico* (11 May 2022) at www.sportico.com/personalities/athletes/2022/worlds-highest-paid-athletes-2022-lebron-1234674858/ (accessed 16 January 2023).

[11] Mellor, S, 'Kanye West is keeping quiet after reportedly losing his coveted billionaire status. Here's the money he's lost' *Fortune* (26 October 2022) at https://fortune.com/2022/10/26/kanye-west-keeping-quiet-losing-billionaire-status-money-he-lost/ (accessed 16 January 2023); Camenkar, J, 'Serena Williams 2022: Net Worth, Salary and Endorsements' *Essentially Sports* (2 September 2022) at www.essentiallysports.com/tag/serena-williams/ (accessed 16 January 2023).

[12] The rules prohibited payment 'to advertise, recommend or promote directly the sale or use of a commercial product or service of any kind'.

[13] Hoskic, A, 'NCAA adopts interim name, image and likeness policy' *NCAA* (30 June 2021) at www.ncaa.org/news/2021/6/30/ncaa-adopts-interim-name-image-and-likeness-policy.aspx (accessed 27 January 2023).

[14] Mellor (2022).

in endorsements,[15] cost his sponsors a decline in their stock value relative to their competitors within days of the breaking of the news of his infidelity scandal.[16] The reward of partnering with a celebrity is perceived as great, but the risk of something going wrong can result in serious consequences for the partner company if the situation is not managed appropriately. This is because the strength of the para-social relationships does not only manifest in unrequited love for a celebrity, but it can also result in strong feelings of disappointment and anger when the celebrity's actions fall below the expected standard.

The commercialisation of persona is a well-established concept, and celebrities want to reap the rewards of their fame, whether acquired through skill and hard work, talent or luck. The USA, hub of the global entertainment industry, is at the forefront of protection of the valuable aspects of persona. The right of publicity was recognised in 1953,[17] and most States now have either statutory or common law protection. This proprietary right confers the ability to prevent unauthorised commercial uses of persona. While fame is not a requirement, celebrities are most likely to benefit from the right, a fact that was stated in the recognition of this right in *Haelan*.[18] Across the pond, the UK, a major consumer of celebrities, has rejected the existence of an equivalent right. In lieu, passing off (unregistered trade mark law) is the most suitable cause of action for celebrities whose personas have been commercialised without their permission. This contrast in the law has led to a host of studies that consider whether the UK should follow the path of the US and introduce this avenue of legal protection. No existing literature has undertaken a comparative of approach of the industries that commercialise persona to determine if the law makes a difference in practice. Based on empirical analysis of four industries – advertising, merchandising, television and movies, and sports video games – this book contends that the differences in the law, while theoretically significant, result in few practical divergences in these industries in the transactional sphere. This is due to the perception that the law could be expanded in the UK, as well as the extra-legal factors of social norms and the desire to collaborate in all industries in both jurisdictions. However, there is indeed a divergence in the dispute resolution sphere, where UK claimants face difficulties seeking redress, despite the aforementioned fears of expansion, whereas US plaintiffs have used existing law to negotiate settlements and pursue legal action.

This chapter will provide an overview of the existing academic discourse on persona protection in the US and UK, and explain why empirical analysis is necessary to give a more realistic picture of the commercial landscape. The empirical methodology, which consisted of interviews in London, New York and California, will then be explained. Finally, the book will be outlined with a focus on the framework that is used to analyse the empirical data.

[15] Knittel, CR and Stango, V, 'Celebrity Endorsements, Firm Value, and Reputation Risk: Evidence from the Tiger Woods Scandal' (2014) 60 *Management Science* 21, 24.

[16] ibid 34.

[17] *Haelan Laboratories Inc v Topps Chewing Gum Inc* 202 F 2d 866 (2d Cir 1953).

[18] ibid.

II. The Doctrinal Approach to the Right of Publicity

Existing literature takes two main approaches to analysing persona protection:[19] an examination of case law relating to persona, and an examination of theoretical justifications for protecting persona. The case law or doctrinal approach highlights the perceived gaps in UK law that make it difficult for individuals to seek redress against unauthorised uses of their personas. Some authors consider the existence of these gaps and piecemeal protection enough to warrant the introduction of persona protection in the UK,[20] while others compare the gaps to the breadth of US protection to argue that the UK approach is insufficient.[21] On the other hand, those opposed to the right of publicity argue that the UK should maintain its current approach because it provides sufficient protection[22] and allows for creative uses of persona,[23] and/or argue that the US approach is too protectionist.[24] Professor Rothman argues that the US approach to the right of publicity should be reconceptualised by tracing its origin into the right of privacy, thus protecting the individual's identity as opposed to the current state of protecting economic value.[25] There are also those who argue that the US approach is unproblematic

[19] There has been one empirical study conducted on the right of publicity, Bellamore, T, 'Is Vanna White Really So Dangerous – An Empirical Assessment of the Impact of *White v Samsung Electronics* on Parody and Advertising' (2003) 11 *U Miami Bus L Rev* 53.

[20] Walsh, C, 'Are personality rights finally on the UK agenda?' (2013) 35 *EIPR* 253; Blackshaw, I, 'Protecting Sports Image Rights in Europe' (2005) 6 *Bus L Intl* 270; Porter, H, 'Character merchandising: does English law recognise a property right in name and likeness?' (1999) 10 *Ent L Rev* 180; Stallard, H, 'The right of Publicity in the United Kingdom' (1997) 18 *Loy LA Ent LJ* 565.

[21] Barajas, ADL, 'Personality rights in the United States and the United Kingdom – is Vanna too much? Is Irvine not enough?' (2009) 20 *Ent L Rev* 253; Bains, S, 'Personality rights: should the UK grant celebrities a proprietary right in their personality? Parts 1' (2007) 18 *Ent L Rev* 164; Klink, J, '50 years of publicity rights in the United States and the never-ending hassle with intellectual property and personality rights in Europe' (2003) 4 *IPQ* 363; Goodenough, OR, 'Retheorising privacy and publicity' (1997) 1 *IPQ* 37.

[22] Ng, C, 'The law of passing off – goodwill beyond goods' (2016) 47(7) *IIC* 817; Carty, H, 'Advertising, publicity rights and English law' (2004) 3 *IPQ* 209.

[23] Tan, D, *The Commercial Appropriation of Fame: A Cultural Analysis of the Right of Publicity and Passing Off* (Cambridge University Press 2017); Tan, D, 'Fame Monster Reloaded: The Contemporary Celebrity, Cultural Studies and Passing Off' (2010) 32 *Sydney L Rev* 291; Deazley, R, 'Introducing Publicity Rights – Breach of Confidence, the Photograph and Commodifying the Image' (2003) 54 *NILQ* 99.

[24] Lemley, M, 'Privacy, Property, and Publicity' (2019) 117 *Mich L Rev* 1153; Tushnet, R, 'Raising Walls against Overlapping Rights: Pre-emption and the Right of Publicity' (2016) 92 *Notre Dame L Rev* 1539; Tushnet, R, 'A Mask That Eats into the Face: Images and the Right of Publicity' (2014) 38 *Colum JL & Arts* 157; Leaffer, M, 'The Right of Publicity: A Comparative Perspective' (2006–2007) 70 *Alb L Rev* 1357; Madow, M, 'Private Ownership of Public Image: Popular Culture and Publicity Rights' (1993) 81 *Cal L Rev* 125; Coombe, RJ, 'Author/izing the Celebrity: Publicity Rights, Postmodern Politics, and Unauthorized Genders' (1991) 10 *Cardozo Arts & Ent LJ* 365.

[25] Rothman, J, *The Right of Publicity: Privacy Reimagined for a Public World* (Harvard University Press 2018).

and/or commensurate to the value attached to celebrity personas.[26] Finally, other authors argue for the further expansion of US publicity rights.[27]

The second approach considers whether various theoretical justifications support persona protection, as well as the conceptual inadequacies of these justifications.[28] Justifications can be classified as moral or economic. The moral justifications that are discussed in the literature include Lockean labour theory, Hegelian personality theory and unjust enrichment. Economic justifications canvassed in the literature include allocative efficiency, incentive theory and consumer protection.

In comparison to the US, there are relatively few materials that provide a comprehensive analysis of persona protection in the UK. The most comprehensive assessments of persona protection in the UK have been undertaken by Black,[29] Beverly-Smith[30] and Carty.[31] Black argues for the introduction of persona protection, Carty argues against it, and Beverly-Smith suggests a range of options, including using existing causes of action and introducing new rights. In the US, Nimmer argues that right of publicity protection is justified on the basis of natural rights.[32] He arrives at this conclusion by recognising the moral and economic interests that an individual has in controlling exploitation of her persona, analysing the possible causes of action that could be manipulated to protect persona, and rejecting them as inadequate to protect these interests.[33] Nimmer's approach to the topic is reflective of the general approach in the UK, where the majority of the literature has focused on analysing case law to find that persona protection is needed, without justifying the protection on theoretical grounds. Authors who have taken this approach to argue in support of persona protection include Bains,[34] Blackshaw,[35]

[26] Tan, D, 'Much Ado about Evocation: A Cultural Analysis of Well-Knownness and the Right of Publicity' (2010) 28 *Cardozo Arts & Ent LJ* 317; Dogan, S and Lemley, M, 'What the right of publicity can learn from trade mark law' (2006) 58 *Stan L Rev* 1161.

[27] Beach, S, 'Fact & Fiction: Amending Right of Publicity Statutes to Include Life Story and Fictional Characters Rights' (2017) 42(1) *Seton Hall Legislative Journal* 131.

[28] Walsh, C, 'The justifications underlying personality rights' (2012) 24 *Ent L Rev* 17; Black, G, *Publicity Rights and Image: Exploitation and Legal Control* (Hart Publishing 2011); Lapter, A and McKenna, M, 'How the Other Half Lives (Revisited): Twenty Years since Midler v Ford – A Global Perspective on the Right of Publicity' (2006) 15 *Tex Intell Prop LJ* 239; McKenna, M, 'The right of publicity and autonomous self-definition' (2005) 67 *University of Pittsburgh Law Review* 225; Beverley-Smith H, *Commercial Appropriation of Personality* (Cambridge University Press 2002); Kwall, R, 'Fame' (1997) 73 *Ind LJ* 1; McCarthy JT, 'The Human Persona as Commercial Property: The Right of Publicity' (1994) 19 *Colum VLA JL & Arts* 129; Grady, M, 'A positive economic theory of the right of publicity' (1994) 1 *UCLA Ent L Rev* 97; Madow (1993); Nimmer, M, 'The Right of Publicity' (1954) 19 *Law & Contemp Probs* 203.

[29] Black (2011).

[30] Beverley-Smith (2002).

[31] Carty (2004).

[32] Nimmer (1954).

[33] ibid.

[34] Bains (2007).

[35] Blackshaw (2005).

Boyd,[36] Stallard,[37] Barajas,[38] Klink,[39] Porter[40] and Goodenough.[41] In opposition to persona protection, Tan[42] and Deazley[43] assume the perspectives of cultural studies and street photography respectively, and argue that persona protection would have chilling effects on the cultural commons.

The reason for the lack of detailed consideration of theoretical justifications in the UK is probably the infancy of the desire for persona protection, which has only really come to the fore since the 1990s, indicated by the prevalence of articles[44] and cases[45] in this period. In comparison, the US right of publicity has matured over 70 years and has been the subject of much legal debate.[46] The strongest proponent of the necessity and desirability of the right of publicity in the US is McCarthy, who has produced a comprehensive treatise entitled *Rights of Publicity and Privacy*.[47] McCarthy argues that the right of publicity is supported by natural rights,[48] incentive,[49] allocative efficiency[50] and self-definition.[51] He considers which interests are protected,[52] duration,[53] elements of infringement,[54] assignments and licensing,[55] and maintains that the right of publicity is a 'common sense' right that everyone should be entitled to. Other authors who have argued in support of publicity rights include Kwall,[56] McKenna,[57] Grady,[58] Posner,[59]

[36] Boyd, S, 'Does English law recognise the concept of an image or personality right?' (2001) 13 *Ent L Rev* 1.
[37] Stallard (1997).
[38] Barajas (2009).
[39] Klink (2003).
[40] Porter (1999).
[41] Goodenough (1997).
[42] Tan (2010).
[43] Deazley (2003).
[44] Goodenough (1997); Porter (1999); Boyd (2001).
[45] *Irvine and another v Talksport Ltd* [2002] EWHC 367 (Ch); *Fenty and others v Arcadia Group Brands Ltd (trading as Topshop) and another* [2015] EWCA Civ 3, [2013] EWHC 1945 (Ch); *Elvis Presley Trade Marks* [1999] RPC 567, [1997] RPC 543; *Executrices of the Estate of Diana, Princess of Wales* [2001] ETMR 25; *Linkin Park LLC's Application* [2006] ETMR 74, [2005] ETMR 17; *Campbell v Mirror Group Newspapers Ltd* [2004] UKHL 22; *Douglas v Hello!* [2007] UKHL 21; *Molson Scottish Courage Ltd* (ASA ruling, 16 December 1996) – action brought under the Committee of Advertising Practices Code.
[46] Halpern considered this maturation over ten years ago and argued in support of the right of publicity – Halpern, S, 'Right of Publicity: Maturation of an Independent Right Protecting the Associative Value of Personality' (1994) 46 *Hastings Law Journal* 853.
[47] McCarthy, T and Schechter, R, *Rights of Publicity and Privacy* (Thomson Reuters 2022).
[48] ibid §§ 2:1–2:5.
[49] ibid § 2:6.
[50] ibid § 2:7.
[51] ibid § 2:9.
[52] ibid ch 4.
[53] ibid ch 9.
[54] ibid ch 3.
[55] ibid ch 10.
[56] Kwall (1997).
[57] McKenna (2005).
[58] Grady (1994).
[59] Posner E, 'The Right of Privacy' (1978) 393 *GA L Rev* 411; Posner, RA, *Economic Analysis of Law* (9th edn, Wolters Kluwer 1992).

Halpern,[60] Shipley[61] and Sims.[62] Madow argues against publicity rights.[63] Dogan & Lemley occupy a middle ground in this debate,[64] as they are in favour of the protection that the right of publicity offers, but think that trade mark law achieves, to an extent, the goals of publicity protection.

The current assessment of persona protection in the literature does not provide a picture of how the commercialisation of persona works in practice. Analysing case law reveals the culmination of a problem but does not inform about what happens in the transactional sphere and how issues that do not reach trial are resolved. This approach also does not consider which other factors drive behaviour. Law does not operate in a vacuum; there are other non-legal considerations that influence the regulation of persona. As for justifications, they can lend support in favour of a right or against it, but they do not consider the practical implications that law has on industry practice.

III. Empirical Methodology

Existing literature assumes that the relevant legal framework has certain implications, based on litigation in the field. In the absence of empirical data, the transactional sphere is left unexamined. This makes it difficult to draw comparisons between jurisdictions because there is little relevant case law in the UK. Furthermore, even in the US, it is difficult to know the true extent of right of publicity implications since not all disputes are adjudicated. In both jurisdictions, permission may be sought to use persona for reasons other than legal requirements. The empirical methodology facilitates an examination of the practical implications of the right of publicity in the US and the absence of an equivalent in UK, in both the transactional and dispute resolution spheres.

The transactional sphere is examined to determine how parties behave, in what circumstances permission is sought to use persona and why, as well as the inverse question as to when and why persona is used without permission. The dispute resolution sphere is examined to determine the course of action that is taken when persona is used without permission, and the impact of the presence or absence of a relationship on dispute resolution practices. Adopting this methodology allows a more comprehensive examination of the impact of different legal frameworks than has previously been undertaken, by facilitating engagement with the practicalities of the law. Furthermore, this empirical methodology also allows for other

[60] Halpern (1994).

[61] Shipley, D, 'Publicity never dies; it just fades away: The right of publicity and federal pre-emption' (1981) 66 *Cornell L Rev* 673.

[62] Sims, A, 'Right of Publicity: Survivability Reconsidered' (1981) 49 *Fordham L Rev* 453.

[63] Madow (1993).

[64] Dogan and Lemley (2006).

influences on behaviour to be considered, namely, social norms and contracts. Law does not operate in a vacuum, and fieldwork elucidates how law, social norms and contracts interact to regulate behaviour, as well as the overlap between these influences.

A. Choice of Jurisdictions

The US is home to the largest entertainment industry in the world,[65] with New York and California as major hubs.[66] Similarly, the UK's entertainment industry is globally competitive, ranking fifth in the world in size.[67] Consequently, there are legal hubs in New York, California and London that serve the entertainment industry and related industries, including advertising and merchandising. In addition to the similarities between the US and the UK, it was thought that conducting a further comparison *within* the US would yield further insights, because of variations in State-based protections of persona. New York and California both have a well-developed body of case law on the protection of persona, and both are hubs for the entertainment industry, hence these two States were selected for fieldwork. Ultimately, New York and California were found to have the same practices, and thus the US is often referred to in subsequent chapters rather than the individual States.

B. Interviews

The method selected to gather empirical information for this book was semi-structured interviews.[68] All interviews were conducted in 2017.[69] The number of years of experience of the interviewees ranged from six years to 50 years, with an average of 25 years. This book benefitted from elite interviews, as many interviewees are prominent practitioners and have worked with renowned celebrities and entities. The interviewees tended to come from large, international law firms in metropolitan cities with developed entertainment industries. This is because these types of firms are most likely to deal in persona protection, as this protection is frequently sought out by high-net-worth individuals. Similarly, entities that pay to use persona tend to have the financial resources that enable them to utilise these large firms. Due to the experience of the interviewees, they were also able

[65] US Department of Commerce, 'Media and Entertainment Spotlight' *Select USA* at www.trade.gov/selectusa-media-and-entertainment-industry (accessed 16 January 2023).

[66] US Department of Commerce, *International Trade Association Top Markets Report – Media and Entertainment* (USA Department of Commerce 2016) 5.

[67] ibid 1.

[68] May, T, *Social Research: Issues, methods and process* (Open University Press 2010) 134–36.

[69] Permission was obtained from the interviewees to use the information gathered in interviews.

to provide information on entities that do not seek permission to use persona, as their clients often complain about such entities.

Semi-structured interviews allowed for flexibility and the adjustment of questions according to the experience of the interviewee.[70] As interviewees expounded on their respective industries, further reading was done to learn more about logistical issues that impact the way persona is commercialised. This further reading is examined in subsequent chapters, and is frequently used to triangulate information provided by interviewees.

Semi-structured interviews were also considered as the optimal data-collection tool because they allow for certain themes to be focused on as they emerge in conversation, as noted by Creswell.[71] Flexibility was needed to direct questioning according to the experience of the interviewee. The expertise of interviewees was determined by the types of clients they represented, as well as the industries with which they worked. These two variables, clients and industry, would have made it difficult to formulate precise questions that would be relevant across the range of interviewees. Hence, semi-structured interviews were preferred over structured interviews.

After all the interviews were conducted and transcribed, the coding process was carried out as described by Hseih and Shannon:[72] all transcripts were read, recurrent words were highlighted, notes were made on concepts in the data and then themes were created based on these concepts.[73] All quotations used in the chapters are taken verbatim from the interviews. As a result, the quotations contain grammatical errors. Individuals did not necessarily speak in a formal, grammatical manner during the interviews. However, it was felt that these errors should be retained as they reflected the nature of the interviews: conversational and semi-structured.

IV. Outline of the Book

This book is divided into two parts. Part 1: The Foundation provides the necessary background against which the empirical work is analysed in Part 2: Rights in Practice.

In Part 1, chapter 2 conducts an in-depth analysis into the legal regulation available in the UK, New York and California. It is important that the existing law is explained to highlight the perceived gaps in the UK system, as well as the

[70] Barbour, R and Schostak, J, 'Interviewing and focus groups' in Somekh, B and Lewin, C (eds), *Research Methods in the Social Sciences* (SAGE Publications 2004) 41.

[71] Creswell, T, *Research Design: Qualitative, Quantitative and Mixed Methods Approaches* (4th edn, Sage 2014) 46.

[72] Hsieh, H-F and Shannon, S, 'Three approaches to qualitative content analysis' (2005) 15(9) *Qualitative Health Research* 1277, 1279.

[73] ibid.

extent of protection in New York and California. There are fewer circumstances in which permission is required to use persona in the UK as compared to the US. This understanding contributes to the subsequent analysis of permission-based behaviours that exist in both jurisdictions.

Chapter 3 presents the framework for analysis. This framework identifies three influences on behaviour: law; desire to collaborate via contract; and social norms. The reasons for compliance with each of these influences is examined. For law, the theories relevant to this book are deterrence and morality.[74] Deterrence theory suggests that individuals comply with the law to avoid perceived legal sanctions.[75] Fieldwork demonstrated that both US and UK systems of legal regulation influence parties to seek permission to use persona to avoid legal action. Morality is only relevant in the US, and it suggests that compliance with law is based on a sense that the law outlines a morally correct course of action.[76] In the inverse, there may be disregard for law after undertaking a cost–benefit analysis,[77] or there may be ignorance of the applicable law.[78]

The framework is first used to address the approach to dispute resolution in light of the different legal regulation. In the presence of a relationship, companies are unlikely to pursue legal action against a celebrity due to the desire to maintain a relationship in accordance with the signalling function of social norms. Conversely, where there is no relationship, celebrities will attempt to pursue legal action. This is where the right of publicity makes the biggest difference: US claimants are likely to induce settlement due to the breadth of the law, potential for expansion and the cost associated with losing a case. Settlement can even occur where the claim is

[74] The legitimacy theory was not examined in fieldwork as it questions the validity of a source of law rather than the law itself, but it is worth noting that the legitimacy theory prompts compliance with the law when individuals feel the law was derived from an authoritative source. See: Tyler, T, 'Psychological Perspectives on Legitimacy and Legitimation' (2006) 57 *Annual Rev of Psychology* 375; Jackson, J et al, 'Why do People Comply with the Law?: Legitimacy and the Influence of Legal Institutions' (2012) 52 *The British Journal of Criminology* 1051.

[75] Blumstein, A, Cohen, J and Nagin, D, *Deterrence and Incapacitation: Estimating the Effects of Criminal Sanctions on Crime Rates* (National Academy of Sciences 1978); Nagin, DS, 'Criminal Deterrence Research at the Outset of the Twenty-First Century' (1998) 23 *Crime and Justice: A Review of Research* 1; Sherman, L, 'Police Crackdowns: Initial and Residual Deterrence' in Tonry, M and Morris, N (eds), *Crime and Justice: A Review of Research* (University of Chicago Press 1990); Sampson, R and Cohen, J, 'Deterrent Effects of Police on Crime: A Replication and Theoretical Extension' (1998) 22 *L & Socy Rev* 163; Kagan, R, 'On the Visibility of Income Tax Law Violations' in Roth, J and Scholz, J (eds), *Taxpayer Compliance*, vol 2 (University of Pennsylvania Press 1989); Levitt, S, 'The Effect of the Prison Population Size on Crime Rates: Evidence from Prison Overcrowding Litigation' (1996) 111 *Quarterly Journal of Economics* 319; Grasmick, H and Bursik, R, 'Significant Others, and Rational Choice: Extending the Deterrence Model' (1990) 24 *L & Socy Rev* 837; Bachman, R, Paternoster, R and Ward, S, 'The Rationality of Sexual Offending: Testing a Deterrence/Rational Choice Conception of Sexual Assault' (1992) 26 *L & Socy Rev* 343; Paternoster, R and Simpson, S, 'Sanction Threats and Appeals to Morality: Testing a Rational Choice Theory of Corporate Crime' (1997) 30 *L & Socy Rev* 549.

[76] Tyler, T, *Why Do People Obey Law?* (Princeton University Press 1990) 178; Manesh, M, 'The Immorality of Theft, the Amorality of Infringement' [2006] *Stan Tech L Rev* 5.

[77] Robinson, P and Darley, J, 'Does Criminal Law Deter? A Behavioural Science Investigation' (2004) 24 *OJLS* 173.

[78] ibid.

groundless, as the entity being sued may want to minimise the time and money that would need to be spent on defending the claim. In contrast, UK claimants are unlikely to seek redress unless they have strong evidence of passing off. Unlike the strict liability right of publicity, the requirements to prove a passing off claim are more onerous, thus fieldwork gives credibility to existing literature that suggests this gap in the law makes a difference.

However, this gap should not be overstated in light of the fact that the predominant behaviour in the transactional sphere in both the UK and the US is to seek permission to commercialise persona. Permission is sought due to legal requirements or fear of expansion of the law. This fear exists in the US, and rightfully so considering the common law development of the right of publicity. But it also exists in the UK in direct contrast to the views that is difficult to bring a claim under passing off. On the one hand, there have only been two cases where an individual has successfully claimed passing off: *Irvine* in 2003 and *Fenty* in 2013. The stringent analysis of the evidence in these cases resulted in the suggestion by interviewees that it is difficult to succeed on a claim. On the other hand, instances of use of persona without permission were considered rare, and one of the reasons that permission is sought is to mitigate against the risk of any claim.

The law plays a clear role in each jurisdiction in inducing permission to be sought, but it is just one influence on behaviour. There is a strong desire to collaborate with celebrities to reap the benefits of association and endorsement. This is why brands pay dearly for the privilege of drawing on the fame and allure of famous individuals. Regardless of the law, this appeal exists, and in fact marketing literature rarely discussed the law when examining celebrity endorsements. Furthermore, developments in technology mean that the brand must work with the celebrity to achieve maximum success. While photographs are still used, consumers are looking for authentic advertising that makes them feel that the celebrity approves of whatever is being sold. To maximise on the para-social relationship, the brand must work with the celebrity. Failing to work with the celebrity leads not only to potential legal consequences but also to financial consequences, as fans will not approve of unauthorised uses of their admired celebrity. Chapter 3 explains this appeal by reference to excerpts from interviews that illuminate the strength of the desire to collaborate via contract.

In addition to the role of law and the desire to collaborate, the final influence that forms the framework for analysis is social norms. Social norms gained traction in the legal sphere in the 1980s with the seminal book, *Order without Law* written by Ellickson in 1994.[79] Social norms dictate the course of action that should be taken to send the right signal to maintain a favourable reputation. If the right signal is not sent, sanctions may be administered. Social norms were observed across industries and, as such, chapter 3 looks at the development of this field before turning to explain the relevance to persona commercialisation.

[79] Ellickson, R, *Order without Law* (Harvard University Press 1994).

The framework shows how the same behaviour can be sustained in different jurisdictions through varying manifestations of compliance theories. In other words, entities may undertake the same action for different reasons. Law is just one of those reasons, and even then, it is the perception of the law more than the actual law that drives permission-based behaviours. Alongside law, the desire to collaborate with celebrities, and the need to adhere to social norms, also drives behaviour.

Following the framework set out in chapter 3, chapter 4 delves into the dispute resolution sphere. Dispute resolution, namely litigation, is the focal point of existing literature because cases are available for analysis. However, not all disputes culminate in litigation. Empirical work revealed that there are two situations to be considered when looking at dispute resolution: (i) the presence of a relationship; (ii) the absence of a relationship. It is the second situation that has been widely discussed. This chapter advances that in the presence of a relationship, there is rarely recourse to legal action because the brand wants to maintain the relationship with the celebrity. Conversely, when there is no relationship, the celebrity will consider legal action. This is where the difference between the US and UK legal frameworks becomes most apparent.

In chapters 5–8, behaviours are identified and analysed against the framework set out in chapter 3. Chapter 5 looks at the advertising industry, chapter 6 focuses on the merchandising industry, chapter 7 explores film and television production, and chapter 8 considers sports video game development. New York and California were found to have the same behaviours despite different approaches to publicity rights. This is partly because false endorsement is federal and can act as a substitute for the right of publicity, but also because most of the lawyers interviewed advised on inter-State commerce. As such, they must consider the 'lowest common denominator'.[80]

Each chapter follows the same format. The use of persona in the relevant industry is explained to provide context to the behaviours that will be examined. Following this, the relevant theories of compliance are assessed according to the influences at play. Deviations from the behaviour are also considered. Where permission is not sought to use persona, there is usually a disregard of the applicable law or ignorance of the law. In some circumstances, there may be no applicable law to govern a situation.

Out of the nine behaviours observed in relation to persona commercialisation, seven occurred in both jurisdictions. This can be attributed to the occurrence of the same theories of compliance for these behaviours. Three of the industries studied shared the same behaviours. Behaviours regulating the film and television production and video game development industries in the UK have been influenced by developments in US law. The merchandising industry operates in a

[80] This term was cited without prompting in 5 out of 19 New York interviews. In other interviews, it was suggested that lawyers have to be aware of the most expansive law because the product or service will not stay within New York.

similar manner despite differences in the law. The advertising industry is the only industry studied that displayed a divergence in behaviours. Humorous and evocative advertisements are made in the UK but not in the US. This is due to the impact of the right of publicity and false endorsement in the US, as compared to the more limited action of passing off in the UK.

The final chapter considers how law marks a divergence in the dispute resolution sphere, but even then social norms and the desire to maintain relationships must be considered. Within the transactional sphere, the perception of the law is manifested in deterrence theory, but improvements in technology and the desire to capitalise on para-social relationships between fans and technology spur on permission-based behaviours.

PART 1

The Foundation

2

Legal Regulation of Persona in the UK, New York and California

Introduction

This chapter examines the legal regulation of persona in the UK, New York and California. The UK has limited protection afforded by various causes of action, with passing off and the Advertising Codes being the most useful. New York has historically provided publicity protection under the guise of the inter vivos right to privacy. In 2020, after years of lobbying, New York extended this commercial protection post-mortem under the right of publicity terminology, which better reflects the commercial interests of the individual and, now, their estate.[1] California has the most expansive laws that cover both inter vivos and post-mortem rights of publicity via statute, which names elements of persona. In addition, the common law protects 'identity', but only for living individuals. Both States are subject to the false endorsement action under the federal Lanham Act, which also extends to 'identity'. While a false endorsement claim requires confusion, the threshold is lower than the UK's formulation of false endorsement under the passing-off action.

The legal framework for protecting persona in each jurisdiction provides the background against which the empirical findings will be discussed in subsequent chapters. The legal regulation examined in this chapter would suggest that there is more leeway for unauthorised use of persona in the UK due to the piecemeal approach and, in particular, the higher threshold for a passing-off claim. It follows that New York and California, with more expansive protection, would have entrenched the need to seek authorisation to use persona to avoid a potential claim. Particularly as the false endorsement action under the Lanham Act can be used alongside the right of privacy/publicity actions, giving litigants a selection of causes of action.

Subsequent chapters reveal that the doctrinal position does not always align with the law in action. In the UK, passing off, which is assessed in this chapter as having limited application, has a greater impact on decision making than anticipated, particularly in the advertising and merchandising industries. The litigation

[1] New York Civil Code, s 50(f).

risk that influences permission to be sought to use persona was arguably overstated by interviewees in chapters 5–8, as the limitations of passing off observed in this chapter are manifested in the lack of use in dispute resolution, which will be discussed in chapter 4. The two perceptions of passing off observed in fieldwork are irreconcilable. Passing off poses a perceived risk that prompts permission to be sought to use persona in certain circumstances, despite being rarely invoked when persona is used without permission.

As for the UK Advertising Codes, while these should be useful for regulating persona in the advertising industry, they are rarely relied upon. Lawyers interviewed did not consider the Codes to be influential in decision making because disputes are not adjudicated in court, and limited remedies are administered by the Advertising Standards Agency (ASA). The limitations of the Codes are recognised in this chapter, so in this instance, theory and reality align.

In the US, the causes of action examined in this chapter influence permission-based behaviours observed in the advertising, merchandising and video game industries. However, these behaviours often developed before the law, and are often supported by other influences, namely, the benefits of collaboration and social norms. In fact, advancements in technology in the advertising and video game industries have made it particularly worthwhile to collaborate with celebrities to create the best product possible. This indicates that even if the law was not present, some behaviours would continue to exist. In contrast, the level of influence of law in the film industry is disproportionate since publicity rights do not protect one's 'life story', yet a behaviour of seeking permission where it is likely to be given has developed because of the poor handling of these types of cases in courts. This is despite the fact that no claim for infringement of the right of publicity against a film producer has been successful, as will be examined in this chapter.

The law analysed in this chapter often influences behaviours of seeking permission discussed in chapters 5–8. Yet these permission-based behaviours are usually governed by contracts that use the law to guard against liability, rather than to grant positive legal rights, as explained in chapter 4. However, when there is no relationship between parties, and persona is used without permission, the available causes of action will be employed in dispute resolution. The higher threshold for a passing-off claim in the UK equates to limited redress for unauthorised use of persona, whereas publicity and false endorsement actions in the US facilitate claims in many circumstances.

This chapter is divided into three sections. Section I examines the piecemeal approach to persona protection in the UK. Emphasis is placed on passing off and the Advertising Codes as these are the most useful causes of action. Trade mark law is somewhat useful as it confers a proprietary right, but it is limited in what aspects of persona can be registered for protection. Other causes of action – copyright, breach of confidence and defamation – are briefly outlined to explain why they are unsuitable for protecting persona. Section II examines persona protection in the US. The federal false endorsement action is examined first. It will be argued that this action is more plaintiff-friendly than passing off because there is no goodwill requirement, and the threshold for confusion is lower than misrepresentation. Following this, the New York right of privacy is examined. Despite its name, the New York right of privacy performs the function of a publicity right.[2] The introduction of a post-mortem right of publicity is also discussed. Subsequently, the California common law and statutory publicity rights are examined. Section III considers the hypothetical impact that all the causes of action discussed in this chapter *should* have on the industries examined in this book against the *actual* impact observed in fieldwork that will be discussed in subsequent chapters.

I. United Kingdom

There is no protection against misappropriation of persona in the UK under common law or statute. Instead, those wishing to protect and/or exploit persona must rely on piecemeal protection. The protection that will be discussed in this section includes:

- passing off
- the Advertising Codes
- trade mark law
- copyright
- breach of confidence
- defamation.

Misuse of private information is not considered, as the focus of this book is the control of persona in the commercial sphere rather than privacy rights:[3] privacy concerns the ability to control personal information and protect against intrusions

[2] Adkins, BA, 'Crying out for Uniformity: Eliminating State Inconsistencies in Right of Publicity Protection through a Uniform Right of Publicity Act ' (2009) 40 *Cumb L Rev* 499, 505: '[T]he current New York statute derives its cause of action for the right of publicity from the right of privacy, as indicated by the "Right of Privacy" title assigned to the statute.'

[3] The approach to misuse of private information in the UK is not examined in this chapter as it is considered an unsuitable avenue from which to protect persona in the commercial sphere. For more information on the misuse of private information, see: Aplin, T, 'Commercialising Privacy and Privatising the Commercial: The Difficulties Arising from the Protection of Privacy via Breach of Confidence' in Kur, A et al (eds), *Intellectual Property, Unfair Competition and Publicity – Convergence and Development* (Edward Elgar 2014) 189; Aplin, T, 'The Future of Breach of Confidence and the Protection of Privacy' (2007) 7 *Oxford U Commw LJ* 137; Morgan, J, 'Privacy, Confidence and Horizontal Effect: Hello Trouble' (2003) 62 *Cambridge LJ* 444. For UK cases, see: *HRH The Duchess of Sussex v Associated Newspapers Ltd* [2021] EWHC 273 (Ch); *Weller v Associated Newspapers Ltd* [2015] EWCA Civ 1176; *Murray v Express Newspapers plc and another* [2008] EWCA 446; *McKennitt v Ash* [2006] EWCA Civ 1714; *A v B & C* [2002] EWCA Civ 337. For cases at the ECtHR, see: *von Hannover v Germany (No 2)* (2012) 55 EHRR 15; *Reklos v Greece* [2009] EMLR 16; *von Hannover v Germany* (2004) 40 EHRR 1.

into the personal sphere; publicity concerns the ability of an individual to regulate commercial exploitation of persona. The UK does not recognise a tort of privacy.[4] Since the introduction of the Human Rights Act 1998, the courts must give effect to the European Convention on Human Rights (ECHR), including Article 8, the right to respect for private life, which is usually weighed against Article 10, freedom of expression.[5] In order to give effect to Article 8, UK courts transformed breach of confidence to include misuse of private information.[6] Misuse of private information is unlikely to be of assistance in protecting persona on a commercial basis in the UK. While news reporting and magazines are 'commercial', in the sense that they are created to generate profit, they are not the type of uses that would be prevented by persona protection. As such, more relevant causes of action that regulate persona in the commercial sphere are focused on in this section.

In this section, it will be argued that passing off and advertising codes offer some persona protection, but there are limitations in the UK legal framework. For passing off, the main difficulty is the misrepresentation requirement, which does not protect persona per se but rather the goodwill of a trader. The Advertising Codes regulate the use of persona, but they do not provide compensation to an aggrieved individual. Further, they do not apply to packaging, labelling or products, and the non-broadcast code urges rather than requires permission for use of 'living persons'.[7] The other causes of action are more limited. Trade mark law can protect against confusing uses of name and signature, and potentially instances of misappropriation where the mark has a reputation,[8] but only these two aspects of persona are likely to be protected due to registration requirements. The exceptional case of *Douglas v Hello!*, under breach of confidence, has potential for persona protection, but its unique facts and unorthodox approach to breach of confidence potentially limit further application.[9] Copyright can only provide protection if the persona is also the copyright holder, and defamation requires the persona's reputation to be damaged in order to bring a claim. Based on the available causes of action, the assessment that will be made is that the avenues for protection do not allow an individual full commercial control over her persona, in contrast to the US approach that confers proprietary rights.

A. Passing Off

The classic trinity, as stated in the *Jif lemon* case,[10] of goodwill, misrepresentation and damage has been expanded to accommodate different types of harm,

[4] *Wainwright v Home Office* [2003] UKHL 53.
[5] *Campbell v Mirror Group Newspapers* Ltd [2004] UKHL 22.
[6] ibid.
[7] Stallard, H, 'Right of Publicity in the United Kingdom' (1997) 18 *Loy LA Ent LJ* 565, 573–74.
[8] Davies, G, 'Celebrity and Trade Marks: The Next Instalment' (2004) 1 *SCRIPTed* 230.
[9] *Douglas & ors v Hello! Ltd & ors (No 3)* [2007] UKHL 21.
[10] *Reckitt & Colman Ltd v Borden Inc* [1990] 1 All ER 873.

including dilution,[11] reverse passing off[12] and, most relevantly for persona protection, false endorsement. However, despite the much-publicised successes of Eddie Irvine in his claim against TalkSport radio for using his photograph on a brochure,[13] and Rihanna against Topshop for using her photograph on a t-shirt,[14] passing off provides limited protection for persona.

Passing off protects against misrepresentation rather than misappropriation. The consumer must be deceived to the effect that the claimant's goodwill is damaged.[15] The misrepresentation requirement poses the most significant hurdle to a passing-off claim. Goodwill can also be difficult to establish since more than mere reputation is required, but it is unlikely to prove a significant hurdle due to advances in the law. Damage may prove problematic in instances where a licence would not have been granted, but damage is usually presumed once there has been a misrepresentation.[16] The issues that arise under each element of passing off will now be discussed. Following this, an overall analysis will be undertaken of the usefulness of passing off in persona protection.

i. Goodwill

Goodwill is the attractive force that brings in custom.[17] It is more than mere reputation.[18] In order to protect persona under passing off, an individual must possess goodwill. To establish goodwill, a claimant must have trading activity in the UK.[19] While a claimant who has goodwill in the UK is likely to have a reputation, the inverse does not apply, as a claimant who has reputation does

[11] *Bollinger v Costa Brava Wine* Co Ltd [1961] RPC 116.

[12] *Bristol Conservatories Ltd v Conservatories Custom Built Ltd* [1989] RPC 455.

[13] 'Eddie Irvine wins £25,000 damages in TalkSPORT appeal' *Campaign* (1 April 2003) at www.campaignlive.co.uk/article/eddie-irvine-wins-25000-damages-talksport appeal/175837?src_site=brandrepublic (accessed 23 July 2017); Cozens, C, 'MacKenzie's TalkSport loses £275,000 to Irvine' *The Guardian* (2 April 2003) at www.theguardian.com/media/2003/apr/02/radio.business (accessed 17 October 2016); Davies, A, 'Formula one ace wins high court battle over "doctored" ad' *The Guardian* (13 March 2002) at www.theguardian.com/media/2002/mar/13/advertising.formulaone (accessed 10 October 2017).

[14] 'Rihanna wins legal battle with Topshop over T-shirt' *The Telegraph* (22 January 2015) at www.telegraph.co.uk/news/celebritynews/11362116/Rihanna-wins-legal-battle-with-Topshop-over-T-shirt.html (accessed 1 February 2017); Bowcott, O, 'Rihanna wins Topshop T-shirt row' *The Guardian* (22 January 2015) at www.theguardian.com/music/2015/jan/22/rihanna-topshop-tshirt-court (accessed 15 November 2017); 'Pop star Rihanna wins image battle' *BBC* (22 January 2015) at www.bbc.co.uk/news/entertainment-arts-30932158 (accessed 13 May 2016).

[15] Davis, J, 'Why the United Kingdom should have a law against misappropriation' (2010) 69 *Cambridge LJ* 561, 563: 'In fact, what is generally held necessary in passing off is not any misrepresentation, but a misrepresentation which damages the claimant's goodwill.'

[16] Davis (2010) 563–64.

[17] *Commissioners of Inland Revenue v Muller & Co Margarine* [1901] AC 217.

[18] Mellor, J et al, *Kerly's Law of Trade Marks and Trade Names* (16th edn, Sweet & Maxwell 2017) § 20-024.

[19] *Hotel Cipriani v Cipriani (Grosvenor Street)* [2010] EWCA Civ 10; *Anheuser-Busch v Budejovicky Budvar* [1984] FRS 413.

not automatically have goodwill.[20] The requirement of goodwill rather than reputation was made clear by the Supreme Court in *Starbucks v British Sky Broadcasting*:

> I consider that we should reaffirm that the law is that a claimant in a passing off claim must establish that it has actual goodwill in this jurisdiction, and that such goodwill involves the presence of clients or customers in the jurisdiction for the products or services in question.[21]

The evidential burden of proving goodwill is a potential stumbling block, but one that should not prove fatal to a claim. This is because the law has developed in response to merchandising and sponsorship activities. In the past, claims that purported to protect persona were thwarted by the 'common field of activity', which required claimants to be in the same business as the defendant.[22] However, this is no longer a requirement.[23] Even if it were, it is unlikely that it would have a substantial impact since claimants generally are involved in merchandising and sponsorship, as evidenced by the *Irvine*[24] and *Fenty*[25] cases, and as recognised in *Stringfellow*[26] and *Mirage Studios v Counterfeat Clothing*.[27]

In both *Irvine* and *Fenty*, the claimants were at the top of their fields. Birss J discussed Rihanna's numerous merchandising and sponsorship deals and concluded that 'The scope of her goodwill was not only as a music artist but also in the world of fashion, as a style leader.'[28] This finding reflects that goodwill must be in the industry in which the claim is based. For celebrities, this will likely be the merchandising and sponsorship industries. There is no guidance on how much trading activity must be carried out before an individual is found to have goodwill. It is likely that 'A-list' celebrities and athletes such as Beyoncé and David Beckham, who have carefully crafted their personal brands over the years, will possess the requisite goodwill. It is less certain whether emerging celebrities and athletes will be able to prove goodwill.

Celebrities who have fans in the UK but do not have many merchandising or sponsorship deals in the jurisdiction may have difficulty proving goodwill. *Stringfellow* indicates that the potential merchandising and endorsement value of

[20] Kerly (2017) § 20-05.

[21] *Starbucks v British Sky Broadcasting Group Plc* [2015] UKSC 31 [47].

[22] *Harrison and Starkey v Polydor* [1977] FSR 1; *Wombles v Womble Skips* [1975] FSR 488, [1977] RPC 99; *McCulloch v Lewis A May* [1947] 2 All ER 845.

[23] *LegoSystems A/S v Lego M Lemelstrich* [1983] FSR 155; Bains, S, 'Personality rights: should the UK grant celebrities a proprietary right in their personality? Part 1' (2007) 18(5) *Ent L Rev* 164, 166; Tan, D, 'Fame Monster Reloaded: The Contemporary Celebrity, Cultural Studies and Passing Off' (2010) 32 *Sydney L Rev* 291, 293; Phillips, J, Coleman, A, 'Passing off and the common field of activity' (1985) 101 *LQR* 242.

[24] *Irvine and another v Talksport Ltd* [2002] EWHC 367 (Ch).

[25] *Fenty and others v Arcadia Group Brands Ltd (trading as Topshop) and another* [2015] EWCA Civ 3.

[26] *Stringfellow v McCain Foods Ltd* [1984] RPC 501 [517].

[27] *Mirage Studios v Counter-Feat Clothing Company Limited* [1991] FSR 145.

[28] *Fenty* [2013] [46].

the name might be enough,[29] but the claimant must have customers in the UK to establish goodwill.[30] The status of the law on preparations to trade is not clear, but *obiter dicta* indicate that the law may be open to such expansion.[31] As such, the use of technology to distribute entertainment media such as albums via streaming services and music videos on YouTube can result in entertainers', for example singers, gaining a reputation in the UK as they prepare to begin trading activities. It is uncertain whether the same can be said for actors and athletes. For actors, the sale of film tickets might be treated as the trading activity of cinemas and the film producer. Similarly, athletes compete in competitions organised by different entities, or are employed by a team. Since goodwill requires trading activity in the UK, famous individuals in the aforementioned fields are likely to be required to show evidence of merchandising and endorsement in the UK, such as brand collaborations and/or the sale of products bearing an aspect of persona.

ii. Misrepresentation

In the UK, passing off protects against deceptive uses of goodwill, rather than against misappropriation. The assessment of misrepresentation depends on whether consumers believe there is a connection between the claimant and the defendant. According to Lord Justice Jacob in *Reed Executive v Reed Business Information*:

> Once the position strays into misleading a substantial number of people (going from "I *wonder* if there is a connection" to "I *assume* there is a connection") there will be passing off, whether the use is as a business name or a trade mark on goods.[32]

[29] *Stringfellow v McCain* [1984] [517]: 'He [referring to an expert witness] assumed that this use by the first defendants in this name was the result of the grant of merchandising rights to the first defendants and it was his view that a use of this character would be damaging to the image, which I think can fairly be equated with the goodwill attaching to the name.'

[30] Kerly (2017) § 20-025.

[31] *Starbucks v British Sky Broadcasting Group Plc* [2015] UKSC 31 [66]: 'Finally, a point which I would leave open is that discussed in the judgment of Sundaresh Menon CJ in *Staywell* … namely whether a passing off claim can be brought by a claimant who has not yet attracted goodwill in the UK, but has launched a substantial advertising campaign within the UK making it clear that it will imminently be marketing its goods or services in the UK under the mark in question. It may be that such a conclusion would not so much be an exception, as an extension, to the "hard line", in that public advertising with an actual and publicised imminent intention to market, coupled with a reputation thereby established may be sufficient to generate a protectable goodwill. On any view, the conclusion would involve overruling *Maxwell v Hogg*, and, if it would be an exception rather than an extension to the "hard line", it would have to be justified by commercial fairness rather than principle. However, it is unnecessary to rule on the point which … has some limited support in this jurisdiction and clear support in Singapore. Modern developments might seem to argue against such an exception … but it may be said that it would be cheap and easy, particularly for a large competitor, to "spike" a pre-marketing advertising campaign in the age of the internet. It would, I think, be better to decide the point in a case where it arises.'

[32] *Reed Executive v Reed Business Information* [2004] RPC 767 [797] (emphasis added).

The misrepresentation must amount to more than mere confusion. While many cases use the terms 'confusion' and 'deception' interchangeably, 'mere confusion does not indicate or establish passing off'.[33] For a successful claim to protect persona, there must be an implied endorsement that constitutes a material misrepresentation as to the connection between the claimant and the defendant.[34] 'Material' means that the claimant's goodwill is damaged.[35] There will be many instances where the issue of misrepresentation is unclear, which might deter the individual featured from bringing a claim, but the user still derives the benefit of the persona. This is reflective of reality, and the perceived difficulties of bringing a successful claim are discussed in chapter 4. An example of a situation that might not be pursued due to the requirements of passing off is where a travel agency sells cricket tours using a photograph of a cricketer. Consumers might be confused as to whether there is a connection, but not necessarily be deceived into thinking there is one. The use of persona in the advertisement would illustrate the purpose of the tour, but it might not amount to an endorsement.[36] Such a use would stay within the realm of 'I wonder' as opposed to 'I assume' articulated by Lord Justice Jacob above.

In the two famously successful UK passing-off cases, *Irvine*[37] and *Fenty*,[38] the use of persona was an image that looked 'official'. The image of Rihanna was from her album artwork and Irvine's photograph was edited to look like he was holding a TalkSport radio. For uses that look less 'official', it is less likely that a claim will be made out in passing off. According to Birss J, 'the less flattering the image the less likely it is that it would thought to be authorised'.[39] It is unlikely that the average consumer would think an individual would authorise a use of persona that casts her in a negative light. For example, the public might not think there was authorisation if an advertisement for alcohol uses the persona of a teetotaller. Similarly, a humorous use would probably not constitute a misrepresentation. Since passing off is meant to protect the consumer, this approach is sensible, but a law that is designed to protect persona would prohibit such uses even in the absence of misrepresentation. The misrepresentation element of passing off can be an insuperable evidential barrier to a successful claim.

iii. Damage

Damage in passing off is assessed as a lost licence fee and/or diversion from the claimant's own business activities. According to Birss J, '[i]f … a substantial

[33] Kerly (2017) § 20-97.
[34] ibid (2017) § 20-26.
[35] Wadlow, C, *The Law of Passing-Off: Unfair Competition by Misrepresentation* (Sweet & Maxwell 2016) § 18-027.
[36] It should be noted, however, that the line between illustrating and endorsement advertisements is blurred. See ch 5, section I for discussion of the different types of advertisements.
[37] *Irvine* [2002].
[38] *Fenty* [2013].
[39] ibid [66].

number of purchasers are likely to be deceived … that will obviously be damaging to the claimant's goodwill.'[40] Once misrepresentation is made out, damage is usually uncontentious. According to Davis, 'in practice, a claimant is rarely, if ever, put to the task of proving it [damage] has occurred.'[41] It remains to be seen whether dilution or tarnishment could be assessed as damage where persona is used without authorisation in a non-flattering way. If these heads of damage were extended to individual claimants, they could be compensated for degrading uses, however, such uses make misrepresentation more difficult to prove.

iv. Assessment of Passing Off

Passing off is a useful tool in protecting persona, but there are limits to the efficacy of this deception-based harm given its consumer focus. The state of the law is adequately reflected in Birss J's statement, 'The mere sale by a trader of a t-shirt bearing an image of a famous person is not, without more, an act of passing off.'[42] As such, misrepresentation will be the turning point in many passing-off cases.[43] Goodwill, while a potential challenge for less established celebrities and athletes, is not insurmountable if trading activity can be shown in the UK. The absence of merchandising and endorsement deals might prove problematic, but other trading activity in the UK, with the potential to venture into merchandising and endorsement, could suffice, according to *Stringfellow*.[44] Once goodwill and misrepresentation are made out, damage will usually be found.[45] While this is the strongest cause of action for persona protection in the UK, it must be emphasised that it does not confer a proprietary right, and it is designed to protect consumers. While it has evolved to protect individuals, the strength of the evidence in *Irvine*[46] and *Fenty*[47] as to misrepresentation should not be understated.

B. Advertising Codes

i. The Codes

There are two Advertising Codes that are enforced by the Advertising Standards Authority (ASA). The UK Code of Broadcast Advertising (BCAP) provides

[40] *Fenty* [2013] [74].
[41] Davis, J, 'Why the United Kingdom should have a law against misappropriation' (2010) 69 *Cambridge LJ* 561, 563–64.
[42] *Fenty* [2013] [75].
[43] Barajas, ADL, 'Personality rights in the United States and the United Kingdom – is Vanna too much? Is Irvine not enough?' (2009) 20 *Ent L Rev* 253, 257.
[44] *Stringfellow* [1984].
[45] Fletcher, S et al, 'Court of Appeal found no love for Topshop tank: the image right that dare not speak its name' (2015) 37 *EIPR* 394, 398.
[46] *Irvine* [2002].
[47] *Fenty* [2013].

guidelines for advertisers using radio and television advertisements. The BCAP defines 'advertisement' as

> publicity by advertisers, including spot advertisements and broadcaster promotions with advertisers (outside programme time), that is broadcast in return for payment or other valuable consideration to a broadcaster or that seeks to sell products to viewers or listeners.[48]

'Broadcasters', defined as 'Ofcom-licensed television and radio services provided by broadcasters within UK jurisdiction',[49] are responsible for ensuring that all advertisements comply with the BCAP.[50] The 'Principle' section of the BCAP states that 'The ASA may decline to investigate where there is a dispute which, in its view, would be better resolved … through the Courts.'[51]

The Code of Non-Broadcast Advertising and Direct and Promotional Marketing (CAP) provides guidance for non-broadcast advertisements, sales promotions and direct marketing communications. The preface to the CAP states that '[t]he Code supplements the law, fills gaps where the law does not reach and often provides an easier way of resolving disputes than by civil litigation'.[52] The CAP suggests that, '[i]n many cases, self-regulation ensures that legislation is not necessary'.[53] While both Codes are based on a compliance approach,[54] the CAP is more forceful in emphasising the value of self-regulation. The ASA intervenes where a complaint has been made, but it is up to the marketers to ensure that their advertisements comply. Nonetheless, the Background to the Code states that '[a]ny matter that principally concerns a legal dispute will normally need to be resolved through law enforcement agencies or the Courts'.[55]

The CAP defines 'marketer' as 'an advertiser, promoter or direct marketer'.[56] More usefully, it provides a list of communications that are regulated by the Code,[57] such as advertisements in newspapers, magazines and other print media,

[48] BCAP, Introduction, b(ii).

[49] BCAP, Introduction, b(i). Ofcom is the UK's communications regulator.

[50] 'Broadcasters are responsible for ensuring that the advertisements they transmit comply with both the spirit and the letter of the Code.' BCAP, Section 1, Compliance, Principle.

[51] ibid.

[52] CAP, Preface.

[53] ibid.

[54] BCAP, Section 1, Compliance; CAP, Section 1, Compliance.

[55] CAP, Section 1, Compliance.

[56] CAP, Scope, III(g).

[57] Under CAP, Scope, I, the communications regulated by the CAP are: (a) advertisements in newspapers, magazines, brochures, leaflets, circulars, mailings, e-mails, text transmissions (including SMS and MMS), fax transmissions, catalogues, follow-up literature and other electronic or printed material; (b) posters and other promotional media in public places, including moving images; (c) cinema, video, DVD and Blu-ray advertisements; (d) advertisements in non-broadcast electronic media, including but not limited to: online advertisements in paid-for space (including banner or pop-up advertisements and online video advertisements); paid-for search listings; preferential listings on price comparison sites; viral advertisements; in-game advertisements; commercial classified advertisements; advergames that feature in display advertisements; advertisements transmitted by Bluetooth; advertisements distributed through web widgets and online promotions and prize promotions; (e) marketing databases containing consumers' personal information; (f) promotions in non-broadcast media; (g) advertorials; and (h) advertisements and other marketing communications by or from

and online advertisements and websites that contain 'paid-for marketing communications from or by marketers targeting people in the UK'.[58] It also provides a list of those that are not regulated by the Code. Most notably, the CAP does not apply to 'packages, wrappers and labels'.[59]

Despite the voluntary nature of the CAP, '[t]he vast majority of advertisers, promoters and direct marketers comply with the Code' according to the ASA.[60] Failure to adhere to the Code can result in sanctions. These sanctions include adverse publicity through the publication of a ruling against a marketer, which may in turn result in the withholding of services by contractors. Furthermore, the ASA can require advertisements to be vetted before circulation, and the marketer can be referred to Trading Standards for further action. Broadcasters face more serious sanctions, as consistent failure to comply with the BCAP can result in fines and/or a withdrawal of their licence.[61] An advertisement that is the subject of complaints may be removed from circulation at the ASA's discretion. While these sanctions apply to the advertiser or the broadcaster, no compensation is granted to the individual who made the complaint.

The basis for an individual complaint for unauthorised use of persona can be found in section 3 ('Misleading advertising') and section 6 ('Privacy') of each Code. The key provisions have been classified according to the following themes for ease of reference:

- Use of living persons and caricatures.
- False endorsement.
- Offensive use.

While BCAP uses definitive language, CAP often uses suggestive language as it 'urges' permission to be sought to use persona.

ii. Use of Living Persons and Caricatures

a. BCAP

Under rule 6.1 BCAP:

> Television only – With limited exceptions, living persons *must not* be featured, caricatured or referred to in advertisements without their permission.[62]

companies, organisations or sole traders on their own websites, or in other non-paid-for space online under their control, that are directly connected with the supply or transfer of goods, services, opportunities and gifts, or which consist of direct solicitations of donations as part of their own fund-raising activities.

[58] CAP, Scope, II(c).

[59] CAP, Scope, II(m).

[60] CAP, Preface.

[61] ASA, 'Codes and Rulings – Sanctions' at www.asa.org.uk/codes-and-rulings/sanctions.html (accessed 7 March 2017).

[62] Rule 6.1 BCAP (emphasis added). Exceptions include brief and incidental appearances, such as crowd scenes, and advertisements that refer to a person featured in publications, programmes,

This stringent approach means that the BCAP goes further than passing off as there is no confusion requirement; rather, the approach prohibits misappropriation.

The rule for radio advertisements is not as stringent as the preceding one. Rule 6.2 instructs that if permission has not been obtained, 'a person featured in an advertisement must not be featured in an offensive, adverse or defamatory way'.[63] As to sound-alikes and impersonation, these are allowed if they are 'instantly recognisable and if it could be reasonably expected that the person concerned has no reason to object'.[64] The Code advises seeking legal advice when producing such advertisements.

b. CAP

Rule 6.1 CAP is not as stringent as the BCAP equivalent. It is similar to rule 6.2 BCAP in that it instructs:

> Marketers must not unfairly portray or refer to anyone in an adverse or offensive way unless the person has given the marketer written permission to allow it.[65]

However, it does not go as far as the prohibition in rule 6.1 BCAP. Rather, it 'urges' marketers to seek permission if

(a) referring to or portraying a member of the public or his or her identifiable possessions;
(b) referring to a person with a public profile.

Unlike the BCAP, the CAP does not prohibit the use of living persons, and advertisements that have been the subject of objections have not been judged consistently. This undermines the CAP's ability to protect persona, but it provides leeway to advertisers to use persona without ramifications in some instances. In a complaint that was upheld by the ASA, a security guard lodged a complaint about the use of his photograph to advertise security services.[66] His ex-employer, J&S Security, used his photograph in a leaflet to promote their services. The ex-employer argued that they had obtained oral consent, but this was denied by the guard. The ASA held that the ex-employer had failed to obtain written consent, so the leaflet breached the Code. In contrast, Major Charles Ingram, made notorious by attempting to cheat on the gameshow *Who Wants to be a Millionaire?*, and his wife Diana complained to the ASA (formerly Ofcom) after easyJet used their photographs in an advertisement with the caption, 'No Major fraud required! Lowest fares to the sun …'. Their claim was unsuccessful, as the ASA stated that the Advertising Code recommends obtaining permission when

films and the like, provided that the reference to or portrayal of that person is neither offensive nor defamatory.

[63] Rule 6.2 BCAP ('Privacy').

[64] ibid.

[65] Rule 6.1 CAP ('Privacy').

[66] *J&S Security* (ASA ruling, 30 September 2009).

portraying individuals but does not require it.[67] Furthermore, the image used was in the public domain and the advertisement 'portrayed the Ingrams in a way that was consistent with the verdicts in their recent court case.'[68]

Not all eventualities are addressed by the CAP. Some issues are tackled by the ASA via articles that are accessible under 'Advice and Resources'. In an article entitled 'Privacy: Use of Impersonators and Caricatures', the ASA advised that 'Cheeky or obviously humorous uses of lookalikes that are unlikely to confuse readers about endorsement and are not derogatory to the original celebrity are likely to be acceptable.'[69] In the complaint of *Bedford v The Number*,[70] David Bedford lodged a complaint about a telephone directory producer for using a look-alike of him in an advertisement. The ASA did not ban the advertisement, but rather ordered a publication of the breach of the CAP and the fact that Bedford had not endorsed *The Number*. In another look-alike complaint, Eric Cantona successfully contested an advertisement in 1996 by Molson Beers that featured a look-alike of Cantona to recreate an incident where Cantona, wearing a Manchester United jersey with the collar turned up and his number on it, kicked a fan.[71] In the Cantona complaint, the ASA noted that 'Although the reference did not imply an endorsement of the product, the advertiser had not sought permission from Cantona to portray him in this way.'[72]

The objection to the use of look-alikes in the aforementioned complaints was successful, yet the use of the Ingrams' actual photographs was allowed. The inconsistency in judgments can be attributed to the suggestive language used in the CAP. While this can be beneficial to advertisers willing to test the limits of the Codes, it makes it difficult for individuals to know whether they can use the Codes to protect persona. The absence of legal damages in light of this uncertainty may deter individuals from relying on the Codes.

iii. False Endorsement

a. BCAP

The 'Principle' of section 6 BCAP ('Privacy') states that '[a]dvertisements featuring an individual should not imply that that individual endorses a product if he or she does not'. False endorsement is also dealt with under rule 3.47, which states:

> Advertisements must not claim that the advertiser (or any other entity referred to in the advertisement), the advertisement or the advertised product or service has been approved, endorsed or authorised by any person or body if it has not or without complying with the terms of the approval, endorsement or authorisation.

[67] Boyd, S, 'Image wrongs: Causes of action for misappropriation – Part 2' (2006) 14 *SATLJ* 4.
[68] ibid 4.
[69] ASA, 'Privacy: Use of impersonators and caricatures, Advice Online' (8 April 2014) at www.asa.org.uk/advice-online/privacy-use-of-impersonators-and-caricatures.html (accessed 31 October 2022).
[70] *Bedford v The Number (UK) Ltd* [2004] ILSR SLR-18.
[71] *Molson Scottish Courage Ltd* (ASA ruling, 16 December 1996).
[72] ASA (2014); *Molson* (1996).

Testimonials must not be featured without permission according to rule 3.46 BCAP. Furthermore, under rule 3.1 BCAP, 'advertisements must not materially mislead or be likely to do so'.[73] A similar provision is featured in the CAP, and the significance of this is explained in section I.B.iii.b.

b. CAP

Rule 6.1 CAP advises that written permission should be obtained before 'implying any personal approval of the advertised product', and advises that 'marketers should recognise that those who do not want to be associated with the product could have a legal claim'.[74] This alludes to passing off. However, there is a caveat, which states that 'Prior permission might not be needed if the marketing communication contains nothing that is inconsistent with the position or views of the featured person.'[75]

With regard to testimonials, rule 3.45 CAP states:

> Marketers must hold documentary evidence that a testimonial or endorsement used in a marketing communication is genuine, unless it is obviously fictitious, and hold contact details for the person who … gives it.[76]

Permission is generally required for testimonials, unless the testimonial consists of

> accurate statements taken from a public source, quotations from a publication or references to a test, trial or professional endorsement, research facility or professional journal, which may be acceptable without express permission.[77]

While not directed at use of persona, rule 3.1 states that advertisements must not be misleading. The significance of this rule can be seen in the complaint against Go Groopie Ltd, which featured an advertisement for a skin serum.[78] The advertisement on the website gogroopie.com claimed '[t]reatment already a favourite with celebrities such as Helen Mirren and Jennifer Lopez'. This claim was found to be a violation of rule 3.1 as it was misleading. The ASA ruled that Go Groopie must not display the ad with the misleading claims unless they could be substantiated. The force of this rule shows that there does not necessarily need to be an endorsement; rather, referring to the preference of an individual may be considered misleading if there is no evidence to support the claim.

It is worth noting that an advertisement that purports to contain an endorsement may not be prevented if it is obvious that the person has not endorsed the

[73] Rule 3.1 BCAP ('Misleading Advertising').
[74] Rule 6.1 CAP ('Privacy').
[75] ibid.
[76] Rule 3.45 CAP ('Misleading Advertising').
[77] Rule 3.48 CAP ('Misleading Advertising').
[78] *Go Groopie Ltd* (ASA ruling, 21 August 2013).

product: the CAP has given the examples of Prince Charles (now King) to promote safety eyewear and Cherie Blair to promote beer.[79]

iv. *Offensive Use*

a. BCAP

Rule 6.2 BCAP states:

> Broadcasters must ensure that, if an advertiser has not sought his or her prior permission, a person featured in an advertisement must not be featured in an offensive, adverse or defamatory way.

b. CAP

Advertisers must not feature people in an offensive or adverse way unless permission has been granted, according to rule 6.1 CAP.

v. *Assessment of the Codes*

The BCAP makes it clear that use of persona without permission is generally prohibited, whereas the CAP is aimed at preventing false endorsement and advertisements that portray individuals in an offensive manner, rather than protecting persona per se. This is evidenced by the absence of definitive language regulating living persons, and inconsistent rulings. Permission is 'urged' rather than required by the CAP. This suggestive language allows leeway to advertisers.

While it might be considered a waste of resources if advertisers were to violate the CAP, as the advertisement could be withdrawn from circulation, the risk of this depends on the purpose of the advertisement. If the advertisement is an isolated one that was created to capitalise on a recent event, the CAP will not act as a deterrent because the advertisement would have served its purpose by the time a complaint was made. Even then, there is no guarantee the complaint will be upheld. An intentional violation is possible under the law as well, as an entity may intentionally commit passing off, but the force of the Code is limited as it provides an extra-legal remedy that does not award damages.[80]

[79] ASA, 'Privacy: Implied endorsements' (3 May 2022) at www.asa.org.uk/advice-online/privacy-implied-endorsements.html (accessed 23 January 2023): 'If it is obvious from the context that the celebrity or personality shown has not endorsed the product, the ASA is unlikely to uphold complaints. Examples have included the use of Cherie Blair to promote beer and Prince Charles to promote safety eyewear. If there is a definite implication that an endorsement exists or if it is unclear whether the personality has endorsed a product or service, marketers are in danger of breaching the Code (*Herbametrics Ltd*, 3 July 2002).'

[80] Stallard (1997) 573.

C. Trade Marks

Trade marks are governed by the Trade Marks Act 1994 (TMA 1994). A trade mark must be registered to receive protection. In order to be registered, a mark must be a sign capable of being represented on the register and capable of distinguishing the services of one undertaking from those of another.[81] Infringement occurs if a defendant uses the mark or a similar mark on goods and services, pursuant to section 10 of the 1994 Act. Trade mark law can be useful in protecting a name and signature against unauthorised use that is confusing under section 10(1)–(2). Additionally, if the mark has a reputation, section 10(3) can protect against use that is detrimental to the distinctive character or repute of the mark, or which takes advantage of the repute. The ability to protect against non-confusing uses under section 10(3) allows trade mark law to go further than passing off in protecting persona. However, section 10(3) does not go as far as to prevent misappropriation in the way that a publicity right would, because the mark must have a reputation for the goods and services for which it is registered. The requirement for a reputation under section 10(3) means that this level of protection will only be available to very famous individuals.

Trade marks can be useful in protecting certain aspects of persona: name and signature. These aspects are likely to meet the requirements for registration. As such, individuals can register their names and signatures to prevent confusing use on similar goods and services under section 10(1) and (2) of the TMA 1994. If the provisions on dilution and tarnishment for non-confusing uses under section 10(3) of the Act are applied, trade marks could fill the gap created by the confusion requirement of passing off with regard to name and persona. The effectiveness of this section depends on whether the trade mark 'has a reputation in the United Kingdom'.[82] It is not awareness of the reputation of the individual, but rather awareness of the trade mark as used in the course of trade that is important. As such, while section 10(3) takes a more misappropriation-based approach than passing off and the CAP, it does not go so far as to prevent use of persona altogether.

The classes for which marks can be registered are potentially limited. Generally, marks will be accepted for a wide range of goods and services, but the *Trade Marks Manual* suggests that marks will not be accepted for 'mere image' carriers. 'Mere image carriers' are goods that are described by the mark in question, such as 'posters, photographs transfers and figurines'.[83] An example of a mark that was rejected on this basis is 'Linkin Park'. The band 'Linkin Park'

[81] TMA 1994, s 1.
[82] TMA 1994, s 10(3).
[83] UK Intellectual Property Office, 'Manual of trade marks practice' (14 January 2019) at www.gov.uk/guidance/trade-marks-manual/the-examination-guide (accessed 31 October 2022). 'The examination guide, Part B: Alphabetical list of examination practice, Image Carriers': 'In respect of image carriers such as posters, calendars, photographs, transfers and figurines, the name of the famous person or group is likely to be seen as the subject matter of such goods …'.

attempted to register the band name for posters, but the registration was rejected on the basis that the mark described the goods in question.[84]

i. Assessment of Trade Marks

Trade marks can be used to protect names and signatures. It is unlikely that other aspects of persona would be protected due to the requirements for registration. Furthermore, attempts to register other aspects of persona, such as likeness, would be futile. Even if an individual were able to register her likeness, only the specific likeness or a confusingly similar likeness would be protected. Despite advances in trade mark law to include sounds, voice would not be protected under this regime; only the specific sound clip would receive protection.

D. Copyright

Copyright is governed by the Copyright, Designs and Patents Act 1988 (CDPA 1988). For copyright to subsist, the work must demonstrate the author's own intellectual creation to meet the requirement of originality.[85] The work must be within the term of protection and also fall within the subject matter listed under the CDPA 1988. The defendant's work must relate to the whole or substantial part of the claimant's work, be derived from the claimant's work and be objectively similar to it in order to infringe.[86]

While a claim in copyright infringement for use of a photograph, film or sound recording could be useful, such a claim would only be in relation to the work in question or a substantially similar work. To illustrate, it is worth considering *Fenty* and *Irvine*. In both cases, the defendants had secured the appropriate copyright licence to use the photographs of the claimants. In *Irvine*, Laddie J dismissed the issue of copyright stating that 'There is no question of copyright infringement because the right to use this photograph was purchased from a sporting photograph agency.'[87] Similarly in *Fenty*, Birss J stated that 'A celebrity may control the distribution of particular images in which they own the copyright but that right is specific to the particular photographs in question.'[88] These statements make the limits of copyright clear: it can only be used to protect persona if the individual owns the copyright in a work that has been substantially copied. It does not protect the attributes of persona.

Even if there is an issue of infringement of a copyright work, this is unlikely to aid in the protection of persona because copyright will be owned by the author, or

[84] *Linkin Park LLC's Application* [2006] ETMR 74. See also *Elvis Presley Trade Marks* [1997] RPC 543.

[85] *Pasternak v Prescott* [2022] EWHC 2695 (Ch); *Martin v Kogan* [2017] EWHC 2927 (IPEC); *SAS Institute Inc v World programming Ltd* [2013] EWCA Civ 1482.

[86] CDAP 1988, ss 16 –21.

[87] *Irvine* [2002] [7].

[88] *Fenty* [2013] [2].

the party that has secured a licence or assignment.[89] In the case of photographs, the subject of the work, rather than the author, will seek to protect her attributes (with the exception of 'selfies', assuming the originality criterion is met, where the subject of the photograph is also the author). An exceptional circumstance would be if the photograph had been privately commissioned. Under section 85 of the CDPA 1988, there is a right to privacy of photographs commissioned as private or domestic photographs. The shortcoming of this provision is that the person in the photograph may not be the commissioner.[90]

Copyright does not add to the persona protection regime because it protects copyright works rather than the attributes of persona, and the individual featured is unlikely to be the owner of the copyright work unless she has secured an assignment.

E. Breach of Confidence

There has only been one breach of confidence case in the UK that considered the commercialisation of persona; the 2007 case of *Douglas v Hello! Ltd*.[91] At trial and on appeal, the Douglases were awarded £3,750 for mental distress for invasion of their privacy by publication of unauthorised wedding photographs. This was not further appealed. In the House of Lords, their Lordships had to consider whether the publication of the photographs by *OK!* should be remedied, in light of *Hello!*'s exclusive licence with the Douglases. The commercial agreement between *OK!* and the Douglases played an influential role in the 3:2 majority judgment. Lord Hoffmann applied the traditional breach of confidence test established in *Coco v Clark*[92] and held that the contract granted exclusivity to the photos. The Douglases were entitled to commercialise this exclusivity since they were in 'control of the information'.[93] Lord Hoffmann noted the concern of Lord Nicholls and Lord Walker in their dissents, as they questioned why information that was never intended to be kept secret should be protected by the law of confidence.[94]

The outcome of *Douglas v Hello!* indicates that a party to an exclusive contract may be able to seek redress against a third party who has undermined their exclusivity. This raises the question of whether an exclusive advertising campaign with a celebrity could be protected. On the one hand, the exclusivity of the relationship and the ability of the celebrity to approve of which photographs are used in a campaign would lend itself to *Douglas*-style protection. On the other hand, the

[89] CDPA 1988, s 11.
[90] Sundara Rajan, MT, *Moral Rights: Principles, Practice and New Technology* (Oxford University Press 2011) 105.
[91] *Douglas v Hello! Ltd* [2007] UKHL 21.
[92] *Coco v AN Clark (Engineers) Ltd* [1969] RPC 41.
[93] *Douglas v Hello!* [2007] [118].
[94] ibid [120].

facts of *Douglas* centred around an essentially private event – the couple's wedding. The House of Lords did not enunciate a new cause of action, and did not outline a new test. As such, this case is very fact-specific and not one it would be recommended to rely on due to the uncertainty of the application to different scenarios. It is the only case of its kind to date, and it has yet to be seen whether the courts will move towards protecting persona through *Douglas*-style breach of confidence. Such a move seems unlikely, as the Lords rejected the opportunity to make it. Lord Hoffmann stated:

> There is in my opinion no question of creating an 'image right' or any other unorthodox form of intellectual property. The information in this case was capable of being protected, not because it concerned the Douglases' image any more than because it concerned their private life, but simply because it was information of commercial value over which the Douglases had sufficient control to enable them to impose an obligation of confidence.[95]

F. Defamation

The law on defamation is governed by the common law and the Defamation Act 2013. This statute was introduced as a result of the impact of the Human Rights Act 1998, as it was found that the UK's approach to defamation stifled freedom of expression.[96] The Act introduced a threshold test for determining whether a statement is defamatory. A statement, which means 'words, pictures, visual images, gestures or any other method of signifying meaning',[97] is defamatory if publication causes serious harm to the reputation of the claimant.[98]

If persona is used in a manner that is defamatory, it is likely to be in contravention of the Advertising Codes, which prohibit the offensive use of individuals in all advertising mediums. An example is an advertisement that uses the persona of someone who has spoken out against the product being advertised, such as cigarettes. If the public thinks this person has collaborated with a cigarette brand, she may be perceived as hypocritical. This may give rise to a claim in defamation if the statement is untrue. Relying on defamation could be more advantageous than the Advertising Codes due to the availability of damages. In the past, amateur golfer Cyril Tolley succeeded in his defamation claim against Fry's chocolate, as the perception of commercial exploitation of his persona would have compromised his amateur status.[99] More recently, Kevin Pietersen claimed against Specsavers for using a photograph of him in an advertisement that suggested he

[95] ibid [134].

[96] Jones, M, Dugdale, A and Simpson, M, (eds), *Clerk and Lindsell on Torts* (21st edn, Sweet & Maxwell 2016) § 22-03.

[97] Defamation Act 2013, s 15.

[98] Defamation Act 2013, s 1.

[99] *Tolley v JS Fry & Sons Ltd CA* [1930] 1 KB 467.

cheated in a cricket match.[100] The claim was settled out of court. There have been no other recent cases of this nature, as most defamation cases tend to deal with the publication of unsavoury stories and photographs.[101] Defamation does not generally protect the individual against unauthorised use of persona. The position of defamation is best explained by Bains, who states:

> Defamation law is however not the best means by which to safeguard a celebrity's personality since it does not protect against appropriation and exploitation of one's personality, but only against the criticism and ridicule of their personality.[102]

G. Summary of the UK Approach to Persona Protection

The most useful cause of action for protecting persona in the UK is passing off, but this only applies where there has been a false endorsement that amounts to deception. Mere confusion of consumers is not enough. The BCAP is useful in protecting persona, but the CAP is less useful because it protects against certain uses of persona rather than persona per se. Furthermore, no damages are awarded for breach of the Codes. Neither of these avenues confers a proprietary right to persona. Trade marks can be used for proprietary rights in name and signature, but these are the only two aspects of persona that are likely to meet the registration requirements. Trade marks can protect against confusing uses, or dilution or tarnishment if the mark has a reputation. Copyright, breach of confidence and defamation are too limited in scope to be considered useful in protecting persona.

The UK's piecemeal approach provides limited protection to persona. There is no strict liability cause of action that protects against unauthorised use of persona. Rather, as explained, various causes of action can be utilised when persona is employed in circumstances that would fit within the existing requirements.

The next section will reveal that the US approach, which confers expansive persona protection, facilitates claims against unauthorised uses of persona in many circumstances as well as granting a proprietary right.

II. US Persona Protection

The right of publicity was first recognised in 1953 in the case of *Haelan Laboratories v Topps Chewing Gum*.[103] This case concerned the use of baseball players' photographs on cards by two rival chewing-gum makers. Haelan's

[100] Bolton, P, 'Specsavers say sorry to Kevin Pietersen for Hot Spot row' *The Telegraph* (2 October 2013).
[101] See, eg: *Horan v Express Newspapers* [2015] EWHC 3550 (QB); *Elliott v Rufus* [2015] EWCA Civ 121; *Cooke & Anor v MGN Ltd & Anor* [2014] EWHC 2831 (QB).
[102] Bains (2007) 167.
[103] *Haelan Laboratories Inc v Topps Chewing Gum Inc* 202 F 2d 866 (2d Cir 1953).

predecessor had secured exclusive licences with the players concerned. Its competitor, Topps, secured licences for the same players and used their images on its cards. Some licences were secured through the defendant's agent. In those instances, the defendant was liable for inducing breach of contract. However, other licences were secured through a third party, Russell Publishing Co, which independently secured grants from the players. Because the defendant secured these grants through Russell, it had not committed the alleged offence of knowingly inducing breach of contract.[104] Furthermore, in some instances, Topps had no licence and no authorisation at all from the players.[105]

The defendant in the case argued that that licences secured by the plaintiff were 'a release of liability, because a man has no legal interest in the publication of his picture other than his right of privacy'.[106] The court disagreed with this argument. Recognising a right of publicity, the 2nd Circuit Court stated:

> We think that, in addition to and independent of the right of privacy (which in New York derives from statute), a man has a right in the publicity value of his photograph, ie, the right to grant the exclusive privilege of publishing his picture, such a grant may be validly made 'in gross,' ie without an accompanying transfer of a business or of anything else … This right may be called a 'right of publicity.' For it is common knowledge that many prominent persons (especially actors and ball-players), far from having their feelings bruised through public exposure of their likenesses, would feel sorely deprived if they no longer received money for authorizing advertisements, popularizing their countenances … This right of publicity would usually yield them no money unless it could be made the subject of an exclusive grant which barred any other advertiser from using the pictures.[107]

The 2nd Circuit applied New York law in coming to its decision. The case was remanded and the plaintiff was successful.[108]

Despite the outcome of *Haelan*, it was not until 1984 that the New York Appeals Court found that the right of publicity was part of New York's privacy statute,[109] thus refuting the idea (in New York) that privacy is only suitable for emotional distress.[110] This incorporation was ironic, as it was the unsuitability of privacy that led to the creation of a publicity right. Yet publicity was subsequently subsumed by privacy in New York. In other States, the common law right of publicity is independent from the common law and/or statutory rights to privacy. It was not until 2021 that New York used the terminology of 'publicity', and this terminology has only been used in recognising a statutory post-mortem right.[111]

[104] ibid [868].
[105] ibid.
[106] ibid.
[107] ibid.
[108] Hylton, J, 'Baseball cards and the birth of the right of publicity: Haelan Laboratories v Topps Chewing Gum' (2001) 12(1) *Marq Sports L Rev* 273, 288.
[109] New York Civil Rights Law, Art 5, ss 50 and 51.
[110] *Stephano v News Group Publications Inc* 474 NE 2d 580 (NY 1984) [584].
[111] McCarthy, T and Schechter, R, *Rights of Publicity and Privacy* (Thomson Reuters 2022) § 6:101.

The common law and statutory rights to privacy and publicity are State-based, protecting against misappropriation of persona and conferring proprietary rights. In addition, false endorsement, under section 43(a) of the Lanham Act,[112] is a federal cause of action that protects against confusing uses of persona. Since this cause of action is federal, it will be examined first. Following this, the approach to persona protection in New York and California will be examined.

A. Federal False Endorsement Action

The Lanham Act was originally enacted in 1946.[113] In 1988, it was amended to include the prohibition of false endorsement, codifying existing judicial interpretations of the Act.[114] Section 43(a) of the Lanham Act prohibits the use by any person in commerce of any word, term, name, symbol or device that is likely to cause confusion as to the 'connection or association of such person with another person, or as to the origin, sponsorship, or approval of his or her goods, services, or commercial activities by another person'.[115] This section of the chapter will compare false endorsement against passing off to make the argument that the requirements of confusion and reputation are less onerous than deception and goodwill. The effect of this is that false endorsement under the US Lanham Act is a more versatile tool in protecting persona than is passing off in the UK.

The current approach to confusion under false endorsement is to apply one of several tests, with similar factors, to determine whether there is a likelihood

[112] Lanham Trade Mark Act 1946.

[113] Hortwitz, E and Levi, B, 'Fifty Years of the Lanham Act: A Retrospective of Section 43(a)' (1996) 7(1) *Fordham Intell Prop Media & Ent LJ* 58.

[114] Senate Judiciary Committee, Report 515 – Trade Mark Law Revision Act of 1988, 100th Congress, 2d Session, 40; *Waits v Frito Lay* 978 F 2d 1093 (9th Cir 1992) [1106].

[115] Lanham Act, s 43(a) ('Civil action') provides:

> (1) Any person who, on or in connection with any goods or services, or any container for goods, uses in commerce any word, term, name, symbol, or device, or any combination thereof, or any false designation of origin, false or misleading description of fact, or false or misleading representation of fact, which—
>
> (A) is likely to cause confusion, or to cause mistake, or to deceive as to the affiliation, connection, or association of such person with another person, or as to the origin, sponsorship, or approval of his or her goods, services, or commercial activities by another person, or
>
> (B) in commercial advertising or promotion, misrepresents the nature, characteristics, qualities, or geographic origin of his or her or another person's goods, services, or commercial activities,
>
> shall be liable in a civil action by any person who believes that he or she is or is likely to be damaged by such act.

of confusion.[116] The 9th Circuit uses the *Sleekcraft* test,[117] and other circuits have used a variation of this. The factors in *Sleekcraft* are:

(a) the level of recognition that the plaintiff has among the segment of the society for whom;
(b) the defendant's product is intended;
(c) the relatedness of the fame or success of the plaintiff to the defendant's product;
(d) the similarity of the likeness used by the defendant to the actual plaintiff;
(e) evidence of actual confusion;
(f) marketing channels used;
(g) likely degree of purchaser care;
(h) defendant's intent on selecting the plaintiff; and
(i) likelihood of expansion of the product lines.[118]

The application of these factors can be illustrated by case of *White v Samsung*.[119] Samsung created an advertisement that featured a robot wearing a red dress and blonde wig, standing beside the 'Wheel of Fortune'. Vanna White, the letter turner on the *Wheel of Fortune* gameshow, sued under the right of publicity and false endorsement. In applying the above factors to assess false endorsement, the court reasoned that the strength of the mark related to the recognition of the celebrity by those at whom the Samsung advertisement was directed, and held that White's 'mark', in the form of her persona, was strong. They then considered White's 'goods' to be similar to Samsung's VCRs. On the third factor (c), the similarity of marks, the court held that there was ambiguity: 'On the one hand, all aspects of the robot ad identify White; on the other, the figure is quite clearly a robot, not a human.'

No evidence of actual confusion was presented to address the fourth factor (d). The marketing channels under the fifth factor (e) were found to be the same, as Vanna White has appeared in magazines and the Samsung advertisement also appeared in magazines. For the sixth factor (f), the court found that consumers would exercise a low level of care in determining who endorses VCRs. The intent of the defendant was particularly relevant in finding confusion:

> We do not disagree that defendants intended to spoof Vanna White and 'Wheel of Fortune'. That does not preclude, however, the possibility that the defendants also intended to confuse consumers regarding endorsement. Another ad in the series depicted Morton Downey Jr as a presidential candidate in the year 2008. Doubtless, defendants intended to spoof presidential elections and Mr Downey through this ad. Consumers, however, would likely believe, and would be correct in so believing, that

[116] Other tests include: *Standard & Poor's Corp v Commodity Exchange Inc* 683 F 2d 704 (2d Cir 1982); *Polaroid Corp v Polarad Electronics Corp* 287 F 2d 492 (2d Cir 1961).

[117] *AMF Inc v Sleekcraft Boats* 599 F 2d 341 (9th Cir 1979).

[118] The *Sleekcraft* test was used in: *Jackson v Odenat* 9 F Supp 3d 342 (2014); *Downing v Abercrombie & Fitch* 265 F 3d 994 (9th Cir 2001); *White v Samsung Electronics America Inc* 971 F 2d 1395 (9th Cir 1992).

[119] *White v Samsung* (1992).

> Mr Downey was paid for his permission and was endorsing Samsung products. Looking at the series of advertisements as a whole, a jury could reasonably conclude that beneath the surface humour of the series lay an intent to persuade consumers that celebrity Vanna White, like celebrity Downey, was endorsing Samsung products.[120]

The use of a robot was of a different nature from the Downey advertisement, which featured an actual photograph of Downey. However, the court found that the use of these figures was comparable, as both uses were implying endorsement.

The holding that Samsung both attempted a spoof of White and wanted to imply endorsement is irreconcilable from a UK perspective, and would probably not have resulted in a successful passing-off claim due to the misrepresentation requirement. This indicates that the US is more lenient when it comes to assessing confusion under false endorsement.[121] In contrast, the UK assesses misrepresentation in passing off by determining whether consumers are deceived that a product has been authorised by the claimant. In *Fenty*, Justice Birrs considered the evidence and assessed that 'Many will buy a product because they think [Rihanna] has approved of it. Others will wish to buy it because of the value of the perceived authorisation itself. In both cases they will have been deceived.'[122] This standard is higher than that of false endorsement because 'mere confusion' is not enough. The approach of passing off has remained rooted in the impact on consumers, while false endorsement considers impact on the persona.

The lower standard for confusion in false endorsement as compared to misrepresentation in passing off is also illustrated by the case of *Burck v Mars*.[123] The well-known Naked Cowboy, a New York street performer, brought a false endorsement claim against Mars Inc for an advertisement featuring a blue M&M dressed in the get-up of the Naked Cowboy.[124] The defendants conceded that they satisfied the first three elements of a false endorsement claim, that is, they used the Naked Cowboy's persona in commerce, falsely or misleadingly, representing a connection with the goods, but they denied that the public would be confused as to whether the Naked Cowboy had an association with M&Ms. The court thought differently and held that 'the complaint has alleged sufficient facts to support a false endorsement claim'.[125]

The success of false endorsement actions in situations where confusion is questionable illustrates how much lower the threshold is when compared to passing off. Another noticeable difference between false endorsement and passing off is that false endorsement requires reputation rather than goodwill. To succeed in a claim, a plaintiff's persona must have 'commercial value'.[126] While reputation

[120] ibid [1401].
[121] ibid [1401]. The last factor was not assessed because it did not 'appear apposite to a celebrity endorsement case such as this'.
[122] *Fenty* [2013] [72].
[123] *Burck v Mars Inc* 571 F Supp 2d 446 (SDNY 2008).
[124] ibid.
[125] ibid [9].
[126] *Condit v Star Editorial Inc* 259 F Supp 2d 1046 (ED Cal 2003) [1051]; Beser, J, 'False Endorsement or First Amendment: An analysis of celebrity trade mark rights and artistic expression' (2004) 41 *San Diego L Rev* 1787, 1808.

is an important factor in false endorsement, it is less onerous than goodwill. An illustration of the role of reputation can be seen in the New York case of *Allen v National Video Inc.*[127] Woody Allen claimed that the use of look-alike photographs in magazine and newspaper advertisements, as well as counter cards, constituted false endorsement.[128] The advertisements used disclaimers to say that a look-alike was used but the counter cards did not. He was successful under section 43(a) of the Lanham Act as the court found that, even with the use of look-alikes, the public would be confused into thinking the defendants were associated with the plaintiff. In applying section 43(a), there was no assessment of whether Allen was a trader. Rather, the court noted Allen's reputation had 'significant, exploitable, commercial value'.[129]

Unlike in *Fenty*,[130] there was no discussion of the plaintiff's merchandising and endorsement deals. This is significant, because Allen succeeded on his claim in 1985, whereas in 1997 in the UK, an interlocutory injunction was denied to the pop group ABBA, which sought to prevent a UK party from selling merchandising bearing the name of the group and likenesses of the singers.[131] The application failed on two grounds. First, ABBA did not have any current trading in the UK, thus defeating the goodwill requirement. The group had arranged for a licence for jigsaw puzzles bearing the singers' names and faces, but that licence would come into effect only after the application. The licence was negotiated in September 1976 and would come into effect on 1 January 1977. The application was heard on 2 November 1976. Second, the use of the singers' images on merchandise would not lead the public to believe that they had endorsed the said merchandise. Oliver J opined:

> I do not think anyone reading the advertisements of which complaint is made or indeed receiving the goods described in them could reasonably imagine that all pop stars named in the advertisements were giving their approval to the goods offered or that the defendants were doing anything more than catering for a popular demand among teenagers for effigies of their ideals … To suggest that there is some proprietary right in the plaintiff's name which entitled them to sue simply for its use is contrary to all the English authorities …[132]

It was not until the 1991 case of *Mirage v Counterfeat Clothing*[133] that character merchandising was recognised in the UK as an established activity, and subsequently the reasoning was expanded to persona in *Irvine* in 2003.[134]

[127] *Allen v National Video Inc* 610 F Supp 612 (SDNY 1985).
[128] Allen also brought a claim under the right of publicity, but the court found the false endorsement action more suitable because a look-alike was used rather than a photograph of Allen.
[129] *Allen* [1985].
[130] *Fenty* [2013].
[131] *Lyngstad v Anabas Products Ltd* [1977] FSR 62.
[132] ibid [68].
[133] *Mirage Studios v Counterfeat Clothing Co* [1991] FSR 145.
[134] *Irvine v TalkSport* [2003] EWCA Civ 423.

The interlocutory application in *Anabas* did not proceed to trial, so the UK courts did not have the opportunity to consider the status of passing off with regard to persona until the *Irvine* case.

i. Assessment of False Endorsement

False endorsement provides a high level of protection for persona because the threshold for confusion is apparently low, even though it is meant to protect against deception,[135] and there is a need to show reputation rather than goodwill. In New York, this means that false endorsement offers potentially more extensive persona protection than the right to privacy (discussed in section II.B), as it is not limited to certain aspects of persona. Indeed, Allen and the Naked Cowboy succeeded under false endorsement but not under the right of publicity (termed 'privacy' in New York). In California, false endorsement is arguably more limited than publicity rights due to the confusion requirement. While this may seem contradictory, as it has been argued that the confusion threshold is more akin to misappropriation, the threshold still exists, whereas the very broad publicity rights in California only require there to be a misappropriation. Overall, false endorsement can be used to protect all aspects of persona once there has been a minimum level of confusion, but it should be noted that is does not grant a proprietary right in persona.

B. New York Persona Protection under the Right to Privacy and the Post-Mortem Right of Publicity

Since 1903, sections 50 and 51 of Article 5 of the New York Civil Rights Law have provided persona protection in the form of a right to privacy. This right to privacy essentially performs the function of a publicity right, despite the terminology. Both sections provide similar protection, the main difference being that a violation of section 50[136] is a misdemeanour, whereas section 51[137] provides a cause of action

[135] *Allen* (1985) [625]: 'Application of the act is limited, however, to potential deception which threatens economic interests analogous to those protected by trademark law.'

[136] Section 50 ('Right of privacy') provides 'A person, firm or corporation that uses for advertising purposes, or for the purposes of trade, the name, portrait or picture of any living person without having first obtained the written consent of such person, or if a minor of his or her parent or guardian, is guilty of a misdemeanour.'

[137] Under s 51 ('Action for injunction and for damages'), 'Any person whose name, portrait, picture or voice is used within this state for advertising purposes or for the purposes of trade without the written consent first obtained as above provided may maintain an equitable action in the supreme court of this state against the person, firm or corporation so using his name, portrait, picture or voice, to prevent and restrain the use thereof; and may also sue and recover damages for any injuries sustained by reason of such use and if the defendant shall have knowingly used such person's name, portrait, picture or voice in such manner as is forbidden or declared to be unlawful by section fifty of this article, the jury, in its discretion, may award exemplary damages …'.

in private law. Section 51 is used more often in protecting persona as it allows for the civil claim. More recently, section 50 was amended to include section 50(f), which introduced a civil claim for a post-mortem right of publicity.

Section 51 states the aspects of persona that are protected. Name, portrait, picture and voice are protected against unauthorised use for advertising and/or purposes of trade. Voice was added to section 51 in 1995.[138] Prior to this, claims based on unauthorised use of voice were unsuccessful.[139] In order to use these attributes, written consent must be obtained from the person. Since the right of privacy protects against misappropriation, the best way to discuss this cause of action is by examining the protection conferred to different elements of persona. Since 2021, protection has been granted post-mortem by means of a right of publicity for the deceased under section 50(f) to prevent unauthorised use of name, voice, signature, photograph, likeness and, if likely to deceive, digital replica. At the time of writing, there have no cases have been brought under the new post-mortem right, so in this section we focus on living individuals.[140]

i. Voice

There have been no voice cases since the amendment in 1995, so the scope of 'voice' is unclear.[141]

ii. Name

New York courts have provided varying interpretations of what can be protected under 'name'. In the case of *Pfaudler v Pfaudler Co*, the plaintiff's surname was used by a company for the purposes of advertising their vacuum fermentation.[142] In interpreting the law, Rodenbeck J stated that 'The word "name", as used in the statute, must mean a person's full name. It was evidently the purpose of the Legislature to prevent the use of the full name of a person, by which alone he could be identified.'[143] The restrictive approach has continued to be observed by New York courts. Claims against unauthorised use of stage names[144] and fictitious[145] names have been rejected as being outside the scope of statutory protection.

[138] 1995 NY Laws 674, § 1, came into effect 1 November 1995.

[139] *Maxwell v NW Ayer Inc* 605 NYS 2d 174 (1993); *Tin Pan Apple v Miller Brewing Co* 737 F Supp 826 (SD NY 1990); *Lahr v Adell Chem Co* 300 F 2d 256 (1st Cir 1962).

[140] See Perot, E, 'Post-mortem rights of publicity – A comparison of New York and California' in Rosati, E and Bosher, H (eds), *Developments and Directions in Intellectual Property Law: 20 Years of the IPKat* (Oxford University Press 2023) 348 for discussion of the implications of introducing the post-mortem right of publicity in New York.

[141] Czarnota, P, 'The right of publicity in New York and California: A critical analysis' (2012) 19 *Jeffrey S Moorad Sports LJ* 481, 498.

[142] *Pfaudler v Pfaudler Co* 186 NYS 725 (Sup 1920).

[143] ibid [726].

[144] *Davis v RKO Radio Pictures* 16 F Supp 195 (SDNY 1936).

[145] *Geisel v Poynter Products Inc* 295 F Supp 331(SDNY 1968) [355].

It is possible that a nickname may be protected, but it would have to be 'so notorious to the public that it had come closely and widely identified with the person who bears it'.[146] There have been no successful nickname cases to date. It should be noted that rapper '50 cent' sued Taco Bell for using his performer name but settled the case before it went to trial.[147] It would have been interesting to see whether the court would have treated '50 cent' as the plaintiff's name within the meaning of section 51, as he is more widely known to the public by this moniker than his legal name.

iii. Portrait and Picture

Portrait and picture have been interpreted by the courts as including a 'recognizable likeness'.[148] Likeness is limited to real people and does not include a 'character created or a role performed by a living person'.[149] This explains why the Naked Cowboy's claim against Mars for depicting his likeness on a billboard was denied under the right of privacy but allowed to proceed under false endorsement (see section II.A). There have been other instances of claims succeeding under false endorsement but not privacy due to the interpretation of likeness.

In *Allen*, the claim under the right of privacy failed as the court considered it better suited to the Lanham Act analysis, and because the remedies available under the Lanham Act would be the same as under the right-of-publicity claim. In dealing with the question of when a look-alike would infringe a right of publicity, the court stated:

> [I]f defendants had used, for example, a clearly recognizable painting or cartoon of the plaintiff, it would certainly constitute a 'portrait or picture' within the meaning of the statute. The case of a look-alike, however, is more problematic. A painting, drawing or manikin has no existence other than as a representation of something or someone; if the subject is recognizable, then the work is a 'portrait.' Defendant Boroff, however, is not a manikin. He is a person with a right to his own identity and his own face. Plaintiff's privacy claim therefore requires the court to answer the almost metaphysical question of when one person's face, presented in a certain context, becomes, as a matter of law, the face of another.[150]

The court went on to state that where a look-alike 'seems indistinguishable from the real person and the context of the advertisement clearly implies that he or she is the real celebrity, a court may hold as a matter of law that the look-alike's face is a "portrait or picture" of the plaintiff', citing the case of *Onassis v Christian Dior*

[146] *DeClemente v Columbia Pictures Industries Inc* 860 F Supp 30 (EDNY 1994) [44].

[147] Ware, H, 'Taco you very much, 50 cent wins suit' *New York Post* (24 November 2009) at http://nypost.com/2009/11/24/taco-you-very-much-50-cent-wins-suit/ (accessed 10 September 2019).

[148] *Burck v Mars, Inc* 571 F Supp 2d 466 (SDNY 2008) [451]; *Onassis v Christian Dior-New York* 472 NYS 2d 254 (NY Sup Ct 1984) [261]; *Young v Greneker Studios* 26 NYS 2d 357 (NY Sup Ct 1941).

[149] *Burck v Mars Inc* (2008) [449].

[150] *Allen* (1985) [622].

NY Inc.[151] In the case of *Onassis*, Jacqueline Kennedy successfully claimed that her right of privacy was infringed by an advertisement that used a look-alike, because that advertisement gave the impression that the plaintiff had actually appeared in it:

> It is the over-all impression being made that counts. The statute necessarily contemplates that a depiction may not be precise, for the words 'portrait or picture' comprehend a sketch, a cartoon, or a caricature which selectively omits some features and accentuates others. There are then points of resemblance and points of difference and distortion, but if done well there is instant recognition. What difference if a sketch is used instead of a look-alike model in connection with a commercial promotion? The end result is the same – trading on the name or features of another and the unwarranted commercial exploitation of a person who has not consented to be commercially exploited.[152]

This explanation may appear counterintuitive, as it indicates that a sketch might be more readily caught under the right of privacy than a look-alike due to the inevitable physical differences of a look-alike, but the *Allen* case explained that

> the question … is not whether some, or even most people will be *reminded* of the plaintiff when they see this advertisement. In order to find that the photograph contains plaintiff's 'portrait or picture,' the court would have to conclude that most persons who could identify an actual photograph of plaintiff would be likely to think that this was actually his picture.[153]

In a recent case concerning likeness, Rockstar Games was sued by Lindsay Lohan and Karen Gravano in New York for using their likenesses to create characters in the *Grand Theft Auto* video game.[154] The claims were rejected in the New York court because the video game did not use their actual likeness and the use did not fall under the statutory definition of 'trade' or 'advertising' in the New York statute, as a video game is a work of fiction and satire.[155]

iv. *Life Story*

The New York right to privacy protects certain aspects of persona. It does not, however, protect the right to 'life story,' as this falls within the ambit of First

[151] *Onassis v Christian Dior NY Inc* 472 NYS 2d 254 (S Ct NY Co 1983).

[152] ibid [262].

[153] *Allen* (1985) [624].

[154] *Lohan v Take-Two Interactive Software Inc* 31 NY3d 111 (2018); *Gravano v Take-Two Interactive Software Inc* 142 AD 3d 776 [1st Dept 2016]; Love, F, 'Lindsay Lohan sues "Grand Theft Auto V" makers for allegedly using her likeness in video game' *Newsday* (2 July 2014) at www.newsday.com/entertainment/celebrities/lindsay-lohan-sues-grand-theft-auto-v-makers-for-allegedly-using-her-likeness-in-video-game-1.8641134 (accessed 29 July 2019).

[155] *Lohan* (2018); *Gravano* (2016); Kain, E, 'Court tosses out Lindsay Lohan's "Grand Theft Auto V" lawsuit' *Forbes* (2 September 2016) at www.forbes.com/forbes/welcome/?/sites/erikkain/2016/09/02/court-tosses-out-lindsay-lohans-grand-theft-auto-v lawsuit/&toURL=http://www.forbes.com/sites/erikkain/2016/09/02/court-tosses-out-lindsay-lohans-grand-theft-auto-v-lawsuit/&refURL=&referrer=#7fc66c7e6f2c (accessed 29 July 2019).

Amendment protection. Nonetheless, a 2013 claim questioned the correct approach to this concept. In the case of *Porco*, Lifetime Entertainment Services made a television film about a murderer but fictionalised some aspects of the account.[156] The convicted murderer, Chris Porco, sued from jail. Lifetime was restrained from airing the movie until the order was reversed in 2014. Lifetime then succeeded on its motion to dismiss in 2015, but this was reversed in 2017. In May 2020, the Supreme Court of New York dismissed both Lifetime and Porco's summary judgment applications. The appellate court cited *Messenger*, which stated that 'a work may be so infected with fiction, dramatization or embellishment that it cannot be said to fulfil the purpose of the newsworthiness exception'.[157] The court ruled that it was a question for the jury whether the film was 'materially and substantially fictitious', so as to bring it outside of the realm of the newsworthiness protection and thus constitute a right of privacy infringement.

An amicus brief was filed in October 2020 by several organisations, including The Authors Guild and the Media Coalition Foundation. The brief argued that the 'materially and substantially fictious' standard established by the trial court 'unduly expanded New York's limited right of privacy/publicity, and thereby chilled the First Amendment rights of authors, publishers, booksellers'.[158] In June 2021, the appellate court reversed the order and granted summary judgment in favour of Lifetime.[159] In applying *Messenger*, the court noted that the newsworthiness exception applied to movies and other types of expressive works.[160] The court stated, however, that where a film is 'substantially fictionalized', it will fall outside the remit of the newsworthiness exception because it would be 'an attempt to trade on the persona of the plaintiff'.[161] The court found that 'the sensational facts of the crime, the investigation and the trial of Christopher Porco are indisputably events of public interest, and the film therefore qualifies as newsworthy',[162] reaffirming the *Messenger* position.

C. California Persona Protection

California has both a statutory and common law right of publicity. As of 1972, section 3344(a) of the California Civil Code protects name, voice, signature, photograph and likeness[163] against use 'in any manner, on or in products, merchandise,

[156] *Porco v Lifetime Entertainment Services* (2017) 147 AD 3d 1253.
[157] *Messenger v Gruner and Jahr Printing and Publishing* 93 NY 2d 948 (1999).
[158] *Porco v Lifetime Entertainment Services LLC* (2020) Appellate Division – Third Department Case No 531681 Brief of American Booksellers Association et al as Amici Curiae.
[159] *Porco v Lifetime Entertainment Services* 150 NYS 3d 380 (2021).
[160] ibid.
[161] ibid [383].
[162] ibid [385].
[163] Greenberg, M and Lovitz, M, 'Right of Publicity and the intersection of copyright and trade mark law' (2012) *GGU Law Digital Commons*, Paper 484, 4.

or goods, or for the purposes of advertising or selling, or soliciting purchases of, products, merchandise, goods or services'. Section 3344(e) clarifies that use in a commercial medium will not require consent 'solely because the material containing such use is commercially sponsored or contains paid advertising'. It is a question of fact as to whether the attribute 'was so directly connected with the commercial sponsorship or with the paid advertising as to constitute a use for which consent is required under subdivision (a)'. The limitations of the right are made clear in section 3344(d), which states that the protected attributes can be used without consent 'in connection with any news, public affairs, or sports broadcast or account, or any political campaign'.

Section 3344.1 provides a post-mortem right of publicity with a term of 70 years after the death of the person. This right is similar to the right of publicity for living persons, but there are two main differences. First, in order to claim damages for infringement, the successor in interest or the licensee must register her claim to the right of publicity of the deceased pursuant to section 3344.1(f). The deceased's publicity rights 'are property rights, freely transferable or descendible, in whole or in part, by contract or by means of any trust or any other testamentary instrument' according to section 3344.1.(b). Second, the attributes of the individual (name, voice, signature, photograph and likeness) must have had commercial value at the time of the person's death, or have become valuable because of her death. It is not required that the person used her attributes commercially during her lifetime.

i. Name

There has been little case law on name, so it is unclear whether fictional names and nicknames are protected under the California statute. However, the case of *Abdul-Jabbar* confirmed that 'name' under the statute 'is not limited to present or current use'.[164] In that case, basketball player Kareem Abdul-Jabbar, formerly known as Lew Alcindor, brought a claim against GMC for using his birth name in an advertisement; GMC claimed that Alcindor could not rely on the right of publicity because he had abandoned his name. The district court accepted this argument, but the court of appeal rejected it, stating that 'To the extent GMC's use of the plaintiff's birth name attracted television viewers' attention, GMC gained a commercial advantage.'[165]

ii. Voice

The statutory right applies only to actual voice and does not include sound-alikes.[166]

[164] *Abdul-Jabbar v GMC* 85 F 3d 407 (9th Cir 1996) (formerly Lew Alcindor).
[165] ibid.
[166] *Midler v Ford Motor Co* 849 F 2d 460 (9th Cir 1988) [463]: 'California Civil Code section 3344 is also of no aid to Midler. The statute affords damages to a person injured by another who uses the person's "name, voice, signature, photograph or likeness, in any manner." The defendants did not

iii. Photograph

A plaintiff claiming infringement of the right of publicity by use of a photograph must be 'readily identifiable' in the photograph. Photograph includes 'any photograph or photographic reproduction, still or moving, or any videotape or live television transmission, of any person, such that the person is readily identifiable'.[167] A person is 'readily identifiable' if 'one who views the photograph with the naked eye can reasonably determine that the person depicted in the photograph is the same person who is complaining of its unauthorized use'.[168]

iv. Likeness

Likeness is difficult to define and must be approached on a case-by-case basis. In *Newcombe v Adolf Coors Co*, Coors Brewing Company published an advertisement that featured a drawing of a pitcher on a baseball field and a glass of beer.[169] Newcombe claimed the drawing was based on his likeness as evidenced by the distinctive stance. Newcombe, a recovering alcoholic, strongly objected to his alleged depiction in the advertisement. The appeal court, considering the summary judgment entered against Newcombe by the trial court, borrowed the definition of 'readily identifiable' used for photographs from the statute: 'in order to constitute Newcombe's likeness, the pitcher depicted in the advertisement must be readily identifiable as Newcombe'.[170] The court held that the use of Newcombe's likeness was a triable issue of fact and thus reversed the summary judgment on this issue.

Another case that considered the meaning of 'likeness' involved a robotic depiction. The court held that a robot could fall within the definition of likeness if sufficiently detailed.[171] In the case of *Wendt v Host International*, the defendants secured a licence from the producers of the television series *Cheers* to create themed airport lounges based on the series. The defendants created robots based on the likenesses of actors from the series and placed them in the lounges.[172] Generally, the level of detail required to be considered 'likeness' is not clear, as the court in *White v Samsung* rejected White's statutory publicity right claim against Samsung for using a robot dressed in her customary red dress and with blonde

use Midler's name or anything else whose use is prohibited by the statute. The voice they used was Hedwig's, not hers. The term "likeness" refers to a visual image not a vocal imitation. The statute, however, does not preclude Midler from pursuing any cause of action she may have at common law; the statute itself implies that such common law causes of action do exist because it says its remedies are merely "cumulative."'.

[167] California Civil Code, s 3344(a)(b).

[168] California Civil Code, s 3344(a)(b)(1).

[169] *Newcombe v Adolf Coors Co* 157 F 3d 686 (9th Cir 1998) [692]–[693].

[170] ibid.

[171] *Wendt v Host Intern Inc* 125 F 3d 806 (9th Cir 1997) [810].

[172] ibid.

hair, for falling outside the scope of the right.[173] However, the court in *Wendt*, in referring to their decision in *White*, noted that 'we specifically held open the possibility that a manikin moulded to Vanna White's precise features, or one that was a caricature or bore an impressionistic resemblance to White might become a likeness for statutory purposes'.[174] The judgments in these cases indicate that likeness is to be assessed according to the degree of resemblance on a case-by-case basis.

In a series of cases concerning use of likeness in video games (*Re NCAA Student-Athlete Name & Licensing Litigation*[175] and *Davis v Electronic Arts*[176]), the likenesses and names of college athletes were virtually depicted. It was clear that the characters in the video games were based on the athletes. Since video games are First Amendment works, the California court applied the 'transformative use test', which considers whether the work in question has 'transformed' the persona to an extent that the use should be 'immunized from liability for right of publicity infringement'.[177] This test, developed in 2001, is used in California to determine whether an expressive work infringes the right of publicity.[178] The video games failed the 'transformative use' test[179] because they recreated the plaintiffs in so far as possible. A similar outcome was arrived at in *No Doubt v Activision*, as the court opined that the depictions of the members of the band were 'pure mimicry' (the case was settled after a second appeal).[180] In contrast, in *Kirby v Sega of America Inc*, a celebrity was unsuccessful in her claim for infringement of her right of publicity because the character in the game was considered transformative as it was not a literal depiction of the plaintiff: there were physical differences, the hair-style and outfits were different, the character in the game was a space-age reporter rather than a singer and the character's dance moves were dissimilar to those of the plaintiff.[181]

In contrast to the statutory right that protects named elements of persona, the common law right of publicity protects 'identity', which has been interpreted more broadly than the statutory right. However, the California common law right is limited to living persons, unlike the statutory right, which exists post-mortem.[182]

[173] *White v Samsung* (1992).
[174] *Wendt v Host* (1997) [810].
[175] *Re NCAA Student-Athlete Name & Licensing Litigation* 724 F 3d 1268 (9th Cir 2013) (*Keller*).
[176] *Davis v Electronic Arts* 775 F 3d 1172 (9th Cir 2015).
[177] McCarthy (2022) § 8:73.
[178] *Comedy III Productions v Saderup* 25 Cal 4th 387 (2001).
[179] There are five factors used by the court to determine whether a use is transformative: (i) Literal depictions are unlikely to be transformative. Conventional artistic choices are not enough. (ii) If the celebrity image is 'the very sum and substance' of the work rather than the 'raw materials from which an original work is synthesized', it is unlikely to be transformative. (iii) Work which is 'primarily the defendant's own expression rather than the celebrity's likeness' is likely to be transformative. (iv) It needs to be considered whether the elements that dominate the work are literal and imitative or creative based on quantitative assessment. (v) If the marketability of the work is primarily a result of the celebrity depicted, it is unlikely to satisfy the test.
[180] *No Doubt v Activision Publishing Inc* 192 Cal App 4th 1018 (2011) [1033].
[181] *Kirby v Sega of America Inc* 144 Cal App 4th 47 (2006).
[182] *Lugosi v Universal Pictures* 603 P 2d 425 (Cal 1979) [428]; *Bruce Lee Enterprises LLC v AVELA Inc* 2011 WL 1327137 (SDNY 2011).

The common law right was first recognised in 1974 in the case of *Motschenbacher v RJ Reynolds Tobacco Co*,[183] two years after the introduction of the statutory right of publicity. The court stated that 'the California appellate courts would, in a case such as this one, afford legal protection to an individual's proprietary interest in his own identity'.[184] However, the court did not label this protection, as it stated it was unsure whether the protection should be termed 'privacy', 'property' or 'publicity'.[185] Identity was given a broad interpretation in this case, as the plaintiff's features were not visible. Rather, the aspect of his identity that was appropriated was his distinctive race car.

The California Court of Appeals subsequently outlined the elements necessary for proving infringement of the common law right of publicity in the case of *Eastwood v Superior Court*:

1. The defendant's use of the plaintiff's identity;
2. The appropriation of the plaintiff's name or likeness to defendant's advantage commercially or otherwise;
3. Lack of consent;
4. Resulting injury.[186]

The broader scope of the common law right of publicity compared to the statutory right of publicity is best illustrated by the case of *White v Samsung*.[187] The Court of Appeal stated:

> The district court dismissed White's claim … reasoning that defendants had not appropriated White's 'name or likeness' with their robot ad. We agree that the robot ad did not make use of White's name or likeness. However, the common law right of publicity is not so confined.[188]

In finding infringement, the Court of Appeal noted other decisions in which one of the attributes protected by the statute was not appropriated but the identity of the plaintiff was used to make a commercial gain. These included the use of a race car,[189] a sound-alike[190] and a catchphrase:[191]

> It is not important how the defendant has appropriated the plaintiff's identity, but whether the defendant has done so. *Motschenbacher*, *Midler*, and *Carson* teach the impossibility of treating the right of publicity as guarding only against a laundry list of specific means of appropriating identity.[192]

[183] *Motschenbacher v RJ Reynolds Tobacco Co* 498 F 2d 821 (9th Cir 1974).
[184] ibid [825].
[185] ibid [827].
[186] *Eastwood v Superior Court for Los Angeles County* 149 Cal App 3d 409(Ct App 1983) [417].
[187] *White v Samsung* (1992).
[188] ibid [1379].
[189] *Motschenbacher* (1974).
[190] *Midler* (1988).
[191] *Carson v Here's Johnny Portable Toilets Inc* 698 F 2d 831 (6th Cir 1983).
[192] *White v Samsung* (1992) [1398].

The court went on to explain the policy aims of the common law right:

> Indeed, if we treated the means of appropriation as dispositive in our analysis of the right of publicity, we would not only weaken the right but effectively eviscerate it. The right would fail to protect those plaintiffs most in need of its protection. Advertisers use celebrities to promote their products. The more popular the celebrity, the greater the number of people who recognize her, and the greater the visibility for the product. The identities of the most popular celebrities are not only the most attractive for advertisers, but also the easiest to evoke without resorting to obvious means such as name, likeness, or voice.[193]

v. Life Story

Neither the common law nor the statutory right of publicity in California protects the right to 'life story'. However, recent cases have questioned how courts should approach these cases. In the case of *Sarver v Chartier*, a war veteran sued the producers of *Hurt Locker*, as he claimed the film was based on his life experiences. The case was dismissed under California's Strategic Lawsuit Against Public Participation statute (SLAPP) as, 'The Hurt Locker is not speech proposing a commercial transaction.'[194] In contrast, the superior court in *De Havilland* denied a motion to strike under SLAPP as the work, a docudrama entitled *Feud*, was not transformative, because 'the Defendants admit that they wanted to make the appearance of Plaintiff as real as possible'.[195]

Like *Porco* in New York (see section II.B.iv), the *De Havilland* case and the failure of the producer's motion to strike caused much tension in the production sector. The International Documentary Association filed an amicus brief in support of the defendants, FX Networks and Pacific 21 Entertainment Group. The brief argued that the failure to find the documentary transformative would impair documentary film making, and cited *Dora v Frontline Video*[196] in support of the proposition that finding infringement would be contrary to the First Amendment. The application of the right of publicity to television and movies was first considered in *Guglielmi*,[197] but this case failed because the claim was brought on behalf of a deceased individual, and post-mortem protection was not available at that point. However, when post-mortem protection was recognised via the California Celebrities Rights Act, an exception was included for audiovisual works, whether fiction or non-fiction.[198] Several cases subsequently confirmed that being portrayed in a film does not infringe the right of publicity.[199]

[193] ibid [1399].

[194] *Sarver v Chartier* 813 F 3d 891 (9th Cir 2016) [905].

[195] *De Havilland v FX Networks LLC* Case No BC667011 (2017) Ruling on Defendant's Motion to Strike (Anti-SLAPP).

[196] *Dora v Frontline Video Inc* 15 Cal App 4th 536 (1993).

[197] *Guglielmi v Spelling-Goldberg Productions* 25 Cal 3d 860 (1979).

[198] California Civil Code, s 3344.1(a)(2).

[199] See *Taylor v Nat'l Broadcasting Co* 22 Media L Rep 2433 (Cal Super Ct 1994); *Hicks v Casablanca Records* 464 F Supp 426 (SDNY 1978); *Tyne v Time Warner Entertainment Co* 901 So 2d 802 (Fla 2005);

The Court of Appeal in California restored the status quo and noted that failure of a production to satisfy the transformative use test 'would render actionable all books, films, plays, and television programs that accurately portray real people. Indeed, the more realistic the portrayal, the more actionable the expressive work would be.'[200] The Court therefore found the film to be entitled to First Amendment protection.[201]

III. Legal Regulation in Theory versus Practice

The common law right of publicity coupled with the statutory right of publicity equate to expansive persona protection in California. While the New York privacy right is more limited, and the contours of the post-mortem right of publicity have not yet been tested, the federal Lanham Act accounts for the difference and results in both States having expansive persona protection. The extent of protection available to potential claimants is comparatively greater than that in the UK. Yet, for the most part, this divergence in protection has not resulted in different behaviours in commercialisation practices. When the divergence becomes impactful is in the approach to dispute resolution: US claimants have more possible causes of action on which to base a claim. The strict liability approach to the right of publicity provides an easily accessible avenue to redress when persona is used without authorisation. Furthermore, the threshold for confusion under false endorsement is lower than misrepresentation under passing off. This lower threshold verges on protection against misappropriation, thus further bolstering the legal avenues for persona protection in the US.

This book proceeds by examining empirical data collected across four industries that have often utilised persona: advertising; merchandising; film and television; and sports video games. To conclude this chapter, the way in which the law should work based on the analysis presented is considered against the findings of the way in which the industries operate in reality.

A. Advertising Industry

In terms of the advertising industry, in the UK, permission only needs to be sought in accordance with the law of passing off where it is clear that the brand is trying to convey that the person is endorsing the product or service. As for the Advertising Codes, permission should be sought if a living person is being used,

Sarver v Chartier 813 F 3d 891 (9th Cir 2016); Wander, P, 'First Amendment supports uncensored fictionalised stories about celebrities: De Havilland v FX Networks LLC' (2018) 29(8) *Ent L Rev* 257.

[200] *De Havilland v FX Networks LLC* 21 Cal App 5th 845 (2018) [850].

[201] ibid [870]–[871].

but permission is not required for non-broadcast advertisements; ASA rulings are inconsistent on this point. Interestingly, chapter 3 will reveal that permission is sought more often than is strictly required by passing off, due to the perception of litigation risk as well as the blurring between endorsement and illustrative advertisements,[202] while little heed is paid to the Advertising Codes as advertisers are unconcerned about potential ASA consequences. Exclusive endorsement deals are respected despite the fact that it is only trade marks that confer a proprietary right that can be licensed and enforced against third parties.

As for the US, permission needs to be sought if using persona in any advertisement. Exclusive endorsement deals are respected because it is not considered worthwhile to undermine these deals, rather than because it would be an infringement to do so. While the law can be used to protect the proprietary rights embodied in such deals, the law was not cited as an influence by the lawyers interviewed.

B. Merchandising Industry

In the UK, passing off is applicable to and influential on modern merchandising, which involves collaborating with individuals to create a branded product.[203] It has limited application in the traditional merchandising industry, which merely requires use of a photograph or signature, yet high-street merchandisers seek permission even when they are not required to do so. Alternative merchandisers, usually smaller entities, who may not have access to legal advice and sell in market stalls or on online marketplaces, do not seek permission and are not concerned about the circumstances in which passing off might apply.

In the US, permission must be sought for using persona on merchandising, but only high-street merchandisers do this. Alternative merchandisers are not influenced by the law, despite its applicability.

C. Film and Television Production and Video-Game Development Industries

For both video games and films, different approaches taken in New York as compared to California can cause confusion as to when permission should be sought to use persona. In New York, a video game was considered as falling outside the remit of the statute; whereas in California, video games have been found to infringe where the use of persona is not transformative. For films, *Porco* in New York indicated that too much fictionalisation would preclude a successful

[202] Different types of advertisements will be discussed in ch 5.

[203] Mooro, A, 'Why 2016 was the year we became obsessed with celeb merch' *Refinery29* (13 December 2016) at www.refinery29.uk/rise-of-celebrity-merchandise-2016 (accessed 12 September 2018). The distinction between traditional and modern merchandising is discussed in ch 6.

'newsworthiness' defence; while in California, the film *Hurt Locker* was protected by anti-SLAPP in *Sarver v Chartier* in 2016, whereas this motion was initially rejected in *De Havilland*. These recent developments and inconsistencies in the law have fed in to the behaviour of obtaining 'life story rights'. Permission is not required in any jurisdiction to use persona in films, yet a behaviour of seeking permission for persona where it is likely to be given has arisen in the US. This behaviour has also permeated the UK because of the global nature of this industry. Conversely, there is a behaviour of not seeking permission where it is unlikely to be given, because it would be futile to do so.

The video game industry is also global in nature. Until recently, there was no obvious legal requirement to seek permission to use persona in video games, yet there is a behaviour of this kind in operation. Recent developments in US case law indicate that permission can be legally required under the right of publicity in California as a result of the *NCAA Litigation*, but there have been no similar developments in New York as *Lohan* was unsuccessful. However, due to the distribution of video games, the California approach must be heeded.

D. Industry Summary

In summary, none of the behaviours that will be observed in the upcoming chapters align precisely with the law in the UK, as they often go beyond what is legally required in terms of seeking permission to use persona, or pay little heed to the Advertising Codes. While the permission requirements are so stringent in the US that behaviours often do reflect the law, they also go beyond what is legally required in certain industries – in particular, the film industry and, until recent changes indicated that permission would be necessary, the video game industry.

3

What Influences Behaviour?

Introduction: Influences on Behaviour

The interviews conducted for this book revealed that behaviours relating to the commercialisation of persona, whether permission-based or not, are influenced by several factors. The legal regulation discussed in the previous chapter plays an undeniable role in decision making, but in addition, the desire to form relationships via contract and the accepted industry practices that have resulted in social norms are also influential. These influences are overlapping and porous, a matter that is elaborated upon more fully in section IV. This chapter will examine these influences with the aim of establishing an analytical framework for the industry chapters that follow.

The legal regulation of persona, the utilisation of contracts and the role of social norms contribute to a complex system of commercialisation of persona. Subsequent chapters will therefore attempt to look behind the practices encountered in fieldwork to consider the influences attached to observed behaviours. Behaviours based on seeking permission are influenced heavily by the desire to collaborate via contract, and would likely subsist regardless of the legal framework because of how developments in technology and marketing necessitate collaboration with individuals to create the best product possible to maximise on para-social relationships. This is not to say that law does not influence contracting, as contracts are also used to minimise liability. Rather, contracts also perform the role of securing desirable benefits that exist independently of the law. Additionally, it is necessary to seek permission to use persona to send a signal that will ensure future collaboration, and a positive reception of the product by the public, in accordance with social norms. On the other hand, behaviours based on not seeking permission exist in both jurisdictions because, in some situations, none of the influences are applicable, the parties instead choosing to take a calculated risk or simply not being subject to the influence.

In the fieldwork, a distinction emerged between the transactional sphere and the dispute resolution sphere. In the transactional sphere, multiple influences may be attributed to a single behaviour. While law is not the sole driver of behaviour in the transactional sphere, in the dispute resolution sphere, the substantive law discussed in chapter 2 and threats of litigation and fear of expansion of existing law are the primary influences. This leads to a sharp difference in the approach to dispute resolution in the UK as contrasted with the US. The examination of dispute resolution in the next chapter reveals that the different legal frameworks result in more avenues for redress for US plaintiffs as compared with their UK counterparts.

This chapter is divided into four further sections. Section I examines theories of why people comply with the law. Section II examines the role of contracts in the commercialisation of persona. While contracts are a legal mechanism, they are treated as distinct from law, as law is used to refer to state-imposed obligations (whether arising in statute or common law), whereas contracts are entered into voluntarily. Often, law may influence the desire to secure a contract, but the perceived benefits of collaboration are arguably as influential. Section III provides an overview of social norms, an influence that has arisen because of industry practices alongside legal regulation. Finally, section IV explains how these influences, while distinct concepts, have porous boundaries.

I. The Influence of Law

'Law', or the 'legal framework', refers to the statutory and common law obligations imposed on individuals and legal persons that were discussed in chapter 2. This chapter instead focuses on a different question: Why do people comply with the law? And on the inverse question: Why do people disobey the law? It is worth exploring this latter question, as the legal framework in chapter 2 is only effective if it is complied with. Furthermore, answering this question sheds light on the different variations of law that can influence behaviour. It is not just substantive law but also the threat of litigation, as well as fear of expansion of the law, that can impact behaviour. While these variations of law will be considered in the context of industries in subsequent chapters, the main theories as to why parties comply with law are deterrence, legitimacy and morality. Deterrence is the most relevant theory in persona regulation, as empirical data revealed that parties in both the US and the UK fear legal sanctions if persona is used without permission. Morality is of relevance to the US with regard to the right of publicity, where there is a feeling that individuals have a right to own their identities and control commercialisation, but no similar finding was made in the UK in connection with the existing legal framework. Legitimacy is not examined, as legitimacy considers the validity of sources of law, whereas the fieldwork focused on the impact of existing law.[1] In contrast to the theories of compliance, parties may disobey the law because: (i) they choose to do so based on a cost–benefit analysis and take a calculated risk; (ii) they think they will not be caught; or (iii) they are ignorant of the law.

[1] For an examination of the legitimacy theory, see: Tyler, T, *Why People Obey the Law* (Princeton University Press 1990); Tyler, T, 'Psychological Perspectives on Legitimacy and Legitimation' (2006) 57 *Annual Review of Psychology* 375; Jackson, J et al, 'Why do People Comply with the Law?: Legitimacy and the Influence of Legal Institutions' (2012) 52 *The British Journal of Criminology* 1051.

A. Law as a Deterrent

Deterrence theory suggests that individuals will comply with the law because they fear legal sanctions.[2] The literature on deterrence theory generally focuses on criminal sanctions,[3] although there has been an examination of sanctions in copyright law and tax evasion.[4] The efficacy of legal sanctions depends on whether there is a perceived risk of litigation. Several studies have found that legal sanctions do not deter copyright infringement.[5] In 2003, Jensen found that Internet users routinely infringed copyright, despite the risks of damages, an account of profits and criminal liability.[6] She noted that the now defunct file-sharing website Napster was utilised by at least 30 million people to gain access to works infringing copyright.[7] In 2014, Burleson noted that 'file sharing has now continued undeterred for over a decade'.[8] The copyright infringement described in the aforementioned studies is committed by the general public, who may be ignorant of the law or be aware of the law but choose to disregard it.

Sanctions are more likely to be effective if there is a perceived risk of litigation. This perceived risk has been termed the 'shadow of the law', because law acts as an influence on behaviour but litigation is rarely resorted to.[9] It is worth noting that this terminology ('shadow of the law') is usually confined to the field of law and social norms, yet there have been several articles on the role of law in trade mark and copyright enforcement that suggest that the force of the law acts

[2] Williams, K and Hawkins, R, 'Perceptual Research on General Deterrence: A Critical Review' (1986) 20 *L & Socy Rev* 545; Tyler, T, 'Procedural fairness and compliance with the law' (1997) 133 *Swiss Journal of Economics and Statistics* 219.

[3] Nagin, DS, 'Criminal Deterrence Research at the Outset of the Twenty-First Century' (1998) 23 *Crime and Justice: A Review of Research* 1; Sampson, R and Cohen, J, 'Deterrent Effects of Police on Crime: A Replication and Theoretical Extension' (1998) 22 *L & Socy Rev* 163; Paternoster, R and Simpson, S, 'Sanction Threats and Appeals to Morality: Testing a Rational Choice Theory of Corporate Crime' (1997) 30 *L & Socy Rev* 549; Levitt, S, 'The Effect of the Prison Population Size on Crime Rates: Evidence from Prison Overcrowding Litigation' (1996) 111 *Quarterly Journal of Economics* 319; Bachman, R, Paternoster, R and Ward, S, 'The Rationality of Sexual Offending: Testing a Deterrence/Rational Choice Conception of Sexual Assault' (1992) 26 *L & Socy Rev* 343; Blumstein, A, Cohen, J and Nagin, D, *Deterrence and Incapacitation: Estimating the Effects of Criminal Sanctions on Crime Rates* (National Academy of Sciences 1978).

[4] Kagan, R, 'On the Visibility of Income Tax Law Violations' in Roth, J and Scholz, J (eds), *Taxpayer Compliance*, vol 2 (University of Pennsylvania Press 1989) 76.

[5] Jensen, C, 'The More Things Change, the More They Stay the Same: Copyright, Digital Technology, and Social Norms Note' (2003) 56 *Stan L Rev* 531; Lunceford, B and Lunceford, S, 'Meh. The Irrelevance of Copyright in the Public Mind' (2008) 7 *Nw J Tech & Intell Prop* 33; Garbharran, A and Thatcher, A, 'A Case for Using a Social Cognitive Model to Explain Intention to Pirate Software' (2009) 7 *eHealth Tech & Application* 87; Burleson, K, 'Learning from Copyright's Failure to Build Its Future' (2014) 89 *Ind LJ* 1299.

[6] Jensen (2003) 538.

[7] ibid.

[8] Burleson (2014) 1300.

[9] Mnookin, RH and Kornhauser, L, 'Bargaining in the Shadow of the Law: The Case of Divorce' (1979) 88 *Yale LJ* 950.

as an influence on behaviour.[10] Gallagher's empirical work on trade mark and copyright enforcement revealed that the threat of the law in the form of a cease-and-desist letter is often sufficient to end an alleged infringement, as parties wish to avoid litigation.[11] Literature on the role of trade mark law in dispute resolution suggests that it is a powerful force, which exceeds the actual limits of the law by supporting unmeritorious claims.[12] As explained by Lemley:

> Defending a trademark case is expensive, the outcome is uncertain, and the payoff is limited … [F]ar too many people and companies with meritorious defences simply drop their parody, satire, complaint, or commentary rather than face the prospect of litigation.[13]

Even before any alleged infringement, parties in the transactional sphere who are aware of legal rights may be hesitant to act in a way that may be considered infringement due to the perceived risk of legal sanctions. They wish to avoid the threat of litigation, even if the potential claim is groundless. Hence, movie producers may take licences for 'life story rights' when portraying an individual, despite no strict legal requirement to do so.[14] According to Gibson, risk-averse entities adhere to 'a practice of securing copyright licenses even when none is needed. Better safe than sued.'[15] This trend has also been observed by Rothman, who explains that litigation-avoidance customs can be observed where risk-averse parties secure rights that are not legally required.[16]

The deterrence theory is important in both jurisdictions as it can affect behaviour, even if the potential for litigation is limited, because 'ultimately deterrence depends on perceptions of the risks (and rewards) of offending'.[17] The force of deterrence is thus twofold: in the transactional sphere, it can prevent offending actions from occurring; in the dispute resolution sphere, it can also be used to stop offending actions, even if the action is not strictly prohibited by law.

[10] Lemley, M, 'Fame, Parody, and Policing in Trademark Law' (2019) 2019 *Mich St L Rev* 1; Tushnet, R, 'Registering Disagreement: Registration in Modern American Trademark Law' (2017) 130 *Harv L Rev* 867; Grinvald, L, 'Policing the Cease-and-Desist Letter' (2015) 49 *Usf L Rev* 409; Kiser, J, 'To Bully or Not to Bully: Understanding the Role of Uncertainty in Trademark Enforcement Decisions' (2014) 37 *Colum JL & Arts* 211; Gibson, J, 'Risk Aversion and Rights Accretion in Intellectual Property Law' (2007) 116 *Yale LJ* 882.

[11] Gallagher, W, 'Trade mark and Copyright Enforcement in the Shadow of IP Law' (2011) 28 *Santa Clara Computer & High Tech LJ* 453.

[12] Lemley, M, 'Fame, Parody, and Policing in Trademark Law' (2019) 2019 *Mich St L Rev* 1.

[13] ibid 5.

[14] There are several influences that dictate whether such rights are taken, but the potential risk of litigation, even if a claim is unmeritorious, is an influence, as discussed in ch 7.

[15] Gibson, J, 'Risk Aversion and Rights Accretion in Intellectual Property Law' (2007) 116 *Yale LJ* 882, 884.

[16] Rothman, J, 'The Questionable Use of Custom in Intellectual Property Law' (2007) 93 *Virginia L Rev* 1899, 1909, 1916.

[17] Nagin (1998).

B. Law as an Indicator of Morality

The second theory that explains compliance with law is the morality theory. Tyler's 1990 work, *Why People Obey the Law*, one of the most cited works in this field, suggests that morality is a significant influence on law-related behaviour.[18] In other words, people obey the law because they consider it the right thing to do. In the criminal sphere, Grasmick and Green found that morality was a greater determinant of whether to commit future crime as compared to the threat of legal sanctions.[19] Nagin and Paternoster found that drug use was not considered to be morally wrong by their respondents, whereas theft was.[20] In the intellectual property sphere, studies reveal that people do not consider online copyright infringement to be morally wrong, whereas they do consider theft to be morally wrong. Manesh explains this position:

> [F]ile-sharers seem to share a subjective belief that copyright infringement is not morally wrong. Copyright owners often liken file sharing to theft. They argue that downloading Abbey Road from the Internet is no different than stealing a CD from the local music store. And yet, both statistical and anecdotal evidence suggests that file sharers see nothing wrong with infringement. To millions, theft is immoral, infringement is not.[21]

The role of morality in achieving compliance with the law can be particularly forceful where the risk of detection of infringement is low. However, morality depends on the opinions held by individuals, which are subject to varying external influences. While no questions that used the word 'morality' were asked, empirical data reveal that US lawyers consider persona protection to be moral. In other words, they feel that permission should be sought to use persona in certain circumstances because individuals rightly deserve the protection afforded by the law. In the UK, lawyers were questioned on their opinions about the US right of publicity, but none of the responses suggested that they felt the law is morally correct. Similarly, no responses on passing off suggested that morality impacted on compliance. As such, subsequent chapters will suggest that morality induces compliance with the law in the US. To compare this theory with the situation in the UK, data on attitudes towards the potential introduction of the right of publicity in the UK will be discussed.

[18] Tyler (1990) 178. Tyler's book focuses on the legitimacy of law but also discusses the role of morality.

[19] Grasmick, H and Green, D, 'Legal Punishment, Social Disapproval and Internalization as Inhibitors of Illegal Behaviour' (1980) 71 *Crim L & Criminology* 325.

[20] Nagin, D and Paternoster, R, 'The preventive effects of the perceived risk of arrest: testing an expanded conception of deterrence' (1991) 29 *Criminology* 561.

[21] Manesh, M, 'The Immorality of Theft, the Amorality of Infringement' [2006] *Stan Tech L Rev* 5, 6.

C. The Limitation of the Influence: Disregard and Ignorance of Law

Where people are aware of the law, but deterrence or morality considerations are not in operation, people may disregard the law. Robinson and Darley explain, in relation to criminal law, that people may undertake a cost–benefit analysis to determine whether to break the law.[22] In undertaking this analysis, they will consider the reasons for compliance so far advanced against the perceived gain of breaking the relevant law. People may choose to break the law rather than comply because they perceive that the likelihood of punishment is rare, indicating an ineffectiveness of deterrence theory.[23] Alternatively, even when legal sanctions are likely to be administered, they may have no effect on behaviour. Paternoster reviewed 14 studies and found a limited correlation between perceived legal sanctions and use of illicit drugs, and concluded that 'perceived certainty plays virtually no role in explaining deviant/criminal conduct'.[24] Tyler came to the same conclusion in his study on attitudes and experiences of citizens of Chicago, in relation to their dealings with legal authorities.[25] With regard to copyright, Jensen explains that 'Despite the impressive arsenal of legal weapons available to copyright owners, disregard for copyright laws remains widespread.'[26]

In deciding against compliance, people may think that the reward outweighs the cost of any legal consequences.[27] The impact of consequences will depend on the position of an individual. For example, the cost imposed by a speeding ticket might have greater deterrence for someone who is poor compared to someone who has a large disposable income. The weighing of risk versus reward is evident in the decisions of newspapers and magazines to publish stories that may infringe the privacy of individuals. They may be aware of the risk but consider that the financial benefit derived from the circulation of a story that will garner mass public attention would outweigh the damages awarded in court.[28]

[22] Robinson, P and Darley, J, 'Does Criminal Law Deter? A Behavioural Science Investigation' (2004) 24 *OJLS* 173, 174.

[23] ibid; Buccafusco, C and Masur, J, 'Innovation and Incarceration: An Economic Analysis of Criminal Intellectual Property Law' (2014) 87 *Southern Calif L Rev* 275; Sugden, P, 'The Power of One! The failure of criminal copyright laws (piracy) to blend into greater cultural consciousness' (2014) 26 *EIPR* 367.

[24] Paternoster, R, 'The Deterrent Effect of Perceived Certainty and Severity of Punishment: A Review of the Evidence and Issues' (1987) 4 *Just Q* 173, 191.

[25] Tyler (1990) ch 12 and 13.

[26] Jensen (2003) 538.

[27] Robin, A, 'Copyright Infringement and the Internet: An Economic Analysis of Crime' (2005) 11 *BU J of Science & Tech Law* 256; Robinson and Darley (2004) 195.

[28] See generally: Petire, N, 'Reforming the Remedy: Getting the Right Remedial Structure to Protect Personal Privacy' (2012) 17 *Deakin L Rev* 121; Witzleb, N, 'Monetary Remedies for Breach of Confidence in Privacy Cases' (2007) 27 *Legal Studies* 430; Wei, G, 'Effectively Protecting Private Facts – Privacy and Confidentiality' (2012) 24 *Sac LJ* 223.

People may also disregard the law if they do not consider it to be morally necessary to comply.[29] Tyler and Darley state that people make judgements about whether 'behaviours prohibited by law are contrary to their moral values'.[30] The morality of an individual can be determined by various external factors, such as societal values, culture and socialisation. In terms of the American view of the morality of intellectual property infringement, Burleson asserts that 'in the realm of intellectual property infringement generally, the consensus is that infringement is not morally wrong and thus the law does not deserve compliance'.[31] This view has also been advanced by Loughlan[32] and O'Flynn,[33] and similar arguments have been made with regard to purchasing luxury counterfeit fashion goods.[34] In contrast, murder is generally considered to be morally wrong. People who subscribe to this view on morality refrain from murder not because it is prohibited by law, but because they think it is morally wrong.[35] However, subsequent chapters will reveal that the view on the right of publicity does not align with the general view on intellectual property infringement, as lawyers suggested that there is a moral obligation to respect the right of publicity. That being said, the position of the interviewees as lawyers who play a vital role in commercialisation of persona, and thus have an acute awareness of the law, must be taken into account.

Entertainment and intellectual property lawyers possess a vast knowledge of the law, but the general public are not always aware of the law governing certain behaviours. In Robinson and Darley's study of criminal law, they note that '[p]otential offenders commonly do not know the legal rules, either directly or indirectly'.[36] Similar findings are advanced in the copyright sphere, where it is suggested the people do not understand the law relating to copyright.[37] Litman argues that in order to reduce copyright infringement, copyright principles would need to be taught in schools, so that people would see copyright infringement as something that is wrong. Here it can be assumed that Litman is referring to inculcating morality through the vehicle of education. However, Litman indicates that there is a key obstacle to teaching copyright in schools, namely, its incomprehensible

[29] Nadler, J, 'Flouting the Law' (2005) 83 *Texas L Rev* 1399, 1431.

[30] Tyler, T and Darley, J, 'Taking Public Views about Morality and the Legitimacy of Legal Authorities into Account when Formulating Substantive Law' (2000) 28 *Hofstra L Rev* 707, 716.

[31] Burleson (2014) 1308.

[32] Loughlan, P, 'You Wouldn't Steal A Car … Intellectual Property and the Language of Theft' (2008) *Legal Studies Research Paper No 08/35* at http://ssrn.com/abstract=1120585.

[33] O'Flynn, T, 'File Sharing: An Holistic Approach To The Problem' (2006) 17 *Ent L Rev* 218.

[34] Ledbury Research, *Counterfeiting Luxury: Exposing the Myths* (2nd edn, Anti-Counterfeiting Group 2007) 21; Large, J, 'Get real, don't buy fakes' (2015) 15(2) *Criminology & Criminal Justice* 169, 174; Large, J and Wall, D, 'Jailhouse Frocks' (2010) 50 *British Journal of Criminology* 1094; Large, J, *Criminality, Consumption and the Counterfeiting of Fashion Items* (PhD Thesis, Leeds University, 2011) 163–68.

[35] Tyler and Darley (2000) 716.

[36] Robinson and Darley (2004) 174.

[37] Litman, J, *Digital Copyright* (2nd edn, Prometheus Books 2006) 26, 72, 111–13, 179; Litman, J, 'The Exclusive Right to Read' (1994) 13 *Cardoza Arts & Ent LR* 29, 51.

character, to the point that copyright lawyers have difficulty in understanding the law.[38] Considering that some areas of law are inaccessible to lay people, it is safe to suggest that sometimes law will not be complied with because people are unaware that law exists or do not understand how it applies. In relation to persona protection, subsequent chapters will discuss that parties who use persona without permission where it is legally required usually do not have access to legal advice and are operating outside the normal, regulated channels of commerce.

II. The Desire to Contract

The desire to create certainty and to avoid litigation is manifested in the formation of contracts that allow brands, merchandisers, video-game developers and movie producers to make defined uses of persona. However, contracts in the field of persona commercialisation go further than simply minimising the risk of liability. Contracts are also used to secure the benefits of collaboration, which exist independently of the law. There are numerous contract theories that consider the role of contracts in society.[39] The field of empirical contract studies[40] has evolved to consider how contracts function in practice, and thus departs from traditional theoretical perspectives on contract law, which are often criticised for failing to reflect reality.[41]

[38] Litman (1994) 51.

[39] Classical contract theory: Atiyah, PS, *The Rise and Fall of Freedom of Contract* (Clarendon Press 1985) 402–05; Collins, H, *The Law of Contract* (4th edn, Cambridge University Press 2003) 8; Cohen, M, 'The Basis of Contract' (1933) 46 *Harv L Rev* 553, 575; Fuller, L and Perdue, W, 'The Reliance Interest on Contract Damages' (1936) 46 *Yale LJ* 52, 58; Ibbeston, D, *A Historical Introduction to the Law of Obligations* (Oxford University Press 2001) chs 12–13; Epstein, L, 'Unconscionability: A Critical Reappraisal' (1975) 18 *J Law & Econ* 293, 293. Neo-classical contract theory: Murray. J, 'Contract Theories and the Rise of Neoformalism' (2002) 71 *Fordham Law Review* 869; Macneil. IR, 'Contracts: Adjustment of Long-Term Economic Relations under Classical, Neoclassical, and Relational Contract Law' (1977) 72 *Nw U L Rev* 854; Feinman, J, 'The Significance of Contract Theory' (1989) 58 *U Cin L Rev* 1283. Promissory theory: Fried, C, *Contract as Promise: A Theory of Contractual Obligation* (Oxford University Press 2015). Reliance theory: Cohen, M, 'The Basis of Contract' (1933) 46 Harv LR 553, 578–80; Fuller and Perdue (1936). Transfer theory: Barnett, R, 'A Consent Theory of Contract' (1986) 86 *Colum L Rev* 269; Benson, P, 'Contract as a Transfer of Ownership' (2007) 48 *Wm & Mary L Rev* 1673; Smith, S, *Contract Theory* (Oxford University Press 2004) 98. Law and economics: Hesselink, MW and de Vries, GJP, *Principles of European Contract Law* (Kluwer 2001) 80; Kronman, A and Posner, R, *Economics of Contract Law* (Little Brown & Co Law & Business 1979); Posner, E, *Economic Analysis of Law* (9th edn, Wolters Kluwer 1992) 66. Relational contract theory: MacNeil, IR, 'Relational Contract Theory: Challenges and Queries' (1999) 94 *NW U L Rev* 877.

[40] Korobkin provides an overview of contract studies from 1987–2002. Korobkin, R, 'Empirical Scholarship in Contract Law: Possibilities and Pitfalls'[2002] *U Ill L Rev* 1033.

[41] Scott, J, 'Empirical studies strike back against the force of contract theory' (1997) 4 *UCL Jurisprudence Rev* 256; Bix, B, 'The Promise and Problems of Universal, General Theories of Contract Law' (2017) 30 *Ratio Juris* 395. For more on contract theory, see: Farber, D and Mattheson, J, 'Beyond Promissory Estoppel: Contract Law and the "Invisible Handshake"' (1985) 52 *Chi L Rev* 903; Hillman, R, 'Questioning the "New Consensus" on Promissory Estoppel: An Empirical and Theoretical Study' (1998) 98 *Colum L Rev* 680; Hillman, R, 'The Unfulfilled Promise of Promissory Estoppel in the Employment Setting' (1999) 31 *Rutgers LJ* 1; Whitmore, P, 'A Statistical Analysis of Noncompetition Clauses in Employment Contracts' (1990) 15 *J Corp L* 483; McChesney, F, 'Tortious Interference with Contract Versus "Efficient" Breach: Theory and Empirical Evidence' (1999) 28 *J Leg Stud* 131.

In terms of dissecting existing studies, Korobkin suggests that empirical contract studies can be classified by reference to the source of the data on which the study is based or how the study uses the data. In terms of sources of data, he examines judicial opinions,[42] actual contracting practices,[43] negotiating experiments[44] and non-expert opinions about the law.[45] As to the use of data, he distinguishes between data used to understand substantive contract law itself,[46] data used to understand how substantive contract law impacts contracting parties[47] and data used to argue for changes in the law.[48] Studies based on actual contracting practices that examine how the law impacts on parties are the most relevant to this book, as they are most closely aligned with the aim of determining how the relevant legal frameworks impact on the commercialisation of persona.

In attempting to reconcile various empirical studies, Scott suggests a 'social market' approach. This approach recognises multiple factors that impact on the use of contract:

> [T]he social market approach means that one must examine the empirical studies in terms of a more socially oriented, sectorally and temporally specific, use of the legal

[42] Farber and Mattheson (1985); Hillman (1998); Hillman (1999); Whitmore (1990); McChesney (1999).

[43] Bernstein (1992); Macaulay, S, 'Non-Contractual Relations in Business – A Preliminary Study' (1963) 28 *Am Soc Rev* 55; Bernstein L, 'Merchant Law in a Merchant Court – Rethinking the Code's Search for Immanent Business Norms' (1996) 144 *U Pa L Rev* 1765; Bernstein, L, 'The Questionable Empirical Basis of Article 2's Incorporation Strategy: A Preliminary Study' (1999) 66 *U Chi L Rev* 710; Keating, D, 'Measuring Sales Law Against Sales Practice: A Reality Check' (1997) 17 *JL & Com* 99; Keating, D, 'Exploring the Battle of the Forms in Action' (2000) 98 *Mich LR* 2678; Weintraub, R, 'A Survey of Contract Practice and Policy' (1992) 1 *Wis L Rev* 1; Verkerke, J, 'An Empirical Perspective on Indefinite Term Employment Contracts: Resolving the Just Cause Debate' (1995) 4 *Wis L Rev* 838; Kahan, M and Klausner, M, 'Antitakeover Provisions in Bonds: Bondholder Protection or Management Entrenchment?' (1993) 40 *UCLA L Rev* 931; Burke, J, 'Contract as a Commodity: A Nonfiction Approach' (2000) 285 *Seton Hall Legis J* 291.

[44] Schwab, S, 'A Coasean Experiment on Contract Presumptions' (1988) 17 *J Leg Stud* 237; Korobkin, R, 'The Status Quo Bias and Contract Default Rules' (1998) 83 *Cornell L Rev* 608; Korobkin, R, 'Inertia and Preference in Contract Negotiation: The Psychological Power of Default Rules and Form Terms' (1998) 51 *Vand L Rev* 1583; Ayres, I, 'Fair Driving: Gender and Race Discrimination in Retail Car Negotiations' (1991) 104 *Harv L Rev* 817.

[45] Kim, P, 'Bargaining with Imperfect Information: A Study of Worker Perceptions of Legal Protection in an At-Will World' (1997) 83 *Cornell L Rev* 105; Keating, D, 'Exploring the Battle of the Forms in Action' (2000) 98 *Mich L Rev* 2678; Baumer, D and Marschall, P, 'Wilful Breach of Contract for the Sale of Goods: Can the Bane of Business Be an Economic Bonanza?' (1992) 65 *Temp L Rev* 159.

[46] Farber and Mattheson (1985); Hillman, R, 'Questioning the 'New Consensus' on Promissory Estoppel: An Empirical and Theoretical Study' (1998) 98 *Colum L Rev* 680; Whitmore, P, 'A Statistical Analysis of Noncompetition Clauses in Employment Contracts' (1990) 15 *J Corp L* 483; Johnston, J, 'The Statute of Frauds and Business Norms: A Testable Game-Theoretic Model' (1996) 144 *U Pa L Rev* 1859;.

[47] Macaulay (1963); Keating, D, 'Measuring Sales Law Against Sales Practice: A Reality Check' (1997) 17 *JL & Com* 99; Keating (2000); Bernstein (1992); White, J, 'Promise Fulfilled and Principle Betrayed' (1988) 1 *Ann Surv Am L* 7; Korobkin, R, 'The Status Quo Bias and Contract Default Rules' (1998) 83 *Cornell L Rev* 608.

[48] Kahan, M and Klausner, M, 'Standardization and Innovation in Corporate Contracting' (1997) 83 *Va L Rev* 713; Verkerke (1995); Ayres, (1991).

> and extra-legal nature of contract law which includes social norms such as competition, co-operation, trust and long-term mutual benefit.[49]

Scott's review of various empirical studies of the diamond industry,[50] business in Wisconsin[51] and engineering firms[52] reveals that contracts are entered into for a variety of reasons, often unrelated to established contractual theories. It is the substance of the agreement rather than the form of the contract that is considered to be of importance. This observation is applicable to the field of persona commercialisation. While contracts in this field may be more formal than those in the studies Scott reviewed, one of the major motivations for entering into the contract is to secure the benefits of collaboration. If no agreement is arrived at between parties, the party wishing to exploit persona will not be able to create the quality of product initially desired. This is because, regardless of the law, the developments in technology and marketing strategies, as well as the need to access information, necessitate cooperation with the famous person. Without this cooperation, certain uses of persona could still be made, but the benefits of obtaining cooperation outweigh the cost of seeking permission. As will be argued in the forthcoming chapters, these benefits exist in both the US and UK, and are independent of the relevant legal framework.

In addition to the benefits secured by contracts, Beale and Dugdale distinguish between two further uses of contracts: the first use is legal recourse for remedies when there is a breach; the second 'use', which is more frequently observed in empirical studies, is regulatory. Beale and Dugdale state that 'the parties may … "use" contract law to regulate their relationship, to plan what is to happen in the future'.[53] Such 'use' avoids litigation.[54] This trend of avoiding use of the court system was observed in Macaulay's study of businesses in Wisconsin.[55] He explains that the threat of litigation can result in resolution without going to court: 'Courts may be involved only marginally: filling a complaint, or even merely writing a letter on an attorney's letterhead, may be enough to provoke serious negotiation.'[56] Similarly, Scott's review of empirical studies further reveals that reliance on legal channels is rare:

> There is certainly no immediate resort to legal remedies when something goes wrong. All the studies identify that the main reason for this, in the case of longer term and ongoing relations, is the desire to do business again in the future and that taking legal action is destructive and expensive.[57]

[49] Scott (1997) 262.
[50] Bernstein (1992).
[51] Macaulay (1963).
[52] Beale, H and Dugdale, T, 'Contracts between businessmen: Planning and the use of contractual remedies' (1975) 2 *Brit J Law & Society* 45.
[53] ibid 45.
[54] ibid.
[55] Macaulay (1963).
[56] Macaulay, S, 'An Empirical View of Contract' (1985) 3 *Wis L Rev* 465.
515. (Macaulay reflects on his 1963 article in this article.).
[57] Scott (1997) 264.

In some circumstances, parties to a contract may create rights that are not legally recognised. A prime example of this occurs in the television format industry. Despite the limited applicability of copyright law to television formats, there is a global trade in formats.[58] Bowrey and Handler suggest that these rights are licensed, even in the absence of legal requirements, because there are benefits that accompany the licence, such as a reduced potential for litigation and consequential production delays and access to merchandise.[59] Similarly, in the UK, in the absence of the right of publicity, parties create their own version of so-called 'image rights' and enter into contracts to secure uses of persona in a similar manner as occurs in the US.

When the benefits of collaboration are solidified by contract, the contracts are more likely to be used as a framework for the relationship rather than a strict set of rules: litigation is avoided because parties generally want to maintain relationships[60] and avoid incurring litigation expenses.[61] However, in the absence of a contract, parties will use litigation where there is a relevant cause of action. The variance in the legal frameworks marks a divergence in dispute resolution, whereas this variance does not affect relationships governed by contract, as parties can negotiate for rights that are not necessarily legally recognised.

A. Benefits of Collaboration: Securing Rights to Use Persona

Contracts in both jurisdictions specify the elements of persona that are the subject of the agreement. However, the term 'right of publicity' is used infrequently to secure rights in the US; rather, it is used to guard against liability. While the term 'image rights' is used in the UK, and has assumed legal significance, 'image rights' are not recognised under UK law. As such, neither jurisdiction places emphasis on existing legal terminology to secure rights to use persona, but rather to secure waivers of liability.

In securing rights to use persona in the US, the contract will specify the aspects of persona to be used. Interestingly, as noted, the term 'right of publicity' is not often used to grant rights to persona for licensing purposes. When questioned whether 'right of publicity' terminology would be used for a licensing agreement, a named partner in a law firm who represented 'A-list' celebrity clients explained:

> It [the contract] would be very specific. The celebrity would have approval of the image; where it goes, the ad itself, where the ad goes. I don't know if it [the contract] would say

[58] Baker & McKenzie and FRAPA, *FRAPA Legal Report 2017: An overview of the legal status of formats* (FRAPA, 2017).

[59] Bowrey, K and Handler, M, *Law and Creativity in the Age of the Entertainment Franchise* (Cambridge University Press 2014) 149.

[60] Keating, D, 'Exploring the Battle of the Forms in Action' (2000) 98 *Mich L Rev* 2678, 2698–99; Macaulay (1963) 62.

[61] Macaulay (1963) 64.

> the words 'right of publicity'. We would specify that we can use the celebrity's name and image to create proposed advertisements.[62]

Another noted that the term 'right of publicity' is used to guard against liability rather than to secure rights to exploit persona. As observed by another interviewee,

> The language of the statute comes up more in litigation. If you are drafting a contract you have reached an agreement on how you are going to use the person's image, name or persona so you don't necessarily have to cite a particular law.[63]

Instead, the specific aspects of persona will be named:

> I would put in that you waive any claim for right of publicity but when you want to cover name, likeness, signature, persona, anything you would need as a marketer, they will be specifically mentioned in the contract.[64]

Similarly:

> The language in all these agreements talk about rights to use someone's name, likeness, image, performance, voice … We are actually very specific about the attributes in the agreements, but we don't generally use the phrase 'right of publicity' when we are referring to those aspects that make a person a person.[65]

Specifying the attributes can allow the persona to be selective, rather than granting a broad licence for the right of publicity. A lawyer stated that for endorsement deals, celebrities enter into a 'name and likeness agreement':

> They govern and speak about rights of publicity but we don't name it a 'right to publicity agreement'. An endorsement deal will have releases allowing the company hiring the endorser to use the name, likeness and those sorts of thing.[66]

To corroborate the information provided by US lawyers above, a standard-form agreement was examined.[67] This agreement provided the following term on securing rights to use persona:

> Celebrity Content. 'Celebrity Content' shall mean Celebrity's full and formal name, nicknames or alias identities (collectively the 'Names') or any shortening, abbreviations, or alternative renderings of the Names, signatures now used or hereafter to be used by Celebrity, and any or all renderings of Celebrity's voice, Celebrity's image and likenesses, and any and all attributes of Celebrity's personality and appearance.[68]

[62] California interview 6.
[63] New York interview 14.
[64] New York interview 2.
[65] New York interview 13.
[66] California interview 23.
[67] Lindey, A, *Lindey on Entertainment, Publishing and the Arts* (3rd edn, Thomson Reuters 2018) § 3:34, 'Personality endorsement agreement'.
[68] ibid § 1.1.

> License. Upon the terms and subject to the conditions of this Agreement, Celebrity and Manager grant to Licensee an exclusive, irrevocable license (the 'License') to make use of, copy, reproduce, modify, adapt, distribute, transmit, broadcast, display, exhibit, project, and to otherwise exploit the Celebrity Content …[69]

As evidenced by the standard term above, each element of persona that is being contracted for will be explicitly described. While this term is boarder than the types of terms described by interviewees, it is worth nothing that the terminology of 'right of publicity' is not used. In fact, lawyers did not feel the US legal framework was significant when there is a relationship between parties. A lawyer who represented celebrities noted:

> I'm not so worried about the law because I'll be limiting [the use of my client's persona] far more than any law would ever permit anywhere. The buyer won't do anything until we have a deal and we'll make the deals as protective as our clients need … Normally limitations would come up in litigation because of unauthorised use.[70]

Similarly, 'Where there is a license there is no real issue … just a matter of negotiating the license.'[71] The licence is negotiated not on the basis of the legal framework but on the needs of the parties. Lawyers were questioned as to why the terminology 'right of publicity' is not asserted in granting rights to use persona. Two reasons were advanced. First, 'publicity' might refer to obligations to make appearances on television shows and radio programmes, so the term may be avoided to prevent confusion as to meaning.[72] An interviewee noted that public appearance might include 'speaking at a conference, opening a supermarket, speaking to a classroom of children'. 'Publicity' when used to refer to public appearance assumes its normal meaning of exposure, as demonstrated by the following standard term:

> ARTIST'S RIGHT TO PRIOR APPROVAL: Notwithstanding any provision in this Agreement to the contrary, in the event of the Purchaser's *use of Artist's name or any Artist Image in any marketing, advertising, publicity, or promotional material* relating to the Artist's Appearances, any such use requires the prior written approval of Artist or Artist's Representative.[73]

Second, the right of publicity is expressed by different terminology in different States. In New York, the inter vivos right is within New York's privacy statute, so using the term 'right of publicity' might not be sufficiently clear. Additionally, there is a lack of consensus as to what is considered within the scope of the right of publicity in different States, as explained in chapter 2 when discussing the applicable law in New York and California.[74]

[69] ibid § 2.1.
[70] California interview 10.
[71] New York interview 1.
[72] California interview 23.
[73] Nichols, CA, *Nichols Cyclopedia of Legal Forms Annotated* (Thomson Reuters 2017) § 71:15:50 (emphasis added).
[74] See ch 2, section II.

As one interviewee stated:

> I would never want to have an argument that you did not understand what right of publicity meant. We have different rights in different states. For clarity purposes, it's more sensible to specify that if you appear in this work, we have the right to use your name, likeness for this purpose.[75]

While the aspects of persona that are licensed are likely to fall within the scope of the right of publicity, the attributes to be licensed are specified instead of using the umbrella term 'right of publicity'.

The situation in the UK, while substantially similar, can be distinguished by the terminology used in contracts for persona commercialisation. Lawyers spoke about 'image rights' when referring to contracts that exploit persona, and this terminology is also used in contracts. The employment of this term in the absence of supporting law is interesting because it indicates that the term 'image rights' has assumed a meaning within industries that use persona. The term has been used by HM Revenue and Customs (HMRC) when addressing payments received by high-profile individuals such as footballers. According to HMRC:

> High-profile individuals, such as professional sportspeople and other celebrities, are often offered payments from those who want to use their name, image or other personal characteristic for commercial purposes. These characteristics are often referred to as 'image rights'.[76]

Furthermore, a court in *Proactive Sports Management Ltd v Wayne Rooney*,[77] in determining arrears of commission due from an 'Image Rights Representation Agreement', set out the term used in the agreement in dispute:

> Image Rights means the right for any commercial or promotional purpose to use the Player's name, nickname, slogan and signatures developed from time to time, image, likeness, voice, logos, get-ups, initials, team or squad number (as may be allocated to the Player from time to time), reputation, video or film portrayal, biographical information, graphical representation, electronic, animated or computer-generated representation and/or any other representation and/or right of association and/or any other right or quasi-right anywhere in the World of the Player in relation to his name, reputation, image, promotional services, and/or his performances together with the right to apply for registration of any such rights.[78]

The above extract illustrates that the phrase 'image rights' has become common parlance among industries that use persona. 'Image rights' contracts are particularly popular in the football arena. A lawyer specialising in sports law explained that when footballers join a club, they will decide whether to retain

[75] California interview 9.

[76] HMRC, 'Tax on payments for use of image rights' (HMRC, 16 August 2017) at www.gov.uk/guidance/tax-on-payments-for-use-of-image-rights (accessed 16 May 2018).

[77] *Proactive Sports Management Ltd v Wayne Rooney* [2010] EWHC 1807 (QB).

[78] ibid [187].

the management of their 'image rights' or to enter into a licence deal for clubs to exploit their 'image rights'.[79] This lawyer noted:

> The Premier League has a template employment contract. There are basic clauses which allow [the] club to use players' images for basic promotional and merchandising purposes. Sometimes a player with a big name will license their club 'enhanced image rights', so their club will pay an additional fee [to use persona]. The rights the club have under template are basic in that you can only use in club context to promote club. Enhanced rights allow club to use image more directly with their sponsor on a more individual level.[80]

The significance of the term 'image rights' was also revealed in interviews when lawyers were questioned about what they mean by 'image rights'. One lawyer responded 'Image rights is a synonym people use for publicity rights, personality rights, endorsement rights … generally all these terms mean the same thing.'[81] When asked to define 'image rights', this lawyer responded 'The right to control the exploitation of your name, image, sound of your voice, signature, and any other means that might identify you as an individual.'[82] Another was asked to define 'persona protection' and responded 'We don't use that term, we would say image rights. There is no such thing in England as an actual image right … but it means anything that you would recognise as being the individual.'[83]

When drafting contracts, aspects of persona that are being licensed will be described in substantively the same manner as in the US. A lawyer conveyed this similarity between jurisdictions:

> You deal with 'image rights' contractually. Tend to have a definition which is very all encompassing – name, image, likeness, voice, sound recording – every element which relates to the celebrity. Since image rights are contractual, UK contracts look the same as US contracts.[84]

In order to compare the licensing of persona in the UK and the US, a standard-form UK term was examined:

> The Company its successors, assignees, and licensees shall have the right to use the names, sobriquet, autograph, likeness, photograph, portrait, caricature, silhouette, voice (both real life and as in the Advertising Material) and all other products of the Services in connection with the Advertising Material or any part of it in connection with any merchandising and/or publishing or music publishing endeavours in connection with the Advertising Material. The Artist shall not be depicted as endorsing any commercial product publicised independently of the Advertising Material where such product is not featured as a special element in the Advertising Material.[85]

[79] UK interview 20.
[80] UK interview 23.
[81] UK interview 4.
[82] UK interview 4.
[83] UK interview 22.
[84] UK interview 14.
[85] Lexis Nexis, *Encyclopaedia of Forms and Precedents, Entertainment and Media*, vol 15(3)(C), pt 2: 'Merchandising, Product Endorsement and Sponsorship', pt 8: 'Product Endorsement Agreement' (LexisNexis 2015).

This standard term illustrates that aspects of persona are named in the UK in a similar fashion to the US. While different terminology may be employed in each jurisdiction, the method of contracting involves specifying the attributes of persona to be licensed. In reality, contracts are more limited than the standard terms referred to, as lawyers indicated they would specify the attributes of persona that are being licensed. When asked whether existing intellectual property rights played a role in persona exploitation in the UK, a lawyer explained:

> IP rights do not play a great role. Contract defines in great details what the brands can do with the celebrity, what they can use, for how long, what countries … no need to go into IP because all spelt out in detail anyway.[86]

As such, even in the absence of a right of publicity, these contracts are similar across jurisdictions.

B. Minimising Liability

It is important to recognise the distinction between minimising the risk of liability and securing rights of exploitation. In the previous section, it was demonstrated that the substantive legal rights are not asserted in securing use of persona, as aspects of persona will be specified. However, the substantive legal rights are used in guarding against liability. In the UK, there is less likely to be a relevant cause of action due to the limitations of passing off as compared to the right of publicity, but intellectual property rights such as copyright and trade marks may be included in a waiver of liability. The difference in guarding against liability is informed by the difference in legal frameworks, as it is futile to guard against a cause of action that is not recognised in the UK. The exception to this would be a UK contract that has selected a US State as the choice of law.

When 'publicity rights' are referred to in US contracts, it is in the form of a waiver of liability. A lawyer, in referring to a 'life story agreement', noted 'It [the contract] will include specific [terms] relating to privacy and publicity waiving [any] claim that any production we make violates any of your rights.'[87] When questioned whether any key provisions in contracts use the term 'right of publicity', a lawyer responded 'Would put in that you waive any claim for right of publicity …'.[88] Similarly, another lawyer commented that the term is used to secure a release of liability: 'An endorsement deal will have releases allowing the company hiring the endorser to use the name, likeness, right of publicity and those sorts of things.'[89]

[86] UK interview 5.
[87] California interview 19.
[88] New York interview 2.
[89] California interview 23.

An example of a US waiver corroborates the information provided by lawyers:

> *Waiver* and Release. Manager and Celebrity hereby waive all rights and release Licensee, its shareholders, partners, officers, directors, employees, agents, and licensees and assigns from, and shall neither sue nor bring any proceeding against any such parties for, any claim or cause of action, whether now known or unknown, for defamation, invasion of right to privacy, *infringement of rights of publicity*, intrusion, false light, or public disclosure of private facts, or any similar matter, or based upon or relating to the use and exploitation of the Celebrity Content.[90]

In the UK, there is no right of publicity and so a waiver of liability of infringement of this right would not be expected. However, an examination of a standard-form agreement revealed that contracts may nonetheless include this terminology:

> The Lender acknowledges that all *rights* of copyright, privacy, *publicity* and all other rights in and to the Commercials and the Photographic Material featuring the Artist and all other products of the Services belong *to the Company absolutely* and that the Company its successors, assignees and licensees shall have the right to exploit any and all of the foregoing in any and all media by any and all manner or means throughout the world together with the right to authorise others so to do.[91]

Failure to obtain a waiver in either jurisdiction can have significant consequences in the rare event that litigation arises. However, consequences relating to the right of publicity are limited to the US where this right exists. An example of the consequence of failing to secure a waiver can be seen in *No Doubt v Activision*.[92] No Doubt entered into an agreement with video-game developer Activision to allow avatars of the musicians to be used in the game *Band Hero*. No Doubt claimed they did not grant permission for the avatars to be used to sing songs by other bands, and in the absence of a waiver, they were able to sue in reliance on the right of publicity and for breach of contract of the 'Professional Services and Character Licensing Agreement'.[93] The significance of this is that the right of publicity statute in California has a fee-shifting provision, as well as multiple heads of damages that can be claimed.[94] In the UK, a party in a similar situation would only be able to sue based on the contract or the existing causes of action such as passing off.

Despite different legal frameworks, contracts work to regulate persona in each jurisdiction. The evidence collected in fieldwork suggests that no obstacles to contracting are posed by the absence of a right of publicity in the UK. In fact, the

[90] Lindey (2018) § 3:37, 'Personality endorsement agreement' (emphasis added).

[91] Lexis Nexis, *Encyclopaedia of Forms and Precedents, Entertainment and Media*, vol 15(3)(C), pt 2: 'Merchandising, Product Endorsement and Sponsorship', pt 13, 'Artist commercials agreement' (LexisNexis 2015) (emphasis added).

[92] *No Doubt v Activision Publishing Inc* 192 Cal App 4th 1018 (2011).

[93] ibid [1023].

[94] The claim was eventually settled – Gardner, E, 'No Doubt, Activision Settle Lawsuit Over Avatars in "Band Hero"' *The Hollywood Reporter* (10 October 2017) at www.hollywoodreporter.com/thr-esq/no-doubt-activision-lawsuit-band-hero-376217.

term 'image rights' has assumed a meaning in industries that use persona and is used in contracts that commercialise persona. The content of the contract in any jurisdiction will depend on the industry in which it is being used and the requirements of parties to the contract. Generally, the contract will specify which aspects of persona are to be used and for what purposes.

The prevalence of contractual relationships across jurisdictions further evidences the benefits of collaboration. It shows that parties will enter relationships regardless of whether permission is legally required, because there are benefits to be gained from collaborating. As noted by an interviewee:

> These deals are much more complicated than just the existence of a sui generis right – they are a bundle of different rights and service obligations, [which] when taken together are much more valuable than what anybody else could do without authorisation. Planning to use someone's image without permission is not the same as sitting down for a 10-day photo shoot which connects them with your product.[95]

In terms of minimising the risk of liability, waivers will be included against relevant causes of action. The divergence in the legal framework is highlighted here since there is no right of publicity against which a waiver needs to be secured in the UK.

III. Social Norms as a Regulator

There is no set definition of social norms, but there is consensus that norms control behaviour, that is, they determine what course of action should be taken by a compliant individual. The control of behaviour is referred to by terms such as 'obligation',[96] 'rules',[97] 'constraint'[98] and 'regulation'.[99] According to Feldman, 'Group norms are the informal rules that groups adopt to regulate and regularise group members' behaviour.'[100] Young states that 'Social norms are rules of behaviour that govern interactions with others.'[101] Similarly, Cooter says that 'a social norm is an obligation backed by a social sanction'.[102] Regardless of the other characteristics that may exist in a given setting, the core aspect of social norms is that that they regulate the manner in which people behave.

[95] UK interview 20.

[96] Cooter, R, 'Expressive Law and Economics' (1998) 27 *J Leg Stud* 585, 585.

[97] Young, P, 'The Evolution of Social Norms' (2014) 7 *Annual Review of Economics* 359, 361.

[98] West, M, 'Legal Rules and Social Norms in Japan's Secret World of Sumo' (1997) 26 *J Leg Stud* 165,167.

[99] Feldman, Y, 'The development and enforcement of group norms' (1984) 9(1) *Acad Manangement Rev* 47, 47.

[100] ibid.

[101] Young (2014).

[102] Cooter, R, 'Three Effects of Social Norms on Law: Expression, Deterrence and Internalization' (2000) 79 *Or L Rev* 1, 4.

This regulation is aided by the evaluation of behaviour by individuals who adhere to the norm, to determine whether other individuals are also in compliance. Compliant individuals approve of those who comply and disapprove of those who defect from the norm. Disapproval can have negative consequences for the defector, known as sanctions, which result from the sending of a negative signal by the defector. The desire to send a positive signal due to the benefits of acceptance and cooperation with compliant parties results in action in accordance with the norm regardless of personal opinions of the norm.[103] This demonstrates a potential strength of norms: individuals are likely to comply because they fear the disapproval of others. However, Fauchart and von Hippel note, '[g]roup members who do not need or care about such social rewards … often conform less than other group members'.[104] Theories of compliance explain why individuals adhere to a norm, similar to the theories of compliance with law.

A. Sanctions Theory

The most common theory of compliance observed in social norms literature is sanctions.[105] Sanctions are the consequences for defecting from the norm, and are usually considered non-legal, including things such as gossip, social exclusion and even threats of physical violence. In Fauchart and von Hippel's case study on social norms regulating the protection of recipes in French cuisine, the sanctions for copying a recipe include shaming, reduced access to information and diminishment of status.[106] One of Fauchart and von Hippel's goals was to determine whether sanctions were actually enforced, and they found that, indeed, chefs were able to give examples of sanctions being administered.[107] One respondent said that chefs would not talk to a chef who copied a recipe exactly.[108] The study also observed an instance of the shaming of a chef on an online message board for

[103] McAdams, R, 'An Attitudinal Theory of Expressive Law' (2000) 79 *Oregon L Rev* 339, 340.
[104] Fauchart, E and von Hippel, E, 'Norms-Based Intellectual Property Systems: The case of French chefs' (2008) 19 *Organization Science* 187,189.
[105] Gibbs, JP, 'Norms: The problem of definition and classification' (1965) 70(5) *Amer J Sociol* 586; Jones, W, 'A Theory of Social Norms' (1994) *U Ill L Rev* 545; Bernstein, L, 'Opting out of the legal system – Extralegal Contractual Relations in the Diamond Industry' (1992) 21 *J Legal Stud* 115; Hansen, R, 'Voting Without Law?' (1996) 144 *U Pa L Rev* 2135; Cooter (1998); Bendor, J and Swistak P, 'The evolution of norms' (2001) 106(6) *Amer J Sociology* 1493; Buccafusco, CJ, 'On the legal consequences of sauces: Should Thomas Keller's Recipe be per se copyrightable?' (2006) 24 *Cardozo Arts & Ent LJ* 1121; Schultz, M, 'What jambands can teach us about persuading people to obey copyright law' (2006) 21 *Berkeley Tech LJ* 651; Fagundes D, 'Talk Derby to me: Emergent intellectual property norms governing roller derby pseudonyms' (2010) 90 *Texas L Rev* 1093.
[106] Fauchart and von Hippel (2008) 187.
[107] ibid 194.
[108] ibid 188.

copying recipes.[109] Another chef noted that he confronted a former employee who failed to attribute a recipe to the creator.[110]

In contrast, Oliar and Sprigman's study of the protection of jokes in stand-up comedy revealed that while sanctions are considered to influence social norms against copying, they are not always enforced. Sanctions include refusal to collaborate, a decrease in comedy club bookings, and even physical violence.[111] Oliar and Sprigman note, 'Many of our interviewees stated that enforcement was relatively unlikely to succeed when the appropriator was a more popular comic than the originator.'[112] Comedy clubs would not sacrifice their income to administer sanctions against a norm defector. As such, the perception of sanctions may exist even if the administration of the sanctions is unlikely.

The effectiveness of sanctions theory in ensuring compliance depends, first, on the availability of sanctions and, second, on the willingness of parties to administer sanctions. Administration of sanctions means treating defecting parties differently from compliant parties through gossip, shaming or other forms of social exclusion and reputational damage, which vary according to the industry being observed.

In the industries that commercialise persona, it was difficult to observe sanctions in fieldwork. Sanctions that might be imposed in this area could include refusal by celebrities to collaborate in the future, negative publicity by the celebrity whose persona is used without permission and a consequential decrease in sales due to boycott by fans of the celebrity. While there was some suggestion that failure to seek permission to use persona in certain circumstances could impact the reputation of a party, no evidence was provided that reputational damage actually resulted in such circumstances. This does not mean that sanctions were not present. Rather, the nature of the data made it difficult to observe sanctions, as the lawyers interviewed generally acted for companies that sought permission to use persona. Those who acted for individuals deployed legal sanctions when persona was used without permission, as required by their role. Interviewing lawyers inevitably provided greater information on legal sanctions than on non-legal ones.

B. Signalling Theory

According to the signalling theory, norms are complied with to send a message about the complier.[113] More specifically, people comply with norms in order to be

[109] ibid 197.

[110] ibid 193.

[111] Oliar, D and Sprigman, C, 'There's no free laugh (anymore): The emergence of intellectual property norms and the transformation of stand-up comedy' (2008) 94(8) *Virginia L Rev* 1789, 1791.

[112] ibid 1824.

[113] Posner, E, 'Symbols, Signals and Social Norms' (1998) 27 *J Legal Stud* 765; McAdams, R, 'Signaling Discount Rates: Law, Norms, and Economic Methodology Book Review' (2000) 110 *Yale LJ* 625; Meares, TL, 'Signalling, Legitimacy, and Compliance: A Comment on Posner's Law and Social Norms and Criminal Law Policy Commentary' (2002) 36 *U Rich L Rev* 407; Druzin, B, 'Law, Selfishness, and Signals: An Expansion of Posner's Signalling Theory of Social Norms' (2011) 24 *Can J L & Jurisprudence* 5.

perceived in a certain way by others who also comply. Posner describes signalling theory as follows:

> In every case, the symbolic behaviour is intended as a signal that the agent has a characteristic that the agent wants the receiver of the signal to believe that the agent has, but that the receiver cannot directly observe.[114]

This theory is based on a law and economics model whereby those who adhere to the norm have a low discount rate and are considered 'the high type', whereas those who defect have a high discount rate and are considered 'the low type'. A 'discount rate' is the value attached to an individual, derived from her willingness to adhere to a norm despite the immediate effort required to do so.[115] A 'low discount rate' is usually attached to an individual who adheres to the norm, because she exerts an effort that may not result in immediate gain. By adhering, she sends a message that she is likely to behave in a similar manner in the future, and thus is likely to benefit from cooperative efforts of others.[116] A signal is costly, so the 'high type' is more likely to be able to send a signal than 'the low type'.[117] Cost in this sense is not necessarily limited to financial value, it can also include time and effort.[118]

Posner applies signalling theory to Bernstein's case study on diamond merchants[119] to explain why contracts for sale utilise a practice of sealing envelopes and the use of certain words.[120] Although more efficient ways of contracting exist, these traditions are sustained because 'no one wants to deviate from the equilibrium signal lest as a consequence others believe that he is a low type'.[121] Posner also uses signalling theory to explain tax compliance.[122] He suggests that people pay taxes because failing to do so, and getting caught, sends a signal that the person is deviant, and determines how the individual is perceived in society.[123] Similarly, Carlson applies signalling theory to roadside recycling programmes. She argues they may have been effective because 'easily identifiable recycling bins … provide participants an opportunity to make a visible statement about their environmentally proper behaviour, and in turn, to see

[114] Posner (1998) 767. Posner developed this theory further in Posner, E, *Law and Social Norms* (Harvard University Press 2000).

[115] McAdams, 'Signaling Discount Rates' (2000) 630.

[116] ibid.

[117] Posner (1998) 768.

[118] McAdams, 'Signaling Discount Rates' (2000) 644.

[119] Bernstein, L, 'Opting out of the legal system – Extralegal Contractual Relations in the Diamond Industry' (1992) 21 *J Legal Stud* 115.

[120] Posner, E, 'Standards, Rules and Social Norms' (1997) 21 *Harv J L & Pub Pol'y* 101, 108–09.

[121] ibid 109.

[122] Posner's use of terminology is inconsistent as he refers to 'good type' and 'bad type' in this article instead of the 'low type' and 'high type' he previously used. The meaning is the same – '"Bad types" have high discount rates, meaning that they value future payoffs relatively little compared to current payoffs. "Good types" have low discount rates.' Posner, E, 'Law and Social Norms: The Case of Tax Compliance' (2000) 86(8) *Virginia L Rev* 1781, 1786–87.

[123] Posner (2000) 1794–95.

who is failing to cooperate'.[124] Also in relation to the approval of neighbours, Rachlinski explains that voting sends a signal that the person is a 'public-spirited member of the community'.[125]

Signalling can be observed in any group setting where there is an incentive to comply with social norms in order to maintain a reputation. The failure to send the right signal, that is, failing to comply with the norm, can have negative consequences; as such, signalling is often intimately linked with sanctions, such as those described in the previous section. The presence of signalling suggests that sanctions may play a role in the regulation of persona. It is possible that the sanctions are perceived risks, and are not actively administered, as occurred in stand-up comedy.[126] The signal of seeking permission to use persona was more readily observed in persona regulation than sanctions.

The literature in this field suggests that signalling exists separate from the law. While this book acknowledges that signalling in social norms is a unique influence, it argues that social norms and law are not mutually exclusive. This is because law can influence the type of signal that is sent, by providing guidance on what behaviour is to be expected. Thus, a connection can be made between the deterrence theory of law, which influences behaviour, and the signalling theory of social norms, which instructs parties on what is considered appropriate behaviour. The perceived risk of litigation can influence the signals that parties want to communicate to one another.

IV. The Interaction of Law, Social Norms and Contract

Law, contract and social norms are three overlapping influences on behaviour in the context of commercialisation of persona. Law is defined as obligations imposed by the state; contracts as agreements freely entered into by parties; and social norms as informal rules of group regulation. Consideration of these different influences on behaviour is interesting in an empirical study on persona regulation, given that persona is heavily legally regulated in the US as compared to the more piecemeal approach in the UK. To what extent does this different legal milieu change the behaviours of individuals in industries that exploit persona? This book suggests that law, while an important influence, is but one of several influences on behaviour. The other influences discussed in this chapter, social norms and contract, are instrumental in the commercialisation of persona. While each influence is discussed as a distinct concept, they are porous, interacting to shape the sphere of persona commercialisation, as illustrated in Figure 3.1.

[124] Carlson, J, 'Recycling Norms' (2001) 89 *Cal L Rev* 1231, 1266.

[125] Rachlinski, JJ, 'The Limits of Social Norms Symposium on Law' (1998) 74 *Chi-Kent L Rev* 1537, 1546.

[126] Oliar and Sprigman (2008).

Figure 3.1 The interaction of law, contract and social norms

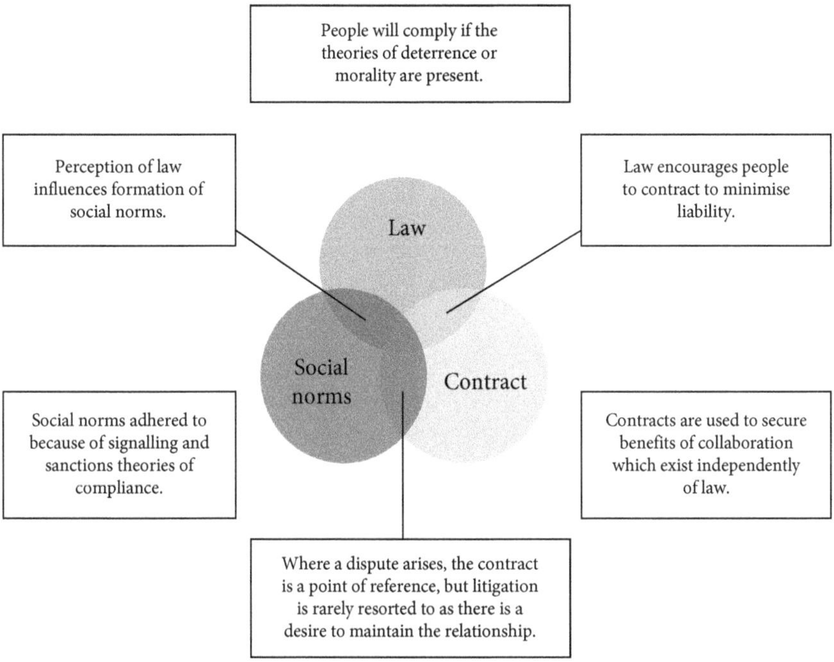

In terms of persona commercialisation, compliance with law translates into the formation of contracts that minimise liability, and may also influence social norms that operate in parallel to the law. Social norms may be reflective of the law but they are complied with because of sanctions and signalling theories of compliance. In complying with social norms, a contract may be entered into by parties. As a result, contracts may be a tool of compliance with social norms and/or the law. However, contract also plays an important independent role in regulating behaviour, as contracts are used to secure benefits of collaboration that may exist independently of the law or social norms.

In examining the interaction of these influences in the context of fieldwork conducted for this book, law appears to have a greater impact than contract and social norms. This is because the law prompts parties to enter into contracts and also shapes social norms. Contracting in itself does not seem to impact the way in which the law operates. The impact of the law on the contract and social norms is greater than the reverse situation. This impact translates into dispute resolution practices. While the transactional sphere is characterised by behaviours subject to multiple, overlapping influences, the dispute resolution sphere is primarily influenced by law. Recognising this distinction is important, as it sheds light on how the different legal frameworks impact potential claimants and defendants when persona is used without permission. Multiple influences may impact why a party does or does not seek permission to use persona, but if this permission is not sought, law will be relied on where possible. The conclusion to be drawn from this is that relationships are multifaceted in terms of the various influences that can be observed, whereas in the absence of a relationship, where persona is used without permission, the law often determines the course of action that is taken. As a result, there is a divergence in dispute resolution practices in the US and the UK, despite the many similarities that will be observed in the transactional sphere in the forthcoming chapters.

PART 2

Rights in Practice

4

Dispute Resolution

Introduction

This chapter examines the dispute resolution practices that are used in the industries studied in this book: advertising, merchandising, film and television, and sports video games. In analysing information collected from interviews, it was found that dispute resolution practices were similar across all the industries where there was a relationship between the parties. Generally, parties are hesitant to sue if there is a breach of contract as they want to maintain a relationship, which gives credence to the role of social norms in persona commercialisation practices. However, in the absence of a relationship, law is the guiding force in determining behaviour. This is the main area where a divergence can be observed between the UK and the US: there is a greater likelihood that a claim will be brought in the US than in the UK. This is an interesting observation, because subsequent chapters will reveal that permission-based behaviours are common in both jurisdictions despite there being a clearer legal requirement in the US to seek permission for persona in certain circumstances.

Despite the absence of a right of publicity, UK interviewees were generally wary of commercialising persona without permission because of the fear of expansion of passing off. Conversely, this fear did not translate into dispute resolution practices as the requirements for passing off are considered onerous. This is an irreconcilable viewpoint. In contrast, in the US, claims will be brought even if there is no basis for doing so because the threat of litigation can induce a settlement. This chapter will proceed by examining the similarities across jurisdictions in the approach to dispute resolution in the presence of a relationship. Then, focus will shift to the approach in the absence of a relationship and argue that the differences in the substantive law discussed in the chapter 2, and the different legal landscapes, have resulted in this divergence.

I. Dispute Resolution in Presence of a Relationship

When there is a relationship between parties, it is rare for litigation to result, because the parties want to maintain the relationship. This relates to the signalling theory of social norms. Litigation is avoided to ensure future cooperation and to maintain a reputation that the entity is good to work with. In sending such a signal, most disputes will be resolved by reference to the contract. According to an interviewee, 'With celebrity endorsement deals, the relationship is based on contract. Issues arise when there is no direct relationship. But when there is a relationship, it all boils down to contract.'[1] Many interviewees noted that celebrities fail to adhere to the obligations of the contract. Yet the entities that have contracted to use persona will not strictly enforce the terms of the contract as they want to remain in a favourable light with the celebrity. One lawyer gave the example that 'You contract with someone to appear at an event and they are too drunk and don't turn up. Technically you can terminate contract and not pay them. We won't enforce this because we don't want to upset celebrities.'[2]

It is common that leeway will be given to celebrities because the party that has contracted to use persona wants to maintain the relationship. Depending on the status of the celebrity, the celebrity is in a stronger negotiating position. As one lawyer noted, 'Celebrities don't need to worry. As long as they are famous, companies will always want to use them.'[3] The status of the celebrity will impact on her negotiating power. A sports lawyer noted:

> The size of an entity makes a difference. A very well-known individual who has commercial awareness, a track record in increasing brand's profile and therefore increasing sales will have a stronger negotiating position than someone who is new to the market.[4]

When an entity is in a more powerful position it may be less lenient about breaches of contract. However, it is still rare that such an entity would resort to litigation. A UK lawyer gave an example of an athlete who breached an agreement that required him to wear branded clothes:

> He told his agent he wasn't going to wear it [the branded clothing] because he could not be bothered. The brand did nothing apart from speaking to him – [the brand] said this [inaction] is not good enough.[5]

Another lawyer gave an example of a celebrity who visited a competitor's store in breach of the exclusivity of her endorsement deal:

> Legal action does not happen that frequently. [Pursuing legal action] can backfire strategically because it can make it look like a bad brand for other celebrities. A celebrity [was photographed] coming out of a shop which was a competing brand. The celebrity was in breach but [the brand] would not want to sue the celeb. It takes a lot for you to want to sue the celebrity because of the adverse publicity.[6]

[1] New York interview 12.
[2] UK interview 6.
[3] UK interview 14.
[4] UK interview 3. It should be noted that a scandal can decrease the bargaining power of a well-known individual; eg, Tiger Wood's affair resulted in the loss of many sponsorship deals. Wie, W, 'Tiger Woods lost $22 Million in Endorsements in 2010' *Sports Illustrated* (21 July 2010).
[5] UK interview 12.
[6] UK interview 14.

A similar observation was made by a brand management specialist:

> [Dispute resolution] is about coming to agreement because no one wants to go to court. Don't want brands to be seen by the fans as attacking the audience that they are trying to get to. Always end up trying to come to an agreement.[7]

The approach to dispute resolution where there is a relationship can be linked to Macaulay's observations on relational contracting, which is situated both within empirical contract theory and social norms literature:

> Adjustment of exchange relationships and dispute settlement by litigation or the threat of it also has many costs. The gain anticipated from using this form of coercion often fails to outweigh these costs, which are both monetary and non-monetary. Threatening to turn matters over to an attorney may cost no more money than postage or a telephone call; yet few are so skilled in making such a threat that will not cost some deterioration of the relationship between the firms.[8]

Resorting to litigation will damage the relationship between the entity and the individual irreparably, so this will occur only where there is no desire for reconciliation. An example of litigation is the dispute between Kat Florence Jewellery and Sarah Jessica Parker.[9] The jewellery brand claimed Parker failed to fulfil her promotional obligations, which included public appearances, photoshoots and interviews. Considering that the brand collaborated with Parker to design the jewellery, Parker's failure to fulfil her promotional obligations undermined the value of the contract. Since no resolution was reached, the brand decided to sue.[10] However, parties generally prefer to reach an amicable solution without resorting to litigation. This is because they do not want to send the wrong signal and they do not want to upset the fans as they are trying to capitalise on the para-social relationship. The value of the contract is that it is a point of reference of what is expected for each party. It is often not fully utilised and it is common that disagreements occur. One interviewee summed up the position as follows:

> [There is] not a contract in the world where someone doesn't complain. The commercial reality is that you will not sue them [the celebrity]. Have to take contracts with a pinch of salt.[11]

This section has examined dispute resolution in the presence of a relationship. It is interesting to note that even if the celebrity is at fault, the onus is on the licensee to maintain the relationship to send the right signal to future collaborators and maintain favour with fans. However, the next section will reveal that where there

[7] UK interview 19.

[8] Macaulay, S, 'Non-Contractual Relations in Business – A Preliminary Study' (1963) 28 *Am Soc Rev* 55, 64.

[9] 'Sarah Jessica Parker sued for not promoting jewellery label' *Harper's Bazaar* (26 March 2018).

[10] A settlement was arrived at: Ell, K, 'Sarah Jessica Parker and Kat Florence reach preliminary settlement' *Women's Wear Daily* (4 February 2019).

[11] UK interview 12.

is an absence of relationship, it is the celebrity who assumes the role of claimant when persona is used without authorisation.

II. Dispute Resolution in the Absence of a Relationship

In the absence of a relationship, the divergence in the legal frameworks in the US and the UK translates to divergent approaches to dispute resolution. The gaps in the UK approach to persona regulation become significant, as fewer potential claimants will have access to a claim, despite the expansion of passing off. In comparison, the breadth of protection in the US provides access to claims in many circumstances. The US approach to dispute resolution will be discussed first, followed by the UK approach.

A. United States

In the US, three main behaviours were observed in dispute resolution in the absence of a relationship: a cease-and-desist letter will be sent; settlement usually occurs; and if not, litigation will ensue. A cease-and-desist letter is considered to be an effective method of addressing the offending action. Even where there is no viable cause of action, or the claim alleged is unlikely to succeed, US lawyers will still send a cease- and-desist letter. As noted by a New York lawyer, 'You can bring a suit on less than compelling grounds because it will be cheaper to settle than to fight.'[12] When asked what action would be taken if a client complained of use of her persona without authorisation, all lawyers responded that they would initially send a letter outlining the complaint. As one lawyer noted:

> When you represent talent, a huge percentage of what you do never gets to court because you don't want it to. If I see someone using my client's image in a bad way, I'll write a nasty letter. Maybe you'll get some money or they'll just stop what they're doing unless there is some legitimate argument … [Y]ou won't see a lot of what is going on in this field by just reading the cases.[13]

In the US, the force of the law behind the letter is often considered strong enough to get the action to stop. According to one interviewee, 'usually if a case is brought there is a decent argument that there is liability'.[14] This is not an accurate reflection of the US legal landscape as it concerns the right of publicity, as groundless claims

[12] New York interview 9.
[13] California interview 15.
[14] New York interview 6.

have been brought against works that should receive First Amendment protection. However, claims might progress through the courts, as occurred in *Porco*[15] and *de Havilland*.[16] While these claims should have been disposed of summarily, the failure of the courts to do this raised concerns across the entertainment industry and resulted in the filing of amicus briefs by interested parties to ensure that a legally sound outcome was arrived at.[17]

The potential for claims to progress even if they do not reach trial stage, the risk of liability if a court makes a questionable decision, combined with the enormous cost of litigation usually induces settlement – unless the party feels she has a strong defence. One lawyer suggested that '98% of cases settle because litigation in this country is so expensive'.[18] The behaviour of settling was referred to by the majority of US lawyers interviewed. A lawyer who represents celebrities noted:

> Out of all the cases we've had, I don't think any of them have gone to trial because the defendant will settle at some point. I've probably had 10 claims that have gone to the point of filing.[19]

Similarly:

> One letter usually settles the case. 50% of the time they'll start negotiating and get rid of it, and the other times they don't, it costs them at least three times as much as it would have.[20]

It is difficult to corroborate the opinions expressed by lawyers on the high cost of litigation in the US because many cases settle on a confidential basis. While it is difficult to ascertain fees spent on lawyers, an attempt was made to investigate damages awarded for infringement of the right of publicity. The Westlaw International Case Evaluator was used to determine damages awarded for publicity rights cases in New York and California from 1994 to the present.[21] This tool was limited in application, as there is no case category for 'right of publicity', so various search terms and case categories had to be used to generate verdicts for publicity rights and false endorsement persona cases. Additionally, web searches were carried out to determine awards for cases that have received media attention, as the jury verdicts are not always published on Westlaw International. The report of the American Bar Association's 39th Annual Forum on Franchising,

[15] *Porco v Lifetime Entertainment Services LLC*147 AD 3d 1253 (2017).

[16] *De Havilland v FX Networks LLC* (2018) 21 Cal App 5th 845 (2018).

[17] 'Lifetime Movie: A Case of Violated Privacy?' *The Authors Guild* (13 October 2020) at https://authorsguild.org/news/lifetime-movie-a-case-of-violated-privacy/ (accessed 2 December 2022); Gottlieb, A, 'IDA Files Amicus Brief in FX Networks and Pacific 2.1 Entertainment vs Olivia de Havilland case' *Documentary.org* (26 January 2018) at www.documentary.org/advocacy/ida-files-amicus-brief-fx-networks-and-pacific-21-entertainment-vs-olivia-de-havilland-case (accessed 2 December 2022).

[18] New York interview 3.

[19] California interview 15.

[20] California interview 12.

[21] 1994 is the earliest start date available.

Right of Publicity Claims in a Digital Age,[22] was a helpful resource. According to this report:

> Celebrities can afford to and will sue to protect unauthorised use of their personal 'brands', and have rung up high damages awards and settlements against companies that have used their identities without permission.[23]

The report noted that Michael Jordan was awarded \$8.9 million in 2015 by a Chicago jury, after a successful summary judgment against Finer Foods LLC for infringement of his Illinois right of publicity by using his name and player number 23 in an advertisement in a commemorative *Sports Illustrated* edition celebrating his career.[24]

Other damages awards include \$403,000 in *White v Samsung*,[25] \$2.5 million in *Waits v Frito-Lay Inc*[26] and \$500,000 for false endorsement in *Beastie Boys v Monster Energy Co*.[27] Settlements include \$5 million in *Woody Allen v American Apparel Inc*,[28] \$1.5 million in *Sirico v Best Buy Co*[29] and \$60 million in *Re NCAA Student-Athlete Name & Likeness Licensing Litigation*.[30] In terms of the cost of litigation:

> A preliminary injunction motion and hearing can easily cost \$100,000. The appeal from that decision can take several months and add an additional cost of legal fees of \$50,000 to \$100,000. Each party to litigation may incur legal fees of \$500,000 to \$1 million or more just to complete trial and there might still be an appeal from the final judgment, adding another \$50,000 to \$100,000 in legal fees.[31]

The highest recorded award in a right of publicity case was the sum of \$15 million in *Doe (aka Twist) v TCI Cablevision*.[32] In that case, a comic-book maker was sued by former hockey player Tony Twist for using his name in a comic. According to Judge Limbaugh:

> The fictional and real Tony Twist bear no physical resemblance to each other and, aside from the common nickname, are similar only in that each can be characterized as having an 'enforcer' or tough-guy persona.[33]

[22] Adler, J and Van der Broek, M, *Right of Publicity Claims in a Digital Age* (American Bar Association 39th Annual Forum on Franchising, 2016).

[23] ibid 48.

[24] *Jordan v Dominick's Finer Foods LLC* 2015 WL 5086730 (NDIll); Adler and Van der Broek (2016) 2.

[25] *White v Samsung Electronics of America Inc* 971 F 2d 1395 (9th Cir 1992).

[26] *Waits v Frito Lay* 33 F Supp 2d 867 (CD Cal 1999), rev'd 255 F 3d 1180 (9th Cir 2001).

[27] *Beastie Boys v Monster Energy Co* 2014 WL 8387093 (SDNY) (Verdict and Settlement Summary).

[28] *Woody Allen v American Apparel* No 08-3179 (SDNY 18 May 2009).

[29] *Sirico v BestBuy* No 08-3179 (SDNY 18 May 2009).

[30] *Re NCAA Student-Athlete Name & Licensing Litigation* 724 F 3d 1268 (9th Cir 2013) (*Keller*); '\$60 Million Settlement Approved in NCAA Video Game Lawsuit' *New York Times* (17 July 2015).

[31] Kurnit, R, 'Right of Publicity' *Lexology* (22 October 2018) at https://gettingthedealthrough.com/area/45/jurisdiction/23/right-publicity-2018-united-states/ (accessed 4 November 2018).

[32] *Doe (aka Twist) v TCI Cablevision* 110 SW 3d 363 (2003).

[33] ibid [366].

The judge went on to state:

> Here, all parties agree that the 'Tony Twist' character is not 'about' him, in that the character does not physically resemble Twist nor does the Spawn story line attempt to track Twist's real life.[34]

However, the court ruled in favour of Twist, as the use of his name and his demeanour was the basis for the character, a fact conceded by the creator of the comic book. Evidence also showed that hockey fans thought that Twist was connected to the character. The court ruled that the use of Twist's name and demeanour was done to establish a connection with the comic book, and to market directly to hockey fans, and thus found that Twist's right of publicity had been infringed.

In addressing whether the comic book was an expressive work and thus protected by the First Amendment, the court rejected both the transformative use test and the *Rogers*[35] test and developed what has become known as the 'predominant use' test. The *Rogers* test was established in 1989; the transformative test was established in the 2001 case of *Comedy III*[36] and used in a comic-book case (*Winter v DC*[37]) in 2003, the same year that *Twist* was decided by the Missouri Supreme Court. As such, the court had points of reference but rejected these existing tests in favour of one formulated by Mark Lee in an article entitled 'Agents of Chaos: Judicial Confusion in Defining the Right of Publicity-Free Speech Interface'.[38] This test was articulated in two lines in *Twist*:

> [T]he metaphorical reference to Twist, though a literary device, has very little literary value compared to its commercial value. On the record here, the use and identity of Twist's name has become predominantly a ploy to sell comic books and related products rather than an artistic or literary expression, and under these circumstances, free speech must give way to the right of publicity.[39]

Less than 10 years later, in 2013, the 3rd Circuit Court in *Hart* described this test as 'subjective at best, arbitrary at worst, and in either case calls upon judges to act as both impartial jurists and discerning art critics'.[40]

The US court system, which allows for judicial activism, is a starkly different legal landscape compared to that in the UK, and thus potential for expansion or differing interpretations of the law legitimises claims that should, on the face, be dismissed. If a trial is lost, the risk of damages can be substantial, whereas settlement allows the defendant greater financial control compared to the risk posed by facing a jury. This contributes to the impact of cease-and-desist letters alleging

[34] ibid [370].
[35] *Rogers v Grimaldi* 857 F 2d 944 (1989).
[36] *Comedy III Productions v Saderup* 25 Cal 4th 387 (2001).
[37] *Winter v DC Comics* 30 Cal 4th 881 (2003).
[38] Lee, M, 'Agents of Chaos: Judicial Confusion in Defining the Right of Publicity-Free Speech Interface' (2003) 23 *Loy LA Ent L Rev* 471.
[39] *Doe (aka Twist) v TCI Cablevision* (2003) [374].
[40] *Hart v Electronic Arts* 717 F 3d 141 (2013) [154].

right of publicity infringement or false endorsement under the Lanham Act. In fact, US lawyers also send cease-and-desist letters even if they have a limited chance of success at trial, if the client has the financial backing to pay for them. This strategy can be successful because of the breadth of the law and lack of clarity as to what uses will not infringe the right of publicity and false endorsement, as facilitated by differing interpretations across States, as evidenced by the outcome of the *Twist* case. One lawyer in California gave an example of a successful cease-and-desist request based on the application of the common law right of publicity to a post-mortem use of persona. The aspect of persona used would not have been protected by the statute, and the common law right of publicity in California does not extend to post-mortem protection. The reputation and financial backing of the lawyer representing the plaintiff's estate nevertheless resulted in a successful settlement.

The impact of sending cease-and-desist letters is most visible in the movie industry, where the right of publicity is used as a money-gouging tool and has directly contributed to the behaviour of seeking permission to use persona in movies; 'life-rights agreements', discussed in chapter 7. It is considered better to avoid the risk of a claim, even if it has a limited chance of success. If a settlement is arrived at upfront, the producer will be negotiating from a more favourable position compared to having to reach a settlement with a hostile defendant.

The trend of sending cease-and-desist letters has been observed in the field of trade mark law.[41] In 2008, Port suggested that unmeritorious claims were made to increase the cost of market entry.[42] Subsequently, Gallagher undertook an empirical study in which he interviewed 58 intellectual property lawyers to determine the role of law in trade mark and copyright disputes. Gallagher's study provides further empirical evidence that the force of the law is often enough to produce a desirable outcome for an aggrieved party, even if the claim is unmeritorious.[43] He concludes that

> aggressive trademark and copyright enforcement efforts often work, as enforcement targets frequently choose to capitulate or settle rather than resist claims on the legal merits, likely due to the costs and uncertainties inherent in IP litigation.[44]

Similar conclusions have been drawn by McGeveran with regard to pursuing parodies of trade marks.[45] Lemly also examined trade-mark litigation practices

[41] See: Grinvald, L, 'Shaming Trademark Bullies' (2011) 90 *Wis L Rev* 625; Manta, I, 'Bearing Down on Trademark Bullies' (2012) 22 *Fordham Intell Prop Media & Ent LJ* 853; Grinvald, L, 'Policing the Cease-and-Desist Letter' (2015) 49 *Usf L Rev* 409.

[42] Port, K, 'Trademark Extortion: The End of Trademark Law' (2008) 65 *Wash & Lee L Rev* 585, 589.

[43] Gallagher, W, 'Trade Mark and Copyright Enforcement in the Shadow of IP Law' (2011) 28 *Santa Clara Computer & High Tech LJ* 453.

[44] ibid 496.

[45] McGeveran, W, 'The Imaginary Trademark Parody Crisis (and the Real One)' (2015) 90(2) *Washington L Rev* 713, 739–45. McGeveran suggests creating exemptions for the use of trade marks in certain categories of work to provide greater clarity for parodists to respond to unmeritorious claims.

and found that 'even claims that are unlikely to win often have the desired effect of scaring off the users'.[46]

Grinvald examined the use of cease-and-desist letters. She noted that the US has a reputation for litigation, and yet 'approximately only three percent of all legal disputes are brough to the judicial system. Of this three percent, only a small fraction of disputes are litigated to a final decision.'[47] She suggests that 'abusive' cease-and-desist letters[48] are used to resolve disputes. Trimble also notes that '[c]ease-and-desist letters are frequently utilized in disputes concerning intellectual property'.[49] These letters often work because of the cost of litigation and the uncertainty of the outcome.[50] In relation to the right of publicity, this uncertainty is arguably even more impactful since the laws are State-based. Even for false endorsement claims under the Lanham Act, courts have given a wide interpretation, as outlined in chapter 2. The conclusions drawn from empirical evidence in this book regarding the trend of sending cease-and-desist letters align with the observations described above.

While cease-and-desist letters are often effective, in the field of persona protection, if a letter does not elicit the desired response of settlement, litigation is likely. Since 2000, there have been 26 notable right-of-publicity cases in the US.[51] This number is probably just a small fraction of the number of complaints that are resolved outside of the court system. However, there is indeed a significant risk of litigation when the law is not complied with. The potential for expansion of the right and the surrounding uncertainty arguably provides more opportunities for claimants, as compared to a more conservative approach taken in the UK, which will now be explained.

B. United Kingdom

The UK approach to dispute resolution is less claimant-friendly than the US approach. Since there is no right of publicity in the UK, threats of litigation would

[46] Lemly, M, 'Fame, Parody, and Policing in Trademark Law' (2019) 1 *Mich St L Rev* 1, 5.

[47] Grinvald (2015) 410, citing Landes, W, 'An Empirical Analysis of Intellectual Property Litigation: Some Preliminary Results' (2004) 41 *Hous L Rev* 749, 761; Port, K, 'Trademar Extortion: The Ned of Trademark Law' (2008) 65 *Wash & Lee L Rev* 585,589; La Belle, M, 'Against Settlement of (Some) Patent Cases' (2014) 67 *Vand L Rev* 375, 377.

[48] Grinvald (2015) 412 defines abusive cease-and-desist letters as follows: 'Cease-and-desist letters are abusive when they contain a threat (implicit or explicit) of litigation if the target does not comply with the letter's demands, as well as one of more of the following items: unnecessary legalese, demands for settlement within a short time frame, demands or immediate payment of some form of fees, and/or weak legal claims.'

[49] Trimble, M, 'Setting Foot on Enemy Ground: Cease and Desist Letters, DMCA Notifications and Personal Jurisdiction in Declaratory Judgment Actions' (2010) 50 *IDEA* 777, 784. See also Kiser, J, 'To Bully or Not to Bully: Understanding the Role of Uncertainty in Trademark Enforcement Decisions'(2013) 37(1) *Col J Law and Arts* 211.

[50] Grindvald (2015) 413.

[51] Faber, J, 'Right of Publicity – Notable Cases' at http://rightofpublicity.com/notable-cases (accessed 10 January 2023).

have to be based on the existing piecemeal causes of action. These causes of action, which include passing off, trade marks, copyright, breach of confidence and defamation, have limited application, as explained in chapter 2, and as a result, there are more instances where persona can be used without consequence. Thus, in the UK, sending a cease-and-desist letter does not carry the same weight as in the US, despite expansions in passing off to accommodate false endorsement. While the behaviours of seeking permission that will be discussed in forthcoming chapters are influenced by the legal framework, there will be instances where persona is used without authorisation and it has to be determined whether the individual has legal recourse.

Lawyers in the UK have less basis from which to pursue unauthorised uses of persona due to the limitations of passing off. Interestingly, the limitations were viewed in the transactional sphere with caution, as permission is likely to be sought to use persona. However, this does not translate into the litigious sphere, as passing off is not as considered as great a threat as is perceived when considering whether to ask permission to use persona. As noted by a lawyer, 'It [passing off] does not protect against casual use. You can't just tell people to stop. You have to prove difficult things such as goodwill, loss …'[52] Another stated, 'One problem we have always had with passing off is that there are hurdles to get through that are quite hard.'[53] Sending a letter without a firm legal basis is unlikely to result in a settlement, in contrast to the US. One UK lawyer noted that he acted for a company that used a rugby player in a humorous advertisement: 'Got a claim letter alleging passing off. Well-crafted letter, but no possibility of implied endorsement.'[54] The lawyer sent a letter responding that there was no basis for passing off and that was the end of the matter. He did not feel impacted by this groundless threat.

Groundless threats were addressed by UK Law Commission reports in 2014[55] and 2015.[56] The Commission noted that passing off was not addressed by these provisions:

> Only threats to bring infringement proceedings for patents, trade marks or design rights come within the provisions. Therefore, a threat to sue on a different right, such as copyright or passing off, will not incur liability.[57]

No changes were made in relation to passing off in the Intellectual Property (Unjustified Threats) Act 2017, which was generated as a result of these reports.

[52] UK interview 12.
[53] UK interview 13.
[54] UK interview 5.
[55] Law Commission, *Patents, Trade Marks and Design Rights: Groundless Threats Report* (Law Com No 346, 5 March 2014).
[56] Law Commission, *Patents, Trade Marks and Designs: Unjustified Threats Report* (Law Com 360, 12 October 2015).
[57] Law Commission (2014) para 3.53.

However, it appears that groundless threats for passing off of persona[58] are not as impactful as groundless publicity rights claims in the US. Passing off still requires misrepresentation to be made out, and UK courts have maintained a strict approach to this element as compared to the expansive approach to false endorsement under the Lanham Act. As expressed by UK interviewee 3, '[You would] have to prove there is an actual endorsement. If there isn't, what is the loss?' When asked how easy or difficult it is to succeed on a passing-off claim, he responded:

> Very difficult. How many passing off cases do you see? Yes, there are some very clear cases where passing off has taken place, but this is one of the issues with the law as it stands. It is difficult to prove passing off.

On one hand, from the perspective of a famous individual, this might be considered disadvantageous. On the other hand, the current status of the law appears to deter frivolous claims. That being said, the legal landscapes must also be considered as contributing to the divergence in dispute resolution practices.

III. Divergence in Dispute Resolution Practices

A. The Different Legal Landscapes

The lack of impact of a letter stating a groundless passing-off claim in the UK compared to the US can be attributed to several factors, which were identified from fieldwork and secondary research. This section seeks to outline the potential factors that contribute to the divergence in dispute resolution practices, but further research would be required on each factor to make definitive findings. This book refers to the work of Beverley-Smith in the comparison of jurisdictions, but does not adopt the position that greater persona protection is needed in the UK. Rather, Beverley-Smith provides a useful explanation as to why the UK law is less susceptible to manipulation by claimants (although he does so in order to explain why persona protection is more developed in the US).

The first factor is that UK judges are more conservative than US judges and are hesitant to depart from precedent.[59] One US lawyer noted:

> My frustration overall is judges love these cases, they think they're really interesting, and they have this tendency to say I know there's law out there and they come up with a new test. It's one of these areas where there are a lot of tests and either a lot of different

[58] This book focuses on persona regulation. It is unclear how frequently groundless threats are made in passing off in general, as the Law Commission impact assessment did not distinguish between passing-off and trade-mark cases – Law Commission, *Simplifying the law of groundless threats of patent, trade mark and design right infringement* (IA No BISIPO010, 13 July 2015).

[59] Beverley-Smith, H, *Commercial Appropriation of Personality* (Cambridge University Press 2002) 191–94.

> courts not talking to each other, or trying to combine the tests to create their own. When it comes down to it as a practitioner, it's difficult to advise on. The more tests there are the less certainty there is to what you can do and what you can't.[60]

In contrast, hesitance to depart from precedent in the UK was evident in *Fenty*, where Justice Birss stated 'Whether an image right can or should be developed is not what this case is concerned with.'[61] Arguably, the nature of the case would have made it suitable to consider whether the UK should recognise a publicity right. The right was recognised in the US case of *Haelan*, where the court considered whether an exclusive licensee had a proprietary interest in the persona of a baseball player.[62] The court held:

> With regard to such situations, we must consider defendant's contention that none of the plaintiff's contracts created more than a release of liability, because a man has no legal interest in the publication of his picture other than his right of privacy, ie a personal and non-assignable right not to have his feelings hurt by such a publication. A majority of this court rejects this contention. We think that, in addition to and independent of that right of privacy (which in New York derives from statute), a man has a right of publicity in the value of his photograph …[63]

The court in *Haelan* distinguished the right of publicity from privacy in a decision that subsequently resulted in the development of the right of publicity that we know today. In *Fenty*, there was no consideration of such a right, and there is unlikely to be consideration in future passing-off cases as misappropriation departs from the core element of misrepresentation. If a case were to consider such a departure, the decision would likely have to come from the Supreme Court. However, even if a case were to reach the Supreme Court, Beverly-Smith notes:

> Unlike American courts, English courts can often assume that reform will be forthcoming from the legislature, if necessary, and the courts are often unwilling to make the changes themselves, reflecting the belief that legislative methods of law reform are superior.[64]

While a general comparison of US and UK judges is beyond the scope of this book, it is undeniable that courts have played a central role in the development of the US right of publicity. In contrast, UK courts have been conservative in their interpretation of existing law, and have declined to recognise a stand-alone 'image right' that could be equated to the right of publicity. Traditionally, common law legal systems have been hesitant to embrace academic writings when compared

[60] California interview 22.
[61] *Fenty and others v Arcadia Group Brands Ltd (trading as Topshop) and another* [2013] EWHC 2310 (Ch) [30].
[62] *Haelan Laboratories Inc v Topps Chewing Gum Inc* 202 F 2d 866 (2d Cir 1953).
[63] ibid [868].
[64] Beverley-Smith (2002) 195.

to civil law systems.[65] In the US, at least regarding the development of privacy and publicity, courts have been more willing to refer to journal articles. Warren and Brandeis's seminal article[66] and Prosser's article[67] both influenced the development of privacy law.[68] The right of publicity was eventually developed to address the perceived inadequacies of the commercial protection of persona under the right to privacy. While the court in *Haelan*[69] did not refer to a journal article in recognising the right, Nimmer's subsequent article[70] was frequently cited as the right of publicity gained recognition across the country.

While both systems are common law, the US having been a former English colony, it must be recalled that the US has a written constitution, a feature of a civil law system.[71] This historical departure from the traditional unwritten constitution of the UK common law could rationalise the apparent difference in the way judges create law in both systems. Similarly, it has been asserted that 'The rule of stare decisis has been applied flexibly in the United States, and more strictly in England.'[72] This could explain the various contours of the right of publicity that have developed on an ad hoc basis. However, more research is needed to make a definitive comparison of the US and UK approaches to judging. It is sufficient at this point to indicate that there has been a comparable difference in the way judges in these jurisdictions have treated the commercial protection of persona.

The second factor that makes seemingly groundless claims forceful in the US, in addition to the potential expansion of the law, is that US civil cases can still be tried by jury if either party so elects,[73] whereas the UK has largely abandoned the jury system in civil claims.[74] According to interviewees, in the US, juries are often favourable to celebrity claimants because 'Americans love their celebrities'.[75] According to one lawyer, 'One lesson of the Vanna White case is you can't go to trial against a celebrity in America. Some people would say that's a lesson from the OJ Simpson case …'[76] The impact of jury- versus judge-rendered

[65] Bowal, P and Kirsch, A, 'The World's Legal Systems' (2010–2011) 35 *LawNow* 23, 25.

[66] Warren, S and Brandeis, D, 'Right to Privacy' (1890) 4 *Harvard L Rev* 193.

[67] Prosser, W, 'Privacy' (1960) 48 *California Law Review* 383.

[68] The right to privacy was first recognised by the common law in the Supreme Court of Georgia in *Pavesich v New England Life Insurance Co* 50 SE 68 (1905), which cited Warren and Brandeis at para 74.

[69] *Haelan v Topps* (1953) [868].

[70] Nimmer, M, 'The Right of Publicity' (1954) 19 *Law & Contemp Probs* 203.

[71] Fernando, O, 'Conceptual Differences between the Civil Law System and the Common Law System' (1990) 19 *Sw U L Rev* 1161, 1162.

[72] Seng, M, 'Aspects of the Common Law System in the United States' (2001) 2 *Common L Rev* 6, 8.

[73] Landes, WM, 'An Empirical Analysis of Intellectual Property Litigation: Some Preliminary Results' (2004) 41 *Hous L Rev* 749, 754.

[74] An exception is defamation, where trial is without a jury unless the court orders otherwise (Defamation Act 2013, s 11).

[75] New York interview 16.

[76] New York interview 16.

decisions is difficult to compare across jurisdictions due to cultural divergences, but US lawyers tended to feel that celebrities have a good chance of success before a jury. As one commented, 'You don't have to know every case ... just get to the jury. Be persuasive.'[77] In fact, one attributed the development of the right of publicity to the popular culture of the US, indicating a preference for celebrity claimants: 'Reverence for celebrities in the US has influenced how the law has developed.'[78]

In a study that examined criminal convictions, Carroll found that celebrities were convicted at a higher rate than non-celebrities.[79] It would be difficult to extrapolate these findings to the right of publicity because trials are usually within the civil realm (although some statutes allow for criminal prosecution, this option is rarely exercised). Furthermore, the right of publicity is most often exercised by celebrity claimants. This renders it infeasible to conduct a comparison of how juries decide in these claims. In addition, the lack of cases in the UK means that it is also difficult to compare US jury trials to non-jury UK trials. Finally, the difficulty in valuing the right of publicity makes it hard to ascertain whether awards are accurate. In discussing the market approach to valuation, Zerehi notes that 'an appropriate comparable for a celebrity's right of publicity is often unavailable'.[80] While fieldwork suggested that juries favour celebrities in right-of-publicity claims, more information is needed to determine the accuracy of these beliefs.

The third factor that contributes to the lack of force of groundless claims in the UK is the breadth of legal protection. Despite similar behaviours across jurisdictions, the law is more restricted and has clearer limits in the UK. This should allow UK lawyers to assess the validity of a claim with more confidence than their US counterparts. The assessment of a claim depends on the perception held by the lawyer drafting or receiving a claim. If a lawyer thinks a claim is invalid, she will advise her client accordingly, whereas in the US, an attempt might still be made at initiating a claim. Similarly, where a UK lawyer receives an invalid claim, she will respond accordingly, and the dispute is likely to end there. In contrast, in the US, a settlement might be reached, because the developmental approach taken by the courts and uncertainty surrounding certain issues means there may be a potential claim, even if it is not currently recognised in the corpus of existing case law. Courts in the US are more receptive to creating law than are UK courts, the latter

[77] California interview 15.

[78] New York interview 6.

[79] Carroll, B, 'Celebrity Adjudication: Comparative Analysis of United States Verdict Rates for Celebrity Defendants' (2013) 11 *ESLJ* 1, 6.

[80] Zerehi, S, 'Valuating a Celebrity's Right of Publicity for Estate Tax Purposes' (2017) 8 *Harv J Sports & Ent L* 125, 132.

tending to show greater deference to Parliament.[81] According to Beverly-Smith, referring to the US legal system:

> Although, in many cases, a relatively small number of authorities will be binding, in other cases there will be a choice from an array of case law which can provide support for almost any legal proposition whatsoever.[82]

This arguably results in US lawyers' perceiving claims more widely than UK lawyers, whose assessment will be more limited by the existing law.

B. The Difference in Legal Frameworks

The most tangible impact of the difference in legal frameworks is the lack of cases in the UK. Considering the law is geared towards persona protection in the US and infringement continues to take place, it is likely that persona is being used without permission in the UK, but there are limited suitable avenues for redress. This divergence is where the gaps in the law become significant. On the one hand, despite the presence of behaviours that regulate persona, non-permission-based behaviours will be difficult to redress under the piecemeal approach in the UK. On the other hand, the power attached to the law in the US can make the approach to dispute resolution unduly stacked in favour of the claimant.

An illustration of how the US approach empowers claimants can be seen in the film industry. While the First Amendment generally protects expressive works such as movies, there have been cases in the US claiming infringement. There have been no similar claims in the UK. The existence of cases in the US may be related to its being perceived as a preferable jurisdiction in which to claim due to factors such as the damages awarded, the use of juries and other variables. However, the UK has no equivalent law that could be manipulated to protect persona in film, unless the use was defamatory or infringed copyright. As a result, there is no opportunity to attempt litigation as the case would likely be struck out for failure to state a claim.[83]

The divergent approaches to dispute resolution demonstrate that the legal framework becomes significant when persona is used without authorisation. While for the most part behaviours are the same across jurisdictions, as will be elucidated in forthcoming chapters, the approach to unauthorised use differs. The implication of the influence of different legal frameworks on the same behaviour

[81] Beverley-Smith (2002) 195.
[82] ibid 192.
[83] Civil Procedure Rules, pt 3, r 3.4.

is best summed up by a UK lawyer, who expressed an opinion on the potential impact of legislation for a right of publicity in the UK:

> [The right of publicity] would not have a huge impact on the number of commercial deals that are done. But it might increase the number of claims because it will be clear that misappropriation is prohibited.[84]

IV. Conclusion

In the absence of a relationship, the US and UK approaches to dispute resolution diverge. Claimants will have difficulty seeking redress in the UK as compared to the US as the law is instrumental in addressing unauthorised uses of persona. In the US, the breadth of the law, the potential for expansion and the perceived ease with which celebrities succeed in front of a jury facilitate the sending of threatening letters regardless of whether there is a valid claim, settlements and actual litigation. The claim may not be valid in the existing case law but courts may decide to depart from precedent and allow the claim to proceed to trial, which can be more costly than obtaining a settlement. In contrast, a letter will be sent in the UK only if there is a strong case for passing off, thus suggesting a more limited avenue for potential claimants. Despite evidence in forthcoming chapters that suggests that passing off is influential in obtaining authorisation, it does not carry the same weight as an avenue of pursuit against unauthorised use of persona.

[84] UK interview 3.

5

Advertising Industry

Introduction

This chapter explains how law, contracts and social norms influence the behaviours that determine how persona is used in the advertising industry. The advertising industry uses persona to promote the sale of products and services. While the use of persona was traditionally limited to print media and radio advertisements, advancements in technology, specifically the rise of social media, have created new avenues for advertising and, consequentially, new ways in which to use persona.[1] This phenomenon has lent itself to greater use of endorsement-style advertisements, as companies want consumers to think that a celebrity has approved of the product or service to maximise on the para-social relationship.

While endorsement-style advertisements are the most popular form of advertisements to use persona,[2] there may be instances where a brand attempts to form an association with a celebrity without a direct endorsement. These types of advertisements are referred to in this book as 'illustrative', and usually occur when a brand depicts a celebrity using its product or service. Since both endorsement and illustrative advertisements imply connections with the celebrity, the line between these styles is blurred. This blurring increases the circumstances in which passing off may occur in the UK, as will be explained in examining influences on behaviour in this chapter.

Alongside endorsement advertisements, companies may seek exclusivity and thus an exclusive endorsement deal.[3] An exclusive endorsement deal requires the chosen persona to promote the company's product or services to the exclusion of competing companies. For example, an exclusive endorsement deal with

[1] See generally Tuten, T, *Advertising 2.0 – Social Media Marketing in a Web 2.0 World* (Greenwood Publishing Group 2008).

[2] There are many types of advertisements, but this book focuses on advertisements that use persona. Of these, the types of advertisements identified by this book – endorsement, illustrative, evocative and topical – endorsement is the most popular, based on the data collected in fieldwork as well as marketing literature: Choi, S and Rifon, N, 'Who is the Celebrity in Advertising? Understanding Dimensions of Celebrity Images' (2007) 40(2) *The Journal of Popular Culture* 304.

[3] Presidio Sports Management, 'Exclusivity Clauses in Endorsement Contracts (Pro Contracts 101 Series) *Presidio Sports Management* (26 February 2018) at www.presidiosportsmgmt.com/blog/exclusivityclauses (accessed 29 July 2019).

a watch maker would require the persona to refrain from promoting any other watch makers. The extent of the exclusivity will be determined by the deal struck between the brand and the persona. Fieldwork suggests that it is rare for exclusive endorsement deals to be undermined, as competitors will not attempt to use the persona of an exclusive licensee.

In contrast to the advertisements discussed above, there are also topical advertisements, which utilise persona to comment on a current event or make a humorous reference, as well as evocative advertisements, which refer to persona indirectly by drawing on a character trait, way of dressing or other mannerism. These types of advertisements are less common but are used by advertisers who want to draw a connection with a celebrity or the meaning associated with a celebrity, but without obtaining an endorsement. Such advertisements are made in the UK, but are not usually made in the US, since the development of the right of publicity from the 1980s onwards made it clear that what constitutes persona is subject to a broad interpretation and goes beyond name, voice and likeness.[4]

The various types of advertisements were studied in the fieldwork for this chapter, which involved 51 interviews with lawyers who had experience with the advertising industry in their respective jurisdictions. Out of these, 15 were based in the UK, 17 in New York and 19 in California. They were able to convey their experiences of working with celebrities, athletes, influencers, brands and advertising firms. From these interviews, key behaviours regarding persona commercialisation in the advertising industry were identified. The behaviours of seeking permission to use persona for endorsement and illustrative advertisements, and respecting exclusive endorsement deals, were observed in the US and the UK. There was a divergence in behaviours in terms of how topical and evocative advertisements are approached, as these are generally made without the permission of the persona in the UK, whereas these types of advertisements are not usually made in the US.

The relevant legal frameworks influence all the aforementioned behaviours, but the desire to collaborate via contract and social norms also offers explanations that will be discussed in this chapter. This is the only industry where there is a divergence in the behaviours observed, as two of the four behaviours are unique to the US and UK respectively. Later chapters will reveal that the same standard behaviours are observed in the industries studied, but the influences on the behaviours vary. This demonstrates that the variance in legal frameworks is not solely accountable for behaviours that commercialise persona.

This chapter is divided into six sections. Section I explains the different types of advertisements that use persona: endorsement, illustrative, topical and evocative. It briefly explains the shift from print advertising to mixed media campaigns,[5]

[4] *White v Samsung Electronics America Inc* 971 F 2d 1395 (9th Cir 1992).

[5] Mixed media campaigns combine print and digital marketing – 'Print vs Digital: How to design mixed media marketing campaigns' *ProActive Marketing* (14 July 2019) at www.proactive.marketing/mixed-media-marketing/ (accessed 14 July 2019).

which are common today due to advances in technology. Following this, each section identifies a behaviour and then considers which of the influences identified in chapter 3 apply: law, contract and/or social norms. In each section, the standard behaviour, as identified by the majority of responses collected from empirical data, is discussed first, followed by the deviation from the standard.

This chapter concludes that the behaviour of seeking permission for endorsement and illustrative uses of persona, which regulates the majority of advertisements in both jurisdictions, would subsist regardless of the legal framework due to the benefits of collaboration. Similarly, the behaviour of respecting exclusive endorsement deals would continue because of the signalling theory of social norms. In contrast, the behaviours with regard to evocative and topical advertisements are most heavily influenced by law, and could change subject to the extent of persona protection available. In the other industries examined in this book, the behaviours are the same despite different legal regulation.

I. Use of Persona in the Advertising Industry

Advertising uses persona to sell a product or service. Traditionally, advertising was done through television, printed billboards, print media and radio advertisements. While all these forms of advertisements still exist, developments in technology have led to the evolution of this industry. Social media is now a key advertising platform. In terms of using persona, many companies want 'brand ambassadors' who will post their product on Instagram and Meta, and who will create YouTube and TikTok videos featuring the product.[6]

Goodenough describes the use of persona in advertising as 'helping to sell products and services … almost any kind of association with a venerated person can be helpful in sales, even if only to draw the attention of prospective buyers to the actual sales message'.[7] There are different types of advertisements that utilise persona. Four categories of advertisement have been identified for the purpose of this book: endorsement, illustrative, topical and evocative. There are other types of advertisements, such as product placement, but they will not be addressed since they were not observed in fieldwork.[8]

Endorsement advertisements attempt to convey a connection between the celebrity and the product or service by using an element of persona. The company wants to convey that the celebrity approves of the product. These types of advertisements are often created through the collaboration of the celebrity and the company.

[6] For an in-depth examination of social media marketing, see Dahl, S, *Social Media Marketing: Theories and Applications* (2nd edn, SAGE Publications 2018).

[7] Goodenough, OR, 'Retheorising privacy and publicity' (1997) 1 *IPQ* 37, 41.

[8] See: Eagle, L and Dahl, S, 'Product Placement in Old and New Media: Examining the Evidence for Concern' (2018) 147 *Journal of Business Ethics* 605; Karrh, JA, McKee, KB and Pardun, CJ, 'Practitioners' Evolving Views on Product Placement Effectiveness' (2003) 43 *Journal of Advertising Research* 138.

For example, Nespresso hired George Clooney as their 'brand ambassador' and created a series of advertisements to promote this connection.[9]

Illustrative advertisements also try to convey a connection by using a defined element of persona, but to a more limited extent. These types of advertisements may use persona to show that a celebrity has used the service or product being advertised. For example, jewellery company Monica Vinader capitalised on Gareth Southgate's wearing one of their bracelets by posting photographs to their Facebook account.[10] The line between endorsement and illustrative advertisements is not clear-cut, as it may be difficult to determine whether an endorsement has indeed been secured. This is because not all endorsement deals require the celebrity to actively promote the brand. Depending on the nature of the deal, a photograph may be used in the more traditional advertising style, or the celebrity might use or wear the product without actively posting on her social media or making definitive statements. While it is clear that a post from a celebrity's own social media account will be an endorsement, it is less clear where the company is in control of the publicity relating to the advertisement. The blurring of these two types of advertising styles has implications for passing off that will be discussed in section II.

Evocative advertisements draw on an element of persona that falls outside of the traditional elements of persona: name, voice, signature and likeness. Distinctive appearance or characteristics can be considered an evocative use. Gareth Southgate's popularity was also capitalised on by 'Sure' body spray, which created an advertisement featuring a bottle of the spray in a blue waistcoat resembling Southgate's iconic World Cup outfit.[11] These types of advertisements are drawing on the 'identity' of the persona, which is protected in some US States, as explained in chapter 2.

Topical advertisements refer to a current event and can take many forms, and may or may not use the traditional elements of persona. They may use the event to draw attention to the product without further comment. For example, John Lewis alluded to the royal wedding in an advertisement that featured wine apparatus dressed as a bride and groom, with the groom in the distinctive red military jacket. The advertisement was strategically placed beside a photograph of the royal couple, Harry and Megan. Topical advertisements may also be humorous or degrading. Online trading platform IG.com used photographs of Donald Trump and Bill Clinton during the US presidential campaign, with the caption 'Trade more than just insults'.

[9] 'George Clooney becomes Nespresso global brand ambassador by extending his relationship with the brand in North America' *Nespresso* (3 November 2015) at www.nestle-nespresso.com/newsandfeatures/george-clooney-becomes-nespresso-global-brand-ambassador-by-extending-his-relationship-with-the-brand-in-north-america (accessed 4 April 2018).

[10] 'Gareth Southgate' *Monica Vinader* at www.monicavinader.com/style-me/gareth-southgate-world-cup-russia (accessed 24 January 2022).

[11] Golob, B, 'Brand alignment brings Sure and Southgate together for world cup semi-finals' *Communicate* (11 July 2018) at www.communicatemagazine.com/news/2018/brand-alignment-brings-sure-and-southgate-together-for-world-cup-semi-finals/ (accessed 25 January 2023).

Empirical investigation suggested that endorsements are the most common type of advertisements, and marketing literature supports this observation, as advertisements that utilise persona tend to convey endorsement.[12] This chapter will now proceed to analyse the behaviours that govern these types of advertisements.

II. Seek Permission to Use Persona in Endorsement and Illustrative Advertisements in the US and UK

This behaviour was observed in all jurisdictions. Lawyers indicated that permission is routinely sought to create endorsement-type advertisements. While less data were available to assess illustrative advertisements, the responses of interviewees indicated that permission would usually be sought for these types of advertisements as well. One lawyer noted, 'By and large, persona is almost always used in a way that conveys endorsement, almost always. Sometimes, if not a direct endorsement, at least an affiliation to give credibility to the third party.'[13] Another noted that permission is sought in order to create an 'association with certain types of products … to enhance the brand's value'.[14] A third explained the permission is sought to achieve 'an association of someone who is successful'.[15] As evidenced by these responses, persona is frequently used to imply a connection between the brand and the celebrity.

The behaviour of seeking permission for endorsement and illustrative uses of persona regulates the majority of advertisements, since these styles of advertisements are the most common ways in which persona is used in this industry.[16] Despite the prevalence of this behaviour, there is no single approach that is used to seek permission. In referring to different approaches, one interviewee noted:

> The best route is the band's manager. Usually the CEO of the band will have a lot of say in what endorsement deals are not done. Actors, usually the agent. Managers don't have the same level of influence. Individuals all have their preferences. One actor may rely primarily on their agent, another on their lawyer.[17]

Another suggested:

> Ad agencies propose the creative side then go to the celebrity's agent. Or they can go to a broker, tell them the idea, and they will approach the celebrity and agent for you. Or the law firm can approach the agent.[18]

[12] Choi, S and Rifon, N, 'Who is the Celebrity in Advertising? Understanding Dimensions of Celebrity Images' (2007) 40(2) *The Journal of Popular Culture* 304.
[13] California interviewee 5.
[14] New York interview 1.
[15] UK interview 23.
[16] Choi and Rifon (2007).
[17] California interview 23.
[18] New York interview 5.

With regard to social media influencers, an interviewee suggested that the fame of the influencer could determine the approach. More famous influencers would be more likely to have agents who handle their advertising deals:

> The approach depends, each brand is different. Brands have an agency that finds the influencers and pairs them up. The big scale ones [influencers] they might go directly to probably have their own agents.[19]

A lawyer whose area of expertise is the representation of athletes noted that English footballers have relationships with their clubs, which could dictate the suitable approach:

> Most of the time [brands] go through the agent. Most football clubs [are] now encouraging brands to go through the club … recently bigger clubs control the deals of the players. Club will say you can't have a personal sponsorship that would conflict with club sponsorship.[20]

These quotations illustrate that celebrities, athletes and influencers may be approached in various ways. It needs to be emphasised that no interviewees suggested that they would use persona for endorsement or illustrative advertisements without permission. Section II.A will consider the influences on the behaviour of seeking permission for endorsement and illustrative uses of persona.

A. Influences on Behaviour

i. Law – Deterrence Theory

Interviews revealed that deterrence theory is the most relevant in prompting parties to seek permission to use persona in endorsement and illustrative advertisements. Deterrence was present in both the US and the UK, despite the differing approaches to legal regulation of persona, explained in chapter 2.

a. United States

The litigation risk is significant in the US due to both the right of publicity and false endorsement under the Lanham Act.[21] Lawyers in California were not very familiar with false endorsement, since the breadth of the publicity right is so wide that they often did not need to rely on it. A California lawyer noted, 'I don't think it [false endorsement] has any greater strength than the California law. In states which don't have a right of publicity, it's more useful.'[22] New York lawyers were

[19] New York interview 13.
[20] UK interview 3.
[21] See ch 2, section II.
[22] California interview 6.

more familiar with false endorsement, as they use this to protect 'identity' in a broader sense than conceived of by the statutory privacy right. When asked what the role of false endorsement was in protecting persona, a New York interviewee stated that it 'Comes up all the time. It can be a separate realm because certain things are not protected under the right of publicity.'[23] Another New York lawyer noted that the California right of publicity must inevitably be considered because 'Most advertisers here are national advertisers. They need to clear the lowest common denominator as clients are risk-averse. [They] tend to steer conservatively in dealing with rights of others.'[24]

When US lawyers were asked whether, in the absence of right of publicity or false endorsement, there would be wider use of persona without authorisation by advertising agencies, there was general consensus that there would be. One lawyer responded, 'If people were not prevented from doing it here by law, they would do it.'[25] Similarly, 'Yes, for sure. The law encourages collaborations.'[26] Arguably, it is not the law directly that encourages collaborations but rather the law that encourages litigation risk management. Permission is sought to avoid legal consequences, but the benefits derived from collaboration also make seeking permission desirable. However, many US lawyers felt the law heavily influenced the behaviour of seeking permission, and the term 'wild west' was utilised by interviewees. A lawyer who represents models commented 'It would be crazy. I couldn't even imagine. It would be worse than the wild, wild west. Models would be completely out of business.'[27] Another stated 'In the absence of the law, it would be the wild west …'[28] In instances where the persona is not considered to be possessed of goodwill, and rather is used because a photograph is needed, the opinions of the aforementioned lawyers might be reflective of what would occur. In particular, models who are not well known, but who are used in stock photography, would probably find their photographs used without permission. However, the endorsement- and illustrative-style advertisements, which draw on the value of well-known individuals, would likely continue to be made with permission in order to obtain the advantages of collaboration.

The breadth of protection afforded puts potential claimants in an advantageous position even if they do not have a valid cause of action. According to a New York interviewee, 'Not many cases go to litigation, most usually settle. A lot of misconception from a legal point is that the law applied but they settle because advertising is not worth going to court for.'[29] An interviewee in California recounted how a senior partner in his firm, with a strong reputation in legal circles, was able to reach

[23] New York interview 1.
[24] New York interview 7.
[25] New York interview 4.
[26] California interview 3.
[27] California interview 12.
[28] California interview 24.
[29] New York interview 5.

a settlement agreement for a use of persona that would not have been covered by the right of publicity and would have been unlikely to succeed under false endorsement.[30] The advertisement featured an aspect of persona of a deceased individual. This aspect was not covered by statute, and the common law right does not apply to post-mortem uses. Furthermore, despite the low threshold for confusion under false endorsement, the aspect was so evocative that it was unlikely this cause of action would have succeeded.

Even if a use of persona would not be caught by false endorsement or the right of publicity, it is safer to get an agreement to avoid the litigation risk. As noted by a New York lawyer:

> I honestly think that the biggest motivation is the avoidance of claims. It's just advertising, yet costs lots of money. Don't risk money and brand reputation over something like an advertisement. Even where you might feel what you are doing has some level of defence, you ask yourself whether you are willing to take the risk. You won't get anything out of it because the ad will be over eventually. If you are investing thousands in a commercial multimedia campaign and you don't get permission [from the persona] and you suddenly get an injunction, the legal cost as well as the interruptive cost to the actual campaign is astronomical. It is just not worth the risk. It is just stupid.[31]

Similarly, another noted 'If you are risk-averse, you don't want someone to hold up an expensive campaign so you'd want to get a release.'[32] The trend of using the uncertainty in US law to induce settlement was discussed in the previous chapter. It is not just the substantive law, but also the risk of expansion that results in risk mitigation practices.

b. United Kingdom

In the UK, deterrence theory is just as impactful because of the nature of these types of advertisements. While the misrepresentation element of passing off is more onerous to prove than the strict liability right of publicity, the nature of endorsement advertisements satisfies this requirement. Illustrative advertisements also run a risk of passing off because the company is still trying to imply a connection with the persona, and it may not be obvious that there is not a direct endorsement. While there was a wealth of evidence that supported the finding of misrepresentation in *Fenty*, essentially persona was used on a t-shirt.[33] This use of persona is akin to the illustrative uses already explained, which further suggests that the line is blurred between illustrative and endorsement uses. As such, there is a legal risk that illustrative uses can fall foul of passing off. Indeed, interviewees perceived the threat of litigation to be an influential factor in seeking permission, even though

[30] California interview 15.
[31] New York interview 5.
[32] California interview 9.
[33] *Fenty and others v Arcadia Group Brands Ltd (trading as Topshop) and another* [2013] EWHC 2310 (Ch).

passing off is rarely utilised against unauthorised uses of persona, as indicated by the infrequency of case law as well as the empirical evidence on dispute resolution practices discussed in chapter 4. Interviewees exhibited risk-averse behaviour and would rather not use persona without permission for endorsement and illustrative advertisements than risk threat of legal action, even if the threat was not valid. One interviewee stated:

> I look after a group of advertising agencies and they will say, before we go too far [developing the advertisement], review the plan and say whether there are any issues. Most will have done a risk assessment. In reality, most organisations will not go ahead without permission because repercussions are above the pay wage of the person who makes the decision.[34]

In considering the effectiveness of passing off in policing unauthorised uses of persona for endorsement and illustrative advertisements, another lawyer claimed 'It is hard [to argue], but usually on a practical level the threat of a passing off action will get the result we need.'[35] Another thought the expansion of passing off to include persona posed a risk to advertisers who do not seek permission: 'I think in the 20 years that I have been practising in this area, there is clearly more protection for celebrities than there used to be, because of things like the Eddie Irvine case.'[36] In assessing the protection available to celebrities, one lawyer commented, 'With passing off and greater commercialisation of celebrities' names, signature, images, they are sufficiently protected.'[37]

It might be suggested that a risk is also posed by breaching the Advertising Codes, but, in accordance with the assessment made in chapter 2, the CAP is perceived as ineffective in addressing unauthorised uses of persona. Only one lawyer suggested that unauthorised use of persona 'tends not to happen because ASA code prevents this'.[38] Another commented:

> With regard to unauthorised references to celebrities, people do not worry with the CAP code because if you are going to have a problem with a celebrity, they will threaten to sue for money. Celebrities will hardly ever go to ASA because they won't get money.[39]

Lawyers who represent clients who have been used without permission also do not feel the Codes to be particularly effective:

> You throw it in as a means to get to the end. It's a complete waste of time, doesn't have any teeth, it's a voluntary code. No sanctions as such. Very light slap on the wrist. It's one of those things you throw in.[40]

[34] UK interview 24.
[35] UK interview 23.
[36] UK interview 4; *Irvine and another v Talksport Ltd* [2002] EWHC 367 (Ch) (Eddie Irvine successfully claimed passing off of his image by use of a photograph in an advertisement).
[37] UK interview 9.
[38] UK interview 6. This interviewee was in-house counsel for an advertising firm, which could explain the conservative approach.
[39] UK interview 4.
[40] UK interview 12.

Another noted 'We do use it a bit but the sanction is a blunt tool. As par for the course we threaten and use it but it's not terribly helpful.'[41]

c. Assessment of Deterrence Theory

The deterrence theory of compliance with law is present in both the US and the UK. It is equally impactful in both jurisdictions, despite the strict liability standard for the right of publicity, which makes it easier to establish than passing off. The nature of endorsement and illustrative advertisements lends itself to potential misrepresentation, particularly as the *Irvine*[42] and *Fenty*[43] cases established that individuals can rely on passing off to protect persona. One lawyer, in assessing how the approach to advertising has changed over the years, stated:

> Until Irvine [the case of *Irvine v TalkSport*], we went through a long period of saying to clients, according to established case law, you can do it [use persona without permission]. But we think the case law is wrong, and sooner or later, someone is going to bring a case [of passing off], and it could be [against] you, so don't just assume you'll get away with it [using persona without permission].[44]

ii. Law – Morality Theory

a. United States

The responses of US lawyers evidenced the morality theory of compliance with law, which suggests that people obey law because it is the right thing to do.[45] While no questions were asked that included the word 'morality', the responses to questions on why permission is sought to use persona and opinions on the right of publicity indicate that morality theory is present. Lawyers feel that permission should be sought to use persona, in accordance with the law, because this is the morally correct course of action. According to one lawyer, 'They're taking advantage of the person's persona. It's bad conduct. It's bad behaviour. Just like when you have torts in society, it's [the law] trying to teach people the same thing.'[46] Another lawyer responded 'Celebrities should have this right. They became famous to profit off their image. They have a right to profit off who they became. It's only fair.'[47] Similarly, 'People should have a right to protect the name and likeness that they built … Who ought to make the money? Some guy who wants to make shirts or the person who made the reputation what it is?'[48] One lawyer directly stated that

[41] UK interview 23.
[42] *Irvine* [2002].
[43] *Fenty* [2013].
[44] UK interviewee 4.
[45] Tyler, T, *Why People Obey the Law* (Princeton University Press 1990) 178.
[46] California interview 12.
[47] New York interview 12.
[48] California interview 14.

morality was at play: 'Morally it makes sense. You don't want people to get stuff free. This is the way they make money. You're stealing from them and this may prevent them from getting another job.'[49]

b. United Kingdom

Similar to the US, no questions that included the word 'morality' were asked in UK interviews. Rather, UK lawyers were asked their opinions on the US right of publicity. Two exceptionally advocated for protection, but the rest felt that the UK system, which focuses on passing off, is preferable to the US system, which protects against misappropriation of persona. In advancing views with regard to passing off, there were no responses that indicated that permission is sought to use persona because it is the right thing to do. Rather, passing off poses a legal risk, in accordance with deterrence theory. In contrast to the US, it appears that morality does not influence the behaviour of seeking permission for endorsement and illustrative uses of persona.

In terms of responses to the question on whether a right of publicity should be introduced in the UK, those who were in favour thought that it would provide legal clarity rather than thinking that it was justified. One lawyer noted:

> When you have the law in place [like in the US where there is the right of publicity], it's much more straightforward to exploit, but also to protect those rights [to persona]. You can call on that law whereas in this country, you have to look at so many different elements. It becomes a jigsaw because you have a piecemeal approach to protecting these rights. I think some legislation should be brought in to protect personality rights to a greater extent.[50]

One thought it would be unnecessary to introduce a right of publicity because it would only protect a small percentage of the population:

> Because we don't have any image rights legislation, if we were to bring it in, who are we trying to protect by bringing in this law? We'd be trying to protect quite a small percentage of the population. The argument against bringing in images rights protection is that there is no need to protect these people [celebrities].[51]

Another felt that the right of publicity does not address a social need and those who would benefit are already adequately compensated:

> I am not in favour of rights for people who already make far too much money anyway. Celebrities are not suffering from an abuse of their personalities ... I think there is a gap [in the law] but there should be a gap. I'm not in favour of publicity rights. I don't see the harm in using aspects of a celebrity when it is not defamatory and there is no false endorsement. Legislation to introduce those rights would be legislating for the rich to

[49] California interview 12.
[50] UK interview 3.
[51] UK interview 9.

> get richer … it's not a social issue that needs to be resolved. The UK approach works perfectly well in practice, and famous personalities are already good at exploiting their image rights, they make a fortune out of it.[52]

Based on the data collected, it is clear that both morality and the deterrence theory of compliance with law influence the behaviour of seeking permission for endorsement and illustrative advertisements in the US, while deterrence theory operates in the UK.

In addition to the absence of morality theory, evidence suggests that there is scepticism surrounding the need for a right of publicity in the UK. Contrary to the literature reviewed in chapter 1, empirical evidence indicates that there is no desire to introduce legislation to improve persona protection. While the law as it stands confers less protection on individuals than does the US legal framework, the gap highlighted by UK interview 5 is only recognised in two circumstances. First, in the advertising industry, where evocative and topical advertisements are made without permission of individuals in the UK. This behaviour will be discussed at section IV, but it is worth noting that this behaviour does not exist in the US as the right of publicity acts as a strong deterrent. Second, dispute resolution practices, discussed in the chapter 4, are informed by the availability of law, resulting in more limited avenues of redress for unauthorised use of persona in the UK.

The views of UK interviewees as regards the potential introduction of a right of publicity should be emphasised, because they acknowledge that gaps in protection exist but do not advocate for greater protection. The evidence provided suggests that such a right is neither desirable nor necessary. When the other influences of the desire to collaborate and social norms are considered, the 'gaps' identified in doctrinal research are often filled.[53] The difference between the legal frameworks in the US and the UK is thus minimised in the transactional sphere due to the other influences observed. However, it should be noted that a difference remains in the dispute resolution sphere, in the rare instances where persona is used without protection.

iii. The Desire to Contract

Permission to use persona is needed to reap the benefits of collaboration to create an advertising campaign that exploits para-social relationships. The benefits are the same in both the US and the UK, as they are unaffected by the differing legal frameworks. Celebrity endorsement is not a new concept.[54] Changes in advertising to include influencers and social media platforms have further entrenched this trend as consumers desire 'genuine' advertising. In other words, they want to

[52] UK interview 5.
[53] See ch 1.
[54] Kaikati, JG, 'Celebrity Advertising – A Review and Synthesis' (1987) 6 *International Journal of Advertising* 93, 93 – 'The use of celebrities in advertising is no recent innovation, of course. Celebrities have been hyping products since the latter part of the last century.'

believe that the person featured actually likes the product being promoted. The trend of using celebrities in advertisements started in the 1960s, but only gained a foothold in the 1980s when the stigma attached to the making of advertisements by celebrities diminished.[55] Now, it is common to see advertising campaigns featuring celebrities.

When permission is sought to use persona, the company can create an authentic campaign by styling the individual and directing the individual on what to say. The individual can control her appearance in the advertising campaign to a certain extent and can determine which products she wants to be associated with. Even in a small-scale collaboration where a single tweet is sent, the company can help determine the type of statement to be delivered and suggest a specific hashtag, and individual celebrities can help alter the statement to make it sound genuine so that they maintain their authenticity in the eyes of their fans. For an Instagram or TikTok post, celebrities can have a large level of control over how they utilise the product in the photograph, and the company gets access to a celebrity's followers. The importance of these benefits influences parties to seek permission to use persona for endorsement and illustrative advertisements.

These benefits have increased in the age of influencer advertising and social media. Most interviewees commented upon changes in the advertising field. One interviewee who has 30 years of experience in the advertising industry remarked that 'Social media is very important now. The level of financing has changed an incredible amount – more money is being spent on social media and less on TV advertising.'[56] Another, when asked the question, 'What would encourage a brand to seek a collaboration rather than just use an image without authorisation?', responded 'The industry is becoming more sophisticated. If you pay for those rights, you can be more sophisticated in how you exploit them. You can get more out of it. They want social media, digital media.'[57]

Collaboration with a celebrity allows for an agreement that can be tailored to suit the needs of the company, as now discussed.

a. Better Quality Advertising Campaign

Collaboration results in access to the individual to create a higher-quality advertisement than might be achieved by using just a photograph. An interviewee noted that, '[f]rom a commercial standpoint, advantages outweigh the disadvantages – quality control … it's beneficial to enter into these deals.'[58] The company can negotiate for the individual to appear at product launches, post on social media, use the product in public and promote the product on talk shows. As noted by an

[55] ibid 94 – 'With the number of film roles declining, and such megastars as the late John Wayne succumbing to big advertising money, the stigma of making commercials has faded.'
[56] UK interview 19.
[57] UK interview 23.
[58] New York interview 8.

interviewee, 'Public appearances form part of a bigger package of rights. Speaking at a conference, opening a supermarket …'[59] While sometimes a photograph is all that is required, collaboration can still be beneficial compared to licensing an image, because the company can style the individual and direct the individual on how to achieve the desired effect. In referring to an influencer, an interviewee noted 'It's one thing to be able to put her face on a t-shirt, it's another thing to have her wear a t-shirt in an Instagram post.'[60]

b. Transfer of Goodwill from the Individual

Celebrities, athletes and influencers have reputations that symbolise certain values. A company will choose an individual whose reputation aligns with the company's desired perception. For example, an 'edgy' brand will want someone who is rebellious, whereas a family brand may prefer someone who is more conservative. One interviewee stated:

> Celebrities have built in recognition and following through their social media presence. It's an attempt to take the recognition and fondness that people have for that individual and have it translate into admiration for the product that is being promoted.[61]

Another commented that '[t]he collaboration allows the personality's goodwill to enhance the brand's goodwill'.[62]

c. Exclusivity

Entering into a deal allows the company to negotiate exclusivity for the relevant industry. When questioned why companies would collaborate rather than using a stock photo, an interviewee responded 'It's exclusive, and sews it back into the brand activity. They want the exclusive rights of this particular persona to be associated with their brand.'[63] The desire for exclusivity is common: as another lawyer noted, 'Anyone who sponsors wants exclusive rights to use image, personal appearance of the individual. The more you pay, the more exclusivity you get.'[64]

d. Authenticity

With the full support of the individual, the company is able to develop a more 'authentic' image, which is particularly valued by millennial and Gen Z consumers.[65] An interviewee stated, 'To help them reach and connect with

[59] UK interview 3.
[60] California interview 23.
[61] California interview 3.
[62] UK interview 24.
[63] UK interview 9.
[64] UK interview 12.
[65] 'From a brand's perspective, they want to be authentic.' (New York interview 13.).

millennial generation, [brands are] doing deals with influencers and YouTubers to meet their objective.'[66] This means the companies might exercise a lower level of control than on more traditional platforms. The company may want the individual to express her own positive thoughts on the product or service rather than using a script. In these types of advertisements, the consumers feel the individual is giving an honest opinion. As noted by a lawyer, 'We want the advertising to feel warm, and sweet, and authentic.'[67] Advertisements are required to be disclosed by both the US FTC[68] and the UK ASA.[69] In assessing the impact on consumers, a lawyer considered 'They [consumers] know they [celebrities] are getting paid but they also think there is an authentic connection between celebrities and the product, and that's what the companies want to capture.'[70]

e. 'Cut Through' – Initial Impact

It is difficult to get the attention of consumers because they are constantly being bombarded with advertisements. Companies work with well-known individuals to achieve this aim. For example, Gillette often collaborates with athletes. An advertisement featuring Roger Federer is more likely to stand out on first viewing than one using an unknown individual. A New York interviewee noted that '[collaboration] breaks through the clutter of advertising because it's someone that people recognise'.[71]

In referring to George Clooney's collaboration with Nespresso, a UK lawyer who specialises in advertising noted:

> What I suppose you get is cut through … noticed … When the ad is fronted up with George Clooney, as a viewer, you are sitting up and taking notice. If you are a woman or a gay man you're thinking I like George Clooney, or if you're a straight man, you're thinking I'd like to be like George Clooney, he's pretty cool. Brands are looking for the cut through.[72]

f. Increase Brand Visibility and Recognition – Lasting Impact

By building an association with a well-known individual, the company's brand becomes more visible and easily recognised, even by people who may not be fans

[66] California interview 3.

[67] New York interview 7.

[68] The FTC requires that individuals 'should clearly and conspicuously disclose their relationships to brands when promoting or endorsing products through social media': Katz, M, 'FTC Staff reminds influencers and brands to clearly disclose relationship' *FTC* (1 April 2017) at www.ftc.gov/news-events/press-releases/2017/04/ftc-staff-reminds-influencers-brands-clearly-disclose (accessed 16 November 2017).

[69] ASA 'Online Affiliate Marketing' (17 August 2021) at www.asa.org.uk/advice-online/affiliate-marketing.html (accessed 23 January 2023).

[70] New York interview 17.

[71] New York interview 5.

[72] UK interview 4.

of the individual. A lawyer commented that collaborations 'increase visibility and recognition of the brand to increase sales'.[73] This effect is similar to that of a famous trade mark. Consumers may not regularly use the goods covered by a famous trade mark but they are aware of the brand. Similarly, consumers may be aware of the individual. If they decide they need a type of product that they have not bought before, they may remember the well-known individual and, by association, the brand. The brand becomes recognisable as a whole and grows beyond the advertisement in a global sense. For example, consumers will use Gillette because they know that athletes endorse the brand.

g. Reach Target Demographic

The individual already has fans who will be influenced by her opinions and admire her style, charisma, talent, etc. The strength of the para-social relationship means that fans desire to emulate the individual by using similar products or wearing the same brand of clothing. For an effective campaign, 'choose person[s] who will have the relevant demographic for your product'.[74] If the individual expresses a preference for a brand, the fans may become interested and extend their feelings of admiration to the brand. To determine a suitable collaboration, companies may approach a 'specialist agency which does a lot of research to identify celebrities where there is a good match with the demographic of the target audience and the individual concerned'.[75] This allows the company to tap into an established client base. According to a lawyer, 'People love celebrities. They just do. Whether they admit it or not, they just do. When a celebrity is associated with a brand, the brand's product sales go up. It's proven.'[76] Sales of Monica Vinader's friendship bracelet rose by 350 per cent after Gareth Southgate was seen wearing one during the 2016 World Cup.[77]

h. Target a New Demographic

A company may want to reach a new demographic that it has not previously been able to connect with. One lawyer commented, 'For established brands, they feel it will enhance their brand … maybe freshen up their image with a younger demographic or reach a different demographic that is becoming increasingly important.'[78] The company will choose an individual who resonates with the demographic, for

[73] UK interview 3.
[74] UK interview 13.
[75] UK interview 4.
[76] California interview 6.
[77] 'Southgate's lucky £115 friendship bracelet to thank for World Cup success?' *BeSoccer* (2018) at www.besoccer.com/new/southgate-s-lucky-pound-115-friendship-bracelet-to-thank-for-world-cup-success-465160#:~:text=In%20the%20lead%2Dup%20to,item%20rose%20by%20350%20percent (accessed 23 January 2023).
[78] New York interview 17.

example 'a Hispanic artist can enhance appeal to Hispanic customers'.[79] The celebrity has a direct influence on the desired consumers, who might otherwise have been difficult to reach through non-collaborative advertising.

i. Quick Distribution of Information through Social Media

Social media campaigns can be fast, effective methods of getting a company's message out. If a company chooses to do a 'sponsored post' on Instagram,[80] it can be as easy as supplying the individual with the product and asking her to say positive things about it. This is much less time-consuming than having to design graphics, edit photoshoots and format. One interviewee noted that 'Influencers can distribute information to a huge number of people very quickly, as effective as publication. Even what they like … [a celebrity posted] a certain tweet about a sweet. Sweet shop could not fulfil orders.'[81]

j. Financial Advantage

While collaborations can be expensive, the reach of social media means that one post could reach more people and have a greater impact than conducting a wide-ranging, multi-platform advertising campaign. A lawyer stated:

> That connection especially through social media can save millions in advertising. If you can get a celebrity to do a social media endorsement, send a tweet or go on a talk show, it brings enormous awareness to a product. Get a lot for less than they would otherwise have spent on advertising.[82]

The benefits of collaboration explain why contracts are entered into in this area, regardless of whether permission to use persona is legally required. Companies and individuals both benefit from these collaborations. Arguably, the persona will more often be at an advantage when they enter into collaboration, because they exercise a level of control over how they are portrayed and will be remunerated regardless of the success of the campaign (except if there is a breach of contract). While companies are keen to enter collaborations because of the benefits already listed, they stand to lose more if sales do not increase, or if the celebrity does something that brings the brand into disrepute.[83] Nonetheless, interviewees firmly

[79] New York interview 17.

[80] Lund, AH, 'What are sponsored photos and video on Instagram?' (Native Advertising Institute, Denmark) at nativeadvertisinginstitute.com/blog/what-are-sponsored-photos-and-videos-on-instagram/ (accessed 10 September 2018).

[81] UK interview 24.

[82] New York interview 17.

[83] In 2022, Kanye West's antisemitic statements led to terminations by Adidas, Balenciaga, Def Jam Records, etc: Guy, Z, 'Every Company That's Dropped Kanye West' *Vulture* (1 December 2022) www.vulture.com/2022/12/kanye-west-dropped-brands-adidas-gap-what-did-ye-say.html (accessed 7 December 2022).

believed that collaboration is usually beneficial. This belief is based on their experience as lawyers in the advertising industry, and is also supported by marketing literature showing that collaboration is reflective of industry practices. The benefits of celebrity endorsement have been confirmed by various case studies in the field of marketing, which have examined how these collaborations leverage para-social relationships and impact on the sale of products.[84] It is worth underscoring that none of the sources referenced in the preceding footnote cite law, demonstrating the strength of these benefits of collaboration as an independent influence on seeking permission to use persona.

iv. Social Norms – Signalling Theory

The final influence on the behaviour of seeking permission to use persona in endorsement and illustrative advertisements is found in the field of social norms, specifically, the signalling theory of compliance. Companies want to maintain a good reputation among famous individuals so that they will want to work with them. Companies that comply with a norm have a low discount rate and will benefit in the long term due to increased likelihood of cooperation. A New York interviewee stated 'If you come across as a bully trying to use someone's name or likeness without permission … that's not a reputation you want to have.'[85] Similarly, a UK interviewee, when asked whether his clients would consider using persona without permission, responded 'Some advertisers will say absolutely not, we don't want reputation damage or negative public relations.'[86]

While signalling theory might explain the behaviour of seeking permission for endorsement and illustrative advertisements, since lawyers suggested that the perception of reputational damage encourages permission to be sought, it is difficult to draw a similar conclusion with regard to sanctions theory. This is despite the fact that these theories go hand in hand as failure to send the right signal could result in sanctions. As explained in chapter 3, it was difficult to observe sanctions in industries that commercialise persona. This could be because non-legal sanctions are administered by parties on which lawyers possessed limited information. For example, fans of a celebrity whose persona has been used without permission may boycott the brand, and thus be third-party enforcers of the behaviour

[84] Ford, JB, 'What Do We Know About Celebrity Endorsement in Advertising?' (2018) 58 *Journal of Advertising Research* 1; Winterich, KP, Gangwar, M and Grewal, R, 'When Celebrities Count: Power Distance Beliefs and Celebrity Endorsements' (2018) 82(3) *Journal of Marketing* 70; Escalas, JE and Bettman, J, 'Managing Brand Meaning through Celebrity Endorsement' in Macinnis, D and Park, CW (eds), *Brand Meaning Management* (Emerald Group Publishing Limited 2015) 29; Tzoumaka, E, Tsiotsou, R and Siomkos, G, 'Delineating the role of endorser's perceived qualities and consumer characteristic in celebrity endorsement effectiveness' (2014) 22(3) *Journal of Marketing Communications* 307; Byrne, A, Whitehead, M and Breen, S, 'The baked truth of celebrity endorsement' (2003) 105 (4/5) *British Food Journal* 288.

[85] New York interview 5.

[86] UK interview 4.

of seeking permission. However, the fans would have to be aware that the use was unauthorised. Similarly, celebrities might refuse to work with companies that use persona without permission, but such information would not necessarily be publicised. Additionally, gossip, one of the most common sanctions, may occur, but lawyers might not occupy the social spaces where such gossip takes place, and thus would not be privy to it. Perhaps in the US the sanctions are more generally legal due to the breadth of protection available, but the more limited protection in the UK leaves space for non-legal sanctions, despite these not being observed.

B. Deviation: Do Not Seek Permission to Use Persona for Endorsement and Illustrative Advertisements

While the standard behaviour is to seek permission for endorsement and illustrative advertisements, there will be deviations when such advertisements are made without permission. According to interviewees, creating endorsement and/or illustrative advertisements without permission is uncommon. Lawyers in the US noted that it was unlikely that reputable companies would use persona without permission, although they considered some instances as surprising:

> It's typically smaller companies [that breach the right of publicity] but I read an article today about the Muhammed Ali estate in a lawsuit against the NFL for using his image to advertise football games. You would think they would know they would have to get a licence so it still happens with large domestic companies that you would think would know better.[87]

When questioned as to why companies would use persona without permission in the US, considering the existence of the right of publicity, interviewees provided evidence that suggest the theories of why people do not comply with law – ignorance and disregard – apply.

i. Law – Ignorance and Disregard

There are several reasons why companies choose to make these types of advertisements without seeking the permission that is legally required in the US context. First, companies are ignorant of the right of publicity. According to an interviewee in New York, 'Most of the cases are from relatively smaller advertisers. They don't know any better. They see things happening and think they can do it [use persona in an advertisement].'[88] Second, even when companies are aware of the law, they

[87] California interview 5. For more on this issue, see Gardner, E, 'Fox Sued for Using Muhammad Ali in Super Bowl Advertisement' *Hollywood Reporter* (10 October 2017). For the advertisement in question, see at www.youtube.com/watch?v=rURPF8C3GyY.

[88] New York interview 5.

choose to disregard it. According to a lawyer who represents many litigious celebrity claimants:

> I think a lot of people claim they were ignorant of the law but 9 out of 10 times they knew. There is this adage – it's easier to ask for forgiveness than ask for permission. A lot of people say sorry, we'll take it down, but behind closed doors they know they got caught.[89]

In choosing to disregard the law, it is likely that a cost–benefit analysis is undertaken. Advertisers may run the advertisement until they get caught, as they can achieve some level of exposure before having to remove the advertisement. The association with the celebrity might be considered worth the risk of getting caught. There will also be instances where they do not get caught, so they can reap the benefit without consequence.

Third, there may be a mistake as to whether the rights were secured. According to one interviewee, 'We've defended clients who have used celebrities in commercials, thinking that they had secured the rights through a third party, but the third party was not authorised to grant those rights.'[90]

A lawyer summed up these reasons:

> [There are] three contexts where I see it come up:
>
> 1. Bad guys;
> 2. People who think it's ok;
> 3. People who mistakenly think they have the rights.[91]

In the UK, ignorance and disregard theories also apply. Endorsement advertisements will fall foul of passing off, and illustrative advertisements run the risk since the line between these types of advertisements is blurred. However, there was no evidence collected in interviews to suggest that such unauthorised uses occur more frequently in the UK. This is significant, as it was presumed that there would be more instances of unauthorised use in the UK given that passing off is more onerous than the strict liability right of publicity, but passing off poses a serious perceived risk, as explained in the discussion of deterrence theory in section II.A.i. As such, advertisers who make endorsement or illustrative advertisements without the permission of the persona are either ignorant of the law, or actively choose to disregard it or do not think it will apply.

Newspaper articles illustrate that these types of advertisements are in fact made. For example, the personas of Holly Willoughby,[92] Chrissy Tiegen,[93] Carrie

[89] California interview 6.

[90] California interview 3.

[91] California interview15.

[92] Evans, M, 'Holly Willoughby dragged into weight loss scam as company uses her to advertise "Keto pills"' *Metro* (8 May 2019) at metro.co.uk/2019/05/08/holly-willoughby-dragged-weight-loss-scam-company-uses-advertise-keto-pills-9448202/ (accessed 12 June 2019).

[93] Fowler B, '"Completely made up bullsh*t." Chrissy Teigen warns fans about fake endorsement scam' *Mama Mia* (14 January 2019) at www.mamamia.com.au/chrissy-teigen-twitter-scam/ (accessed 12 February 2019).

Bickmore[94] and Ruth Langsford were all used alongside fake testimonials and interviews seemingly endorsing pills.[95] Beyoncé, Jennifer Lopez, Joy Behar and Whoopi Goldberg's personas have been used to advertise skincare products.[96] These advertisements serve as examples of disregard/ignorance of the law considering that unauthorised uses of persona seem to be popular among diet pill and beauty product producers. Ignorance might occur where diet pill producers are unaware of the relevant legal framework, but there may also be instances of disregard where they are aware that such types of advertisements are prohibited and yet choose to proceed in order to reap the benefits of associating with a celebrity.

III. Respect Exclusive Endorsement Deals in All Jurisdictions

The second behaviour observed in the advertising industry in both the US and the UK is that exclusive endorsement deals are respected. Exclusive endorsement deals are agreements between a celebrity and a company that the celebrity will promote the goods/services of the company's brand to the exclusion of competitors. For example, David Beckham exclusively promotes Adidas sports goods and will not enter into other deals with competing sports companies.[97] These deals are respected in that competitors are unlikely to use the persona that is exclusively licensed to a company.

Interviewees were asked about how they secure their exclusive endorsement deals against third parties. In the UK, there is no legal basis for addressing unauthorised uses by third parties as there is no proprietary right that protects persona, whereas in the US, exclusive licensees of the right of publicity can sue for infringement.[98] Interestingly, only one US lawyer cited compliance with the law as a reason for respecting exclusive deals. When asked whether in the absence of the right of publicity there would be more widespread unauthorised use of persona, the response was 'Yes, it would be like the wild west. It's not good for the companies that are exploiting the talent because they want the exclusive rights. It's not fair.'[99]

[94] ibid.

[95] Ward, F, 'Ruth Langsford forced to address slimming endorsement claims' *Hello!* (23 March 2019) at www.hellomagazine.com/healthandbeauty/health-and-fitness/2019032371209/ruth-langsford-addresses-health-slimming-claims/ (accessed 29 July 2019).

[96] Wash, S and Benitez, G, 'BBB: Deceptive "free trial" offers and fake celebrity endorsements are a billion dollar problem' *GMA* (12 December 2018) at www.goodmorningamerica.com/culture/story/bbb-deceptive-free-trial-offers-fake-celebrity-endorsements-59754945 (accessed 19 January 2020).

[97] Khalil, M, 'Adidas celebrate 20-year partnership with footballing icon avid Beckham' *Esquire* (9 November 2017) at www.esquireme.com/content/24703-adidas-celebrate-20-year-partnership-with-footballing-icon-david-beckham (accessed 29 July 2019).

[98] *Hillerich & Bradsby Co v Christian Bros Inc* 943 F Supp 1136 (D Minn 1996); *Haelan Laboratories Inc v Topps Chewing Gum Inc* 202 F 2d 866 (2d Cir 1953).

[99] California interview 16.

The signalling theory of social norms appears to influence the behaviour of respecting exclusive endorsement deals. Lawyers in both jurisdictions suggested that it is uncommon for exclusive deals to be undermined. A New York lawyer, when questioned about a third party breaching an exclusive licence, responded, 'Does not really happen … we do not see brands interfering with other endorsements.' Similarly, a UK lawyer stated that 'Very few clients … would want to do it [undermine exclusive licences].'[100] The previously discussed behaviour of seeking permission for endorsement and illustrative advertisements in turn supports the behaviour of respecting exclusive endorsement deals, as companies use persona without permission only in limited circumstances.

A. Influences on Behaviour

i. Social Norms – Signalling

Signalling theory of social norms supports the behaviour of respecting exclusive deals. A lawyer in the UK noted 'Brands respect others' deals. I advise against it [using persona where there is an exclusive licence] because it would probably damage your brand rather than enhance it. It is discourteous.'[101] The lawyer went on to say 'Generally what goes around comes around. If you start playing with fire you are going to get burned.'[102] An individual who works on brand campaigns stated 'I work with big brands and their competitors won't normally do that [breach the exclusivity]. If brand has an exclusive deal, another won't breach it. It's quite frowned upon.'[103] A New York lawyer commented 'It would not give the brand a strategic edge.'[104]

Industry practice dictates that exclusive deals are respected to maintain a favourable reputation and so that deals are in turn respected. While companies will not usually undermine an exclusive deal, there may be a situation where a company is unaware of the exclusivity. A lawyer described a situation where a famous singer was meant to do an exclusive performance in London for a company during an exclusivity window. The singer announced a performance for a competing company in New York. Lawyers for the singer, the London company and the New York company had to get involved to rectify this situation. When asked whether the New York company was aware of the deal, the interviewee said 'It's not for them to know, it's for the artist to know they are already in a deal. The blame was with the artist's manager who was meant to be upfront about the deal.'

[100] UK interview 6.
[101] UK interview 6.
[102] UK interview 6.
[103] UK interview 19.
[104] New York interview 13.

The interviewee noted this was an exceptional circumstance and not something encountered often.[105] Those who practice this behaviour do not get an immediate benefit, but the signalling function works to encourage competitors to show the same respect in turn.

B. Deviation: Undermine Exclusive Endorsement Deals

Due to the nature of the interviewees, who generally worked for reputable companies, no empirical evidence was collected on the deviant behaviour of undermining third-party deals. As such, a US case review was conducted to make observations on this deviant behaviour. The limitation of this case review is that not all disputes culminate in trial, so there may have been instances of this behaviour that are not covered in this review. However, the review is still useful, as it provides evidence of this behaviour and shows how the behaviour appears to have become less prevalent in recent years. A handful of cases were observed in the US of the undermining by companies of third-party deals, with the most recent case occurring in 2000.[106] Since cases are being used as a proxy for prevalence of the behaviour, the absence of recent cases suggests that the standard behaviour of respecting exclusive deals has gained further traction in recent years. Alternatively, companies may require the celebrity to address the situation. As the interviewee noted, 'If a competing company uses the persona, the exclusive licensee will urge the celebrity to take action.'[107] When questioned why there are so few cases of this nature, one lawyer responded 'The individual is really in a sense more hurt than the licensee. If everyone starts using their face, it becomes of no value.'[108] This is not necessarily accurate, as the exclusive licensee will not get the benefit that they paid for if this occurs. However, cases often settle before they reach trial. Using persona without permission for a commercial purpose in the US would be a clear-cut case, and thus settlement would be likely.

There were no cases in the UK because there is no proprietary right of publicity that forms the basis of a claim. However, it was noted that 'Some do respect it [exclusivity], some don't. Advertising by association is a lot cheaper than

[105] UK interview 19.

[106] Cases: *Gridiron.com Inc v National Football League Player's Ass'n Inc* 106 F Supp 2d 1309 (SD Fla 2000); *MJ & Partners Restaurant Ltd Partnership v Zadikoff* 10 F Supp 2d 922 (ND Ill 1998); *Hillerich & Bradsby Co v Christian Bros Inc* 943 F Supp 1136 (D Minn 1996); *Winterland Concessions Co v MacIntosh* 1992 WL 170897 (ED Pa 1992); *Winterland Concessions Co v Sileo* 528 F Supp 1201 (ND Ill 1981), judgment aff'd, 830 F 2d 195 (7th Cir 1987); *Bi-Rite Enterprises Inc v Bruce Miner Co Inc* 757 F 2d 440 (1st Cir 1985); *Bi-Rite Enterprises Inc v Button Master* 555 F Supp 1188 (SD NY 1983); *Winterland Concessions Co v Creative Screen Design Ltd* 214 USPQ 188 (ND Ill 1981); *Factors Etc Inc v Pro Arts Inc* 444 F Supp 288 (SD NY 1977), judgment aff'd and remanded.

[107] New York interview 2.

[108] California interview 4.

advertising by payment.'[109] Another stated it occurs most often among alcohol companies. A lawyer gave this scenario:

> Brands complain about other brands particularly in the alcohol world. You have a brand ambassador. The Oscars after party is sponsored by a competing brand. Your celebrity stands in front of the 'Step and repeat' board with the logos of competing brands. Or, they are drinking the competing brand. That can cause embarrassment. It's a problem in the food and drink sector.[110]

This interviewee noted that there have been instances where another company had to be confronted:

> Celebrity was in breach but brand would not want to sue the celebrity. It takes a lot for you to want to sue the celebrity because of the adverse publicity. We called the other brand and said you know that X is contracted to us, what are you doing? The situation was resolved amicably.[111]

i. Law – Disregard and/or Ignorance

Neither US nor UK lawyers provided responses that could be used to support an analysis of ignorance or disregard of the law. This is despite the fact that there is relevant law in the US. In the UK, there is no similar relevant law as there is no proprietary right that an exclusive licensee can enforce.[112] The reason why US lawyers may not have cited ignorance or disregard of the law in this behaviour is because there appeared to be a lack of clarity about whether a company can enforce the right of publicity as an exclusive licensee. While a California lawyer explained that, '[t]ypically, if someone has been given an exclusive right they can sue,'[113] New York lawyers generally thought that only the persona could bring a claim. This could be due to the nature of the right of publicity in New York, which is couched in terms of privacy.

The perceived personal nature of the right was explained by a lawyer who stated 'The right itself is only held by the individual so the individual has to enforce it.'[114] Similarly, 'The brand would not have the right to go after the other brand because they do not own the persona. Unless there is an assignment, the licensee cannot make the claim.'[115] Another stated the limits of contract law in explaining why a company might not pursue a breach of an exclusive licence by a competitor: 'The brand does not have privity with the other brand … These are things you

[109] UK interview 13.
[110] UK interview 14.
[111] ibid.
[112] While inducement of breach of contract is a possible cause of action if the persona breaches the exclusive contract, this section is considering situations where persona has been used without permission. As such, inducement of breach of contract would not be relevant.
[113] California interview 16.
[114] New York interview 15.
[115] New York interview 2.

may not be able to control.'[116] On the other hand, in the New York case of *Bi-Rite Enterprises v Button Master*,[117] District Judge Sofaer confirmed the proprietary nature of the right of publicity:

> Unlike privacy rights, which protect personality and feelings and are therefore not assignable, the right of publicity gives rise to a 'proprietary' interest in the commercial value of one's persona which is assignable and may be freely licensed. This proprietary interest is much like a copyright; … it embodies a bundle of exclusive marketing rights which its holder may transfer in its entirety by an assignment or in part by exclusive licenses. Holders of exclusive licenses gain standing to protect their interests against all who would encroach on the exclusive rights embodied in the licenses.[118]

Soafer cited *Haelan Laboratories v Topps Chewing Gum*,[119] the case in which the right of publicity was first recognised, as authority: 'This right of publicity would usually yield them no money unless it could be made the subject of an exclusive grant which barred any other advertisers from using their pictures.'[120] The lack of certainty on the part of lawyers about the right of an exclusive licensee to sue for infringement of the right of publicity explains why ignorance and disregard for the law were not advanced as reasons for the behaviour of undermining exclusive deals. More interestingly, it also reveals that parties may act in accordance with the law despite being unaware of it, thus indicating the presence of a social norm.

IV. Do Not Seek Permission for Topical or Evocative Advertisements – UK Only

The third behaviour observed in the advertising industry is unique to the UK. The legal framework is a major factor that influences this behaviour, as well as the opposite behaviour that occurs in the US, discussed in section V. A lawyer noted that 'If someone wants to make tactical advertising to take advantage of current event eg Wimbledon final, they won't ask permission. There's no time, and it's a one off ad.'[121] Similarly, another stated that permission is not sought, instead 'Just say sorry, we won't do it again, and that will be good enough for them.'[122] These types of advertisements occur in the UK, but are not as common as endorsement or illustrative advertisements, both of which are governed by the behaviour of seeking permission discussed so far. These topical or evocative advertisements tend to be rare and are often centred on an event. Lawyers were able to provide a

[116] New York interview 19.
[117] *Bi-Rite Enterprises Inc v Button Master* (1983).
[118] ibid [1999]–[2000].
[119] *Haelan v Topps* (1953).
[120] ibid [868].
[121] UK interview 5.
[122] UK interview 12.

few examples of these types of advertisements, which included easyJet's use of the Ingrams and Specsavers' use of Kevin Pietersen, both discussed in chapter 2. While there is still a behaviour of creating such advertisements without seeking permission, these types of advertisements seem to be created infrequently. Because of the nature of the advertisements, it would be unusual for someone to seek permission, as there is little risk of legal consequences and there is no need to secure collaboration as there would be limited benefit in doing so.

A. Influences on Behaviour – Legally Permissible

Advertisers that make these types of advertisements are not concerned about the fear of litigation, which is minimal in the UK compared to the risk that would be run in the US where the right of publicity is covered by strict liability. As noted by a lawyer, 'At the moment, you are free to make humorous ads as long as you don't defame anyone or falsely imply their endorsement.'[123] While there may be a risk of defamation in a handful of circumstances if the advertisement is degrading, the advertisers choose to proceed despite this knowledge, because they are trying to capitalise on media exposure after undertaking a cost–benefit analysis. For example, in referring to the Specsavers advertisement, which implied that cricketer Kevin Pietersen cheated during The Ashes tournament,[124] one lawyer suggested:

> I am certain Specsavers knew that he would sue them. [They] would probably have been bitterly disappointed if he didn't sue them. They only bought a very small amount of media, knew they could not run it [the advertisement] for very long, and the photograph would have cost them next to nothing. They would have been thinking they really wanted public relations, so they wanted him to sue.[125]

In many instances, there will be no risk of litigation if there is no basis for defamation. As a result, the Advertising Codes would be the only recourse, but as noted in the discussion of deterrence theory in section II, in assessing seeking permission for endorsement and illustrative uses of persona, the Advertising Codes are not considered a serious threat by advertisers. Companies such as Paddy Power and easyJet enjoy creative freedom in the absence of a UK publicity right and create advertisements featuring living individuals that do not imply endorsement.

Paddy Power is notorious for breaching the Advertising Codes, its Oscar Pistorius advert earning the title of 'most complained about advertisement' in 2015.[126] The company's 2015 advertisement promoted a bet on the outcome of

[123] UK interview 5.

[124] Bolton, P, 'Specsavers say sorry to Kevin Pietersen for Hot Spot row' *The Telegraph* (2 October 2013).

[125] UK interview 4.

[126] Baird, D, 'Paddy Power's Oscar Pistorius ad named most complained-about of 2014' *The Guardian* (20 February 2015). Paddy Power has breached numerous sections of the Advertising Code: 'Paddy Power's 10 most controversial adverts' *The Telegraph* (29 August 2012).

the Pistorius murder trial, featuring a likeness of Pistorius as a gold statue, accompanied by the words, 'It's Oscar Time'. Pistorius himself did not complain about the advertisement; rather, the public complained about its impropriety. EasyJet used photographs of David Beckham twice in 2003 without his permission.[127] In one instance, the airline used a photograph of Beckham with his hair styled in cornrows to make fun of his frequent changes of hairstyle, with the caption 'Hair today, gone tomorrow'.[128] In another instance, it used a photograph of Beckham in an advertisement that offered to fly his family from the USA every week for a year to alleviate potential homesickness caused by their move to Los Angeles.[129] Beckham complained to easyJet on both occasions, but no legal action was ever taken nor were the Advertising Codes relied on. In fact, a spokesperson for easyJet said legal action was not threatened: 'They wrote us a very polite, friendly letter asking us to consider making a donation to the NSPCC … We are considering their request. But there was absolutely no threat of legal action. None whatsoever.'[130]

The failure of someone with the resources of Beckham to take legal action explains why this behaviour persists; there are no real disadvantages to the advertisers who choose this style of advertisement. It is highly unlikely that passing off would succeed, as noted by head of corporate affairs of easyJet at the time: 'We do not believe that anyone would look at our ad and believe that Beckham is endorsing easyJet.'[131] Furthermore, the Advertising Codes are subject to the adjudication of the ASA. Many complaints have been held to be without merit by the Authority.[132] It should be recalled that permission is not required but rather recommended, as explained in chapter 2. As such, use of persona does not automatically result in a ruling against the advertisement, so often, individuals may not bother to pursue the Codes unless they are affronted by the advertisement. As noted by a lawyer:

> We quite like the ability to use people in ads. Current affairs would not be acceptable in the US, while often they are quite good ads. Humorous, clever … people enjoy them. The only thing we can do are humorous ads. Otherwise, encouraged to collaborate for the benefits.[133]

[127] Day, J, 'EasyJet risks further Beckham wrath' *The Guardian* (16 June 2003) at www.theguardian.com/media/2003/jun/16/marketingandpr.advertising (accessed 7 July 2017).

[128] Whitehead, J, 'David Beckham unwitting star of another EasyJet ad' *Campaign* (23 June 2003) at www.campaignlive.co.uk/article/david-beckham-unwitting-star-easyjet-ad/183582 (accessed 24 September 2017).

[129] ibid.

[130] Day, J, 'Beckham asks for EasyJet donation' *The Guardian* (28 May 2003) at www.theguardian.com/media/2003/may/28/marketingandpr.advertising (accessed 24 September 2017).

[131] Kleinman, M, 'Beckham agents threaten EasyJet over image use' *Campaign* (28 May 2003) at www.campaignlive.co.uk/article/beckham-agents-threaten-easyjet-image-use/181185 (accessed 29 July 2019).

[132] ASA, 'Privacy: Permission' (11 June 2018) at www.asa.org.uk/advice-online/privacy-permission.html (accessed 23 January 2023).

[133] UK interview 6.

While the risk of running foul of the Advertising Codes and the threat of litigation are not major concerns, advertisers may run advertisements of this nature[134] strategically in order to avoid a complaint or any legal action. They often capitalise on a current event and rely on the media buzz for the advertisement. As such, the advertisement will run for a short period of time. The time frame may be so short that the individual will not notice the advertisement until it has ceased circulation. One interviewee noted 'Keep production costs to a minimum, keep media schedules as short as possible, set aside some money to pay legal fees, and see what happens.'[135] Another commented:

> If you are running an advertisement, before the advert goes out, advise client it is close to the line. Prepare to risk running it for three weeks. It will take at least this much time before someone complains. Won't have to pay any damages for a complaint [under Advertising Codes] anyway.[136]

i. Social Norms – Signalling

It can also be suggested that signalling theory influences this behaviour. While these types of advertisements are rare, the companies that are likely to make them may want to send a signal to their consumers that they are the cheeky type and like to act on the edge of the law. Since these advertisements are made after cost–benefit analysis has been undertaken, the companies that decide to run the risk of a complaint by the celebrity, whether through legal action or media publicity, probably consider the nature of the advertisement to be beneficial to their brand. Generally, only certain kinds of companies, such as those named previously, Paddy Power and easyJet, venture to make these types of advertisements. Companies that enter into exclusive licensing deals, such as Adidas and Nespresso, are unlikely to produce evocative and topical advertisements without the permission of the persona featured.

V. Do Not Evoke Persona or Create Topical Advertisements – US Only

In contrast to the behaviour discussed in section IV, the opposite occurs in the US, where the behaviour observed was that advertisements do not evoke persona

[134] See, eg, the advertisements created by various brands after footballer Luis Suarez bit Giorgio Chiellini during the 2014 World Cup – Hooton, C, 'Luis Suarez bites again: Nando's, Snickers, McDonald's and other brands sink their teeth in on Twitter' *The Independent* (26 June 2014) at www.independent.co.uk/sport/football/international/luis-suarez-bites-again-nandos-snickers-mcdonalds-and-other-brands-weigh-in-with-twitter-memes-9561637.html (accessed 11 September 2018).

[135] UK interview 4.

[136] UK interview 9.

or use persona for topical advertisements without permission. When asked when persona could be used without seeking permission, lawyers referred to situations where freedom of speech would be engaged, such as in news media.[137] However, no one referred to advertisements. Rather, it was indicated that the norm is to seek permission to use persona, and as a consequence, evocative and topical advertisements are not generally made, according to the lawyers interviewed. This is largely due to developments in case law, as will be explained in section V.A.i on deterrence theory. When questioned about law's impact on the inability to make these types of advertisements, one lawyer responded:

> Those are commercial uses [of persona]. We've advised in that way for years. The Vanna White case is something our clients don't complain much about anymore because it's settled law. Since then we've had the Cheers case that makes it clear that even if you have a fictionalised character that is controlled by copyright, the individuals depicting those fictional characters can have a right of publicity claim. All of that is well-settled law and it's not controversial.[138]

In commenting that such advertisements are commercial, the lawyer was referring to the applicability of the right of publicity to commercial uses of persona. Another, referring to *Jordan v Dominick's Finer Foods*,[139] where a topical advertisement was at issue, stated 'Congrats on a victory type of ads are not allowed. There was a big case with Michael Jordan. This is not allowed in the US.'[140] Similarly, 'There is no exception against the prohibition for using someone's name for advertising for the purpose of saying congratulations.'[141] Another addressed evocative advertisements:

> If you wore one white glove and did certain moves, the Michael Jackson estate could probably sue you for that … That's a symbol of him, and if you use that in a commercial you're trying to play on him. If you use any kind of indicia of persona, then you're in trouble.[142]

Before cases ruled that evocative uses could infringe on an individual's right of publicity, topical and evocative advertisements were made in the US. This is evidenced by advertising magazine advice that was published when the first cases on this issue were being tried.[143] Advertising agencies made these types of advertisements without consequence for a period of time. However, this behaviour was eradicated in the US and replaced with the current behaviour of not creating these

[137] California interview 13.

[138] California interview 3. Other lawyers expressed the same thought regarding the settled status of the law prohibiting evocative and topical advertisements: New York interviews 3, 7, 10, 13, 15; California interviews 12, 13, 22, 24, 25; *White v Samsung Electronics America Inc* (1992); *Wendt v Host Intern Inc (aka Cheers)* 125 F 3d 806 (9th Cir 1997).

[139] *Jordan v Dominick's Finer Foods LLC* 115 F Supp 3d 950 (2015).

[140] New York interview 7.

[141] New York interview 5.

[142] New York interview 10.

[143] Kaikati (1987) 95.

types of advertisements due to developments in case law that made it clear that persona extended to identity, which could include likeness, distinctive characteristics and voice, as discussed in chapter 2.

The lawyers consistently claimed that they would advise against creating evocative or topical advertisements, and correspondingly, such advertisements are rarely created. It should be noted that UK lawyers were opposed to this US behaviour. One said, 'Speaking as an English lawyer, I find it ridiculous that they [US] have such wide rights. It becomes impossible to refer to celebrities in any way.'[144] However, US lawyers accepted this behaviour and did not consider it problematic: 'I feel freedom to be able to advertise product is a lot less meritorious than the ability to control the use of name and likeness. Even if I'm not in the market, it shouldn't be fair game like that.'[145] This feeling is reflective of the morality theory of law discussed in section II.A.iii, which exists in the US but not in the UK.

A. Influences on Behaviour

i. Law – Deterrence Theory

This behaviour is influenced by litigation risk and thus can be explained by the deterrence theory of compliance with law. When asked 'How do advertisers avoid the right of publicity?', an interviewee in California stated 'Either you get rights or you sometimes rewrite it [the advertisement] so that it doesn't involve any particular person or you just avoid it.'[146] Another stated 'If you are using someone in a commercial without their authorisation, you are exposed to a claim and that is appropriately so.'[147] According to interviewees in both New York and California, they would not advise clients to make these types of advertisements unless they were willing to run the risk of litigation. However, the cost of litigation is considered to outweigh the benefits of such advertisements, especially since the risk is very significant, as discussed in the previous chapter.

B. Deviation: Evoke Persona or Create Topical Advertisements

i. Law – Disregard and/or Ignorance

Entities that follow this behaviour may not have been properly advised, so they are ignorant of the restrictions imposed by the right of publicity. For smaller

[144] UK interview 6.
[145] California interview 10.
[146] California interview 21.
[147] California interview 3.

advertising agencies without legal advice, it may be less apparent that permission should be sought for uses of persona that do not convey endorsement, particularly if the use is merely evocative. No recent examples of this behaviour were given by interviewees, as lawyers tended to refer to cases prior to 2000.

VI. Conclusion

This chapter used data gathered from fieldwork to examine four standard behaviours in the advertising industry that regulate the use of persona in the US and the UK, as well as deviations from these behaviours. In both jurisdictions, the behaviour that impacts a majority of advertisements is seeking permission to use persona in endorsement and illustrative advertisements. Endorsement-style advertisements are the most common types of advertisements that use celebrities, and in order to create these advertisements effectively, collaboration with celebrities is necessary. As such, while the deterrence theory of compliance with law influences behaviour in both jurisdictions, as well as morality theory in the US, the strength of the perceived benefits of collaboration means that this behaviour would subsist even in the absence of the legal frameworks. This is particularly so in the age of social media and influencer advertising where para-social relationships are targeted, as consumers want to feel connected to the product or service they are buying. Social norms also play a role through signalling theory, as companies want to be seen as good partners to work with. The benefit of collaboration and the need to send the right signal demonstrate that law is not the only driving force in determining how persona is commercialised.

Signalling theory was most relevant to the behaviour of respecting exclusive endorsement deals with individuals. Interviewees felt that it would be disadvantageous to undermine exclusive endorsement deals. The presence of signalling theory has resulted in the same behaviour occurring in both the US and the UK, despite the fact that exclusive licensees in the US have legal rights that are unavailable to exclusive licensees in the UK. Interviewees in the US seemed unclear as to the proprietary nature of the right of publicity, which could explain why none of the compliance with law theories was revealed as influencing the permission-based behaviour. This demonstrates that even though law may apparently be complied with, the reason for compliance may be attributed to another factor – in this case, social norms.

The two aforementioned standard behaviours were observed in both jurisdictions, but there was a divergence in behaviour with regard to evocative and topical advertisements. In the UK, there is a standard behaviour of creating these types of advertisements without seeking permission of the persona, whereas in the US these types of advertisements are not usually created. This divergence can be attributed directly to the difference in legal frameworks, as the deterrence theory of compliance with law was present in the US but not the UK. However, it is important to note that this is the only behaviour divergence observed across the four industries studied in this book. In the next three chapters, it will be demonstrated that the behaviours are the same in the merchandising, film and video game industries, despite differences in legal frameworks.

6

Merchandising Industry

Introduction

This chapter explains how law, contract and social norms influence the commercialisation of persona in the merchandising industry. The use of persona in merchandising can be divided into traditional and modern forms. In its traditional form, producers apply indicia of persona – often images and photographs – to mass-produced goods such as mugs, pillowcases, phone cases and t-shirts. In contrast, modern merchandising uses 'celebrity branded products',[1] where celebrities play an active role in both creating and promoting the product. This modern form of merchandising thus requires even greater involvement of the celebrity than the endorsement advertisements discussed in chapter 5.

In addition to the distinction drawn between traditional and modern merchandising,[2] a distinction is also drawn between the status of merchandisers based on empirical data. Interviewees differentiated between the types of merchandisers that tend to seek permission to use persona and those that do not. 'High-street merchandisers' are those that routinely enter into licences. They are sizeable entities that want to sell their products in high-street stores, are likely to have access to legal advice and may produce high-quality products. In contrast, 'alternative merchandisers' are those that do not seek permission to use persona, are usually smaller entities, which may not have access to legal advice, and sell in market stalls or online marketplaces. High-street merchandisers produce both traditional and modern merchandise, whereas alternative merchandisers are limited to traditional merchandise.

Modern merchandise cannot be produced without the permission and indeed cooperation of the celebrity, which is why only high-street merchandisers are able to venture into production. The need to obtain permission is a commercial issue,

[1] Keel, A, Nataraajan, R, 'Celebrity Endorsements and Beyond: New Avenues for Celebrity Branding' (2012) 29(9) *Psychology and Marketing* 690, 694.

[2] This distinction is based on secondary sources: ibid; Mooro, A, 'Why 2016 was the year we became obsessed with celeb merch' *Refinery29* (13 December 2016) at www.refinery29.uk/rise-of-celebrity-merchandise-2016 (accessed 12 September 2018); Khanom, R, *The Evolution of Celebrity Endorsement in Beauty* (Mintel Academic 2016); Mau, D, 'Justin Bieber Merch Boosts Sales and Social Engagement for Urban Outfits' *Fashionista* (23 November 2016) at https://fashionista.com/2016/11/justin-bieber-merch-urban-outfitters (accessed 13 September 2018).

as the nature of the merchandise requires cooperation to create and promote the product. Additionally, there is generally a legal requirement to obtain permission in both jurisdictions, as the US right of publicity is subject to strict liability and the manner in which persona is used in modern merchandise is likely to satisfy misrepresentation for passing off in the UK. As such, the common behaviour observed with regard to modern merchandisers is that high-street merchandisers seek permission to use persona in both jurisdictions. There are also social norms that have to be considered in the UK that influence the permission to be sought. Interestingly, no equivalent social norms were observed in the US. This does not mean that no social norms operate, but rather the data did not lend themselves to a social norms analysis.

While the influences of law, contract and, in the UK, social norms, influence high-street merchandisers to seek permission to create modern merchandise, high-street merchandisers also seek permission to create traditional merchandise. This is interesting, because the influences should arguably be less relevant when producing traditional merchandise, which usually involves a photograph or a signature applied to mass-produced goods. Yet the data suggest that there are perceived benefits to collaborating to create traditional merchandise. While the US law should be equally influential regardless of the type of merchandise, it can be argued that passing off should have a more limited effect, as it would be more difficult to satisfy the misrepresentation criteria for traditional merchandise. However, the law still acts as a deterrent to high-street merchandisers. Furthermore, social norms operate and influence compliance with this behaviour in the UK.

While high-street merchandisers seek permission to make both modern and traditional merchandise due to the influences discussed above, these influences do not apply to alternative merchandisers. As such, alternative merchandisers use persona without permission to create traditional merchandise in both the US and the UK, regardless of the US strict-liability right of publicity. There may be no applicable law in the UK with regard to traditional merchandise, as passing off would be difficult to satisfy, but the strict-liability right of publicity in the US would apply. Yet alternative merchandisers are either ignorant of or disregard the right of publicity.

A key observation to come from the fieldwork is that, in the merchandising industry, the differing legal frameworks in the US and the UK have not resulted in the observance of different behaviours. This can be contrasted with the advertising industry, where a divergence in behaviour was noted with regard to evocative and topical advertisements. The uniformity of behaviours in the merchandising industry in both jurisdictions suggests that behaviour is not solely determined by the relevant legal framework. While law is indeed influential, the benefits espoused by contracts are arguably equally so, and may exceed the influence of law with regard to modern merchandise due to the collaborative nature of this endeavour. Additionally, the law does not influence alternative merchandisers in the US, which renders the behaviour observed similar to that in the UK where there is limited applicability of existing laws.

The findings in this chapter are derived from 35 interviews with individuals who have experience in the merchandising industry: 11 in the UK, 5 in New York and 19 in California. While the majority of those interviewed were lawyers, three UK interviews were conducted with other persons in the industry. The lawyers interviewed had experience working with both merchandisers who seek licences to use persona and individuals who license their personas. The trend of seeking permission to make traditional merchandising in the UK is a surprise, as it was thought that this practice might not be common, at least prior to *Fenty*.[3] However, many interviewees stated that Topshop's decision to proceed with only a copyright licence was unusual, as will be explained in section II.

No lawyers had experience of advising merchandisers who use persona without permission – an activity that did not seem to be uncommon, based on reports in the fieldwork – although they were able to convey their experiences of representing clients whose personas were being used in such situations. This may be because, as seen in section III, merchandise produced without permission is usually created by 'alternative' merchandisers, which often do not access legal advice.

This chapter is divided into three sections. Section I provides an overview of the use of persona in the merchandising industry. Section II analyses the behaviour of high-street merchandisers seeking permission for both modern and traditional merchandising. Section III analyses the behaviour of alternative merchandisers using persona without permission to produce traditional merchandise.

I. Use of Persona in the Merchandising Industry

Merchandising concerns the production of goods. Whereas advertising encompasses strategies used to sell goods, merchandising focuses on the goods themselves. There is no limit to the type of product to which persona can be applied. Typical goods include mugs, t-shirts, keychains and caps, but product ranges have also included phone cases, pencil cases, pillow cases, dolls, etc. Merchandising that uses persona was traditionally focused on mass-produced, low-cost items. A 1994 report by the World Intellectual Property Organization (WIPO), in describing 'personality merchandising', stated:

> This … form of merchandising involves the use of the essential attributes (name, image, voice and other personality features) of real persons (in other words, the true identity of an individual) in the marketing and/or advertising of goods or services … [M]erchandisers believe that the main reason for a person to buy low-priced mass goods (mugs, scarves, badges, T-shirts, etc) is not because of the product itself but because the name or image of a celebrity appealing to that person is reproduced on the product.[4]

[3] *Fenty and others v Arcadia Group Brands Ltd (trading as Topshop) and another* [2013] EWHC 1945 (Ch).

[4] International Bureau, *Character Merchandising* (WIPO 1994) 9.

It was therefore said that consumers purchase these goods because they '[allow] fans to express their passion for a particular star'.[5]

According to one of the merchandising representatives interviewed, 'Licensing is still fairly young. It grew up in the 1950s. [It is] not yet a mature business. But it has been around 60 odd years now, so it is well structured.'[6] This interviewee was referring to merchandise produced under licence,[7] which initially began in 1930 with the Walt Disney Corporation's licensing of their intellectual property.[8] It is unclear when the practice of licensing persona (rather than characters) began. In the UK, licensing persona was not considered to be an established practice by the UK High Court in the 1977 case of *Lyngstad v Anabas*.[9] In contrast, the 1953 case that recognised the right of publicity in the US, *Haelan Laboratories v Topps Chewing Gum*, found that a licence to use the names and likenesses of baseball players should be protected by the law.[10] There are also examples in the US of persona licensing that significantly pre-date *Haelan*, such as Shirley Temple's licensing her name and likeness in the US for the creation of dolls in 1936,[11] and Amelia Earhart's licensing her name to a company that produced luggage featuring her name from 1933 to 1970.[12] These licences preceded the recognition of the right of publicity, so the law was not instrumental in securing them. It might be asked why traditional merchandisers would have started obtaining licences to use persona, when such merchandise could be made without the collaboration seen in modern merchandising.

A. Types of Merchandise: Traditional and Modern

The terms 'traditional' and 'modern' are used in this book to distinguish between (i) mass-produced goods that use persona as an aspect of the goods, and (ii) goods that use persona as an aspect of the goods, whether by incorporating its attributes

[5] Walker, P, 'The Facts and the Fiction' in Lam, C, Raphael, J and Weber, M (eds), *Disassembling the Celebrity Figure: Credibility and the Incredible* (Brill Rodopi 2018) 164.

[6] UK interviewee 16.

[7] The history of the merchandise industry prior to licensing can be traced back to the 19th century. For more information. see Baillie, I, 'Merchandising: an historical survey' in Adams, Hickey and Tritton (eds), *Merchandising Intellectual Property* (Butterworths Law 1987) xxv.

[8] ibid.

[9] *Lyngstad v Anabas* [1977] FSR 62 [68]: 'So far as it goes it suggests no more than that some people might think that the plaintiffs might have granted some sort of licence for the use of the name, although why they should do so has never been explained, since it is not alleged, and indeed I do not think could be alleged on the evidence, that there is any general custom for such licences to be granted by pop singers. Indeed, the available evidence is quite to the contrary.'

[10] *Haelan Laboratories Inc v Topps Chewing Gum Inc* 202 F 2d 866 (2d Cir 1953) [868] – 'This right of publicity would usually yield them no money unless it could be made the subject of an exclusive grant which barred any other advertiser from using their pictures.'

[11] Battersby, G and Grimes, G, *2016 Licensing Update* (Wolters Kluwer 2016) 6–37.

[12] Morson, J, 'The first celebrity fashion line was Amelia Earhart's' *Racked* (24 July 2017) at www.racked.com/2017/7/24/16000612/amelia-earhart-clothing-line (accessed 12 September 2018).

or by helping with the design of the product, as well as in promoting the sale of these goods. The latter, modern approach to merchandising requires celebrity involvement, whereas the traditional approach can be undertaken without direct assistance from the celebrity. The modern approach to merchandising[13] can be seen in parallel with the advancements in the advertising industry around celebrity endorsements. A Mintel report on the *Evolution of Celebrity Endorsement in Beauty* notes:

> Celebrity endorsements have been central to the advertising sector for decades … By the 1980s, with the rise of celebrity power, the use of celebrities in product endorsement changed with companies making new products especially for celebrities … [M]ore successful examples in recent years have seen celebrities being used for more than just a face of a name. MAC's collaborations, for example, continue to be popular. Following the success of Mariah Carey's Christmas collaboration in 2015, the celebrity has worked on a new range with the brand for Christmas 2016.[14]

Just as companies collaborate with a celebrity to create effective advertising campaigns, modern merchandising involves working with a celebrity to create branded material that is promoted in partnership with the celebrity; 'in recent years, there has been an increase in celebrity-branded products, such as perfumes and clothing lines'.[15] This modern style of merchandising may assume different forms. Keel and Nataraajan identify different models of celebrity-branded products. Celebrity mono-branding products feature only the name of the celebrity, whereas co-branded celebrity products carry the names of both the celebrity and the brand that produces the good.[16] Keel and Nataraajan describe Elizabeth Arden's production of Britney Spears' branded fragrance as an example of mono-branding, where only the celebrity's name is used in connection with product.[17] In terms of co-branding, Adidas produces a line of 'David Beckham' shoes that are promoted by both Beckham and Adidas.[18]

While the aspects of persona used in modern merchandising are often the same as those in traditional merchandising (such as name, photograph and/or signature), the creation and marketing of these products depart from traditional merchandising as celebrity involvement is required. As a result, high-street merchandisers that produce modern merchandise generally seek permission to use persona due to commercial considerations. While the need for collaboration is not as great for traditional merchandise, empirical data show that high-street merchandisers nonetheless generally seek permission for both types of merchandise due both to the desire to collaborate and to the deterrence of the legal framework. In contrast,

[13] Mooro (2016).
[14] Khanom, R, *The Evolution of Celebrity Endorsement in Beauty* (Mintel Academic 2016).
[15] Keel and Nataraajan (2012) 690.
[16] ibid 695–96.
[17] ibid 695.
[18] ibid 696.

alternative merchandisers do not seek permission to create traditional merchandise, as they disregard the law or are ignorant of it.

II. High-Street Merchandisers Seek Permission to Use Persona for Modern and Traditional Merchandise

According to interviewees, high-street merchandisers seek permission to use persona for both traditional and modern merchandise. One merchandising representative said 'I'm coming at this from practical experience of 35 years in the field. In the day to day trade of licensing and merchandising, for the most part, celebrity rights are respected, and contracts are sought.'[19] A lawyer who represents celebrities noted:

> In my experience, it's more usual that people will seek permission than not because the kind of licence proposals that are presented to my clients are fairly elaborate. The licensee is putting a lot of resources behind the proposed usage.[20]

By 'elaborate', the licensee referred to a range of high-quality products. It was indicated that licences were sought in order to secure the investment being made in the production of merchandise. Other interviewees noted the desire of high-street merchandisers to produce 'official' merchandise. A lawyer stated that clients 'want to produce merchandise that is authorised – official merchandise.'[21]

Most high-street merchandisers will seek permission to use persona for modern merchandise, because it is difficult to produce this type of merchandise without cooperation from the celebrity. As for traditional merchandise, the trend of seeking permission has become entrenched in recent years. As noted by one interviewee, 'Retail has really upped the game with regard to requirements from their [merchandise] partner to make sure it is licenced.'[22] In terms of securing a licence for modern merchandise, a merchandiser might directly address the celebrity, her lawyer or her agent, similar to how endorsements are sought. As for traditional merchandise, licences may be sought from the celebrity or a licensing body. A lawyer who exclusively worked with the estate of a deceased celebrity explained the process for approving a licence:

> [Negotiations take] one to three months. How big the deal is determines how long the approval takes. A small apparel deal can happen in three emails. We have a standard merchandising agreement. Basically, we change the royalty rate and a couple of things here and there and it's cut and dry.[23]

[19] UK interview 16.
[20] New York interview 8.
[21] UK interview 5.
[22] California interview 14.
[23] California interview 14.

The licence to use persona may be obtained through a third party that has secured the rights for certain uses, for example to produce merchandise relating to a film the celebrity has acted in. Another merchandising representative explained:

> Many celebrities are licensed in a roundabout fashion. For instance, someone recently bought rights from Disney to make a product based on Pirates of the Caribbean. That will almost certainly include the right to use actors and descriptions of the characters. In that sense, the actors are being licensed as well.[24]

An in-house lawyer for a film and television studio explained 'It's something the studio always wants to secure if they're using a person – they always want to have the right to use the right of publicity in marketing content.'[25] By 'marketing content', the lawyer was referring to merchandise that is produced to promote the film. Another provided this example, 'Let's say that Disney reaches an agreement with Kim Kardashian to do the Kim Kardashian story. We're going to have exclusive rights to merchandising. Clothing, T-shirts, everything …'[26] One lawyer noted that the practice of securing merchandising deals with actors was standard, and only in exceptional circumstances would this not be done:

> It [permission to use persona] should be covered by whatever the agreement is with the talent. The concern comes up with lower budget films where you don't have a team of sophisticated lawyers and you're not anticipating a secondary market in terms of merchandising. Low budget runaway successes like the Blair Witch Project might be an example. I think there is a very good possibility that the actors didn't have an agreement that covered merchandising.[27]

A. Theories of Compliance

i. Law – Deterrence Theory

a. United States

The presence of the right of publicity was considered instrumental in prompting merchandisers to seek permission for use of persona in the US. As noted by one interviewee:

> In the 90s you had Abercrombie and Fitch and big nationals who created t-shirts with someone's likeness, but people realise if they do that now, they can get sued. People are more cautious because of past litigation.[28]

Another also felt that this behaviour had developed within the last two decades. He stated that, 'In conversations with clients about what they can and cannot

[24] UK interview 16.
[25] California interview 25.
[26] California interview 7.
[27] California interview 7.
[28] California interview 1.

do, they understand you cannot use someone's name or image [without permission]. Twenty years ago people did not understand that.'[29] It is interesting that these lawyers suggested greater awareness about the reach of the right of publicity in more recent times. The right of publicity was recognised in 1953 in the case of *Haelan Laboratories v Topps Chewing Gum*,[30] a 2nd Circuit case decided on New York law. The right of publicity was codified in California in 1972,[31] and the California common law right was recognised in 1974 in the case of *Motschenbacher v RJ Reynolds Tobacco Co.*[32] Reasons were not given for the increased respect for the law, but it can be speculated that media coverage of numerous right of publicity cases in the 1990s could have contributed to this. Regardless, at present, it was felt that the law is influential on the behaviour of high-street merchandisers seeking permission to use persona in modern and traditional merchandising.

In drawing a distinction between high-street and alternative merchandisers, a lawyer remarked that 'bigger brands don't want to get sued'.[33] Another stated:

> The law does have a deterrent effect. It's sort of an economic tool that puts a value on something that people value anyway. It creates a value and gives the persona the right to share in that. It's small shops that go out and violate the law.[34]

This viewpoint advanced is interesting because it alludes to the desire to collaborate via contract, which exists independently of, and yet is spurred on by, the law. As will be explained in section III, the behaviour of alternative merchandisers not seeking permission exists because of ignorance and disregard for the law. Since high-street brands have access to legal advice, they are less likely to infringe the right of publicity. As explained by a New York lawyer, 'We have situations with small companies or individuals who are unaware or don't know how to begin dealing with the issues, so that happens, but if it's a bigger company, they know [the law].'[35]

b. United Kingdom

Fear of litigation in the US exists because of the right of publicity, but the situation is different in the UK. Until *Fenty*,[36] the status and scope of passing off with regard to persona merchandise was uncertain as there had been no successful prior cases in the UK. Past cases that considered persona merchandising, namely

[29] New York interview 15.
[30] *Haelan v Topps* (1953).
[31] Greenberg, M and Lovitz, M, 'Right of publicity and the intersection of copyright and trade mark law' (2012) *GGU Law Digital Commons, Paper No 484*, 4.
[32] *Motschenbacher v RJ Reynolds Tobacco Co* 498 F 2d 821 (9th Cir 1974).
[33] New York interview 19.
[34] California interview 23.
[35] New York interview 17.
[36] *Fenty* [2013].

Lyngstad v Anabas[37] and *McCulloch v May*,[38] were unsuccessful, as the claimants did not satisfy the former 'common field of activity' requirement. *Irvine*,[39] which successfully used passing off to protect persona, concerned advertising rather than merchandising. The court distinguished between these two industries:

> When someone endorses a product or service he tells the relevant public that he approves of the product or service or is happy to be associated with it. In effect he adds his name as an encouragement to members of the relevant public to buy or use the service or product. Merchandising is rather different. It involves exploiting images, themes or articles which have become famous. It is not a necessary feature of merchandising that members of the public will think the products are in any sense endorsed by the film makers or actors in the film. Merchandised products will include some where there is a perception of endorsement and some where there may not be … An example of merchandising is the sale of memorabilia relating to the late Diana, Princess of Wales. A porcelain plate bearing her image could hardly be thought of as being endorsed by her, but the enhanced sales which may be achieved by virtue of the presence of the image is a form of merchandising.[40]

The *Fenty* case[41] acknowledged that mere use of an image on merchandise is not enough to constitute passing off, but confirmed that the approach to passing off was the same for advertising and merchandising. It was the first UK case to find passing off for use of persona on merchandise, and thus arguably expanded the reach of passing off.[42]

As for trade marks, it was noted in chapter 2 that registration would not be granted for a 'mere image carrier', as these marks would be considered descriptive.[43] For example, 'Elvis Presley' was rejected as a mark because it was incapable of acting as a designator of origin.[44] Nonetheless, many celebrities have successfully registered their names as trade marks.[45] It is unclear why marks that may be considered descriptive have been successfully registered, but it is suggested that descriptiveness is more likely to be an issue if the mark is opposed. If no opposition proceedings are brought, the mark may be successfully registered if the Registry does not detect a problem with the absolute or relative grounds for refusal.

Passing off and trade mark law are tools that can be deployed against unauthorised uses of persona on merchandise. An interviewee who represents celebrities stated that 'Individuals will say their image is being used. I look at how I can

[37] *Lyngstad v Anabas* [1977] FSR 62.
[38] *McCulloch v Lewis A May* [1947] 2 All ER 845.
[39] *Irvine and another v Talksport Ltd* [2002] EWHC 367 (Ch).
[40] ibid [9].
[41] *Fenty* [2013].
[42] It should be noted that Australian law moved in this direction before the UK. See Catanzariti, T, 'Swimmers, surfers and Sue Smith – personality rights in Australia' (2002) 13 *Ent L Rev* 135.
[43] UK Intellectual Property Office, 'Manual of trade marks practice' (14 January 2019) at www.gov.uk/guidance/trade-marks-manual/the-examination-guide (accessed 31 October 2022).
[44] *Elvis Presley Trade Marks* [1999] RPC 567.
[45] A search of the UK Trade Mark Registry reveals many celebrity names.

enforce their rights and most commonly [I] look at trade marks and passing off.'[46] Since passing off and trade marks are the two most applicable causes of action in addressing merchandising,[47] UK interviewees were questioned on how these causes of action impact the merchandising industry. It emerged from the data that the deterrence theory of law is also present in the UK. Responses with regards to passing off will be discussed first, followed by trade marks.

Interviewees in the UK were asked what impact the *Fenty* decision had on the merchandising industry, if any. Lawyers stated that the outcome of *Fenty* reduced unauthorised merchandising: 'The Rihanna case curtailed this – most big brands won't take the risk.'[48] Another interviewee noted:

> I think the case has made people be more careful when they are sourcing product. If you're ordering a T-shirt with someone's image who you'd immediately recognise, that should raise an alarm bell to check if there is any agreement [with the featured persona].[49]

Whether the impact of *Fenty* was to make brands more careful in securing rights, or whether it reinforced an existing practice, the decision contributed to the behaviour of seeking permission for merchandising in the UK.

In addition to passing off, lawyers were also questioned on the role of trade marks in merchandising. When asked about the benefits of registering a mark, a lawyer responded:

> The ideal advice is to file early as possible. The problem is people may not spend money on filing when they don't know how successful their career is going to be. Might be worth filing in the key merchandise classes such as footwear and clothing at an early stage in certain jurisdictions. If you get your first merchandise deal, you should definitely file.[50]

Another interviewee stated that having a trade mark 'enhances merchandise and endorsement deals. [If you are] selling a T-shirt with a celebrity's name on it, and you have licensed a registered trade mark, you can prevent your competitor [from using the mark].'[51]

Trade marks could be valuable when contracting for use of persona in merchandising, as they might be considered as enhancing the value of the deal. However, the role of trade marks in deterring unauthorised use was thought to be limited by the requirements of registration and grounds for infringement, which were set out in chapter 2.[52] In addressing the limitations of trade marks, a

[46] UK interview 22.
[47] The Advertising Codes do not apply to merchandising.
[48] UK interview 3.
[49] UK interview 9.
[50] UK interview 13.
[51] UK interview 24.
[52] See ch 2, section I.C.

lawyer commented that 'Trade marks are not really suited to protecting personality rights because when people exploit someone's personality they are not doing it to guarantee the origin of goods. They are doing it for other reasons.'[53] It should be noted that section 10(2) of the TMA 1994 provides that infringement can occur if there is a likelihood of confusion, which includes likelihood of association. As such, the reason for using persona is irrelevant, as the assessment to be made is based on confusion on the part of the public. In addressing the confusion requirement, one lawyer stated that 'You can apply for an image as a trade mark but it's associated with a particular product or service. There will only be infringement if it is used on similar goods or services.'[54] This statement does not consider the possibility of infringement under section 10(3) of the TMA 1994, which will be discussed next.

Surprisingly, only one interviewee mentioned the possibility of protecting against misappropriation under section 10(3) of the 1994 Act: 'Trade marks [legislation] has a misappropriation action in it. Where the trade mark has a reputation and the use of the sign, without due cause, takes unfair advantage of the repute of the trade mark [there is infringement].'[55] This section confers protection on marks with a reputation where an identical or similar mark has been used in a way that takes advantage of or damages the reputation or distinctive character of the mark.[56] While section 10(3) avoids the pitfall of the confusion requirement, a lawyer commented that '[t]rade mark law is not suitable for protecting images of people',[57] but no reasons were provided for this suggestion. The effectiveness of trade marks is likely to be limited to names if successfully registered, but would not be suitable for protecting likenesses, as variations of likeness may be used that may not satisfy the similarity requirement. This is because even if a likeness is registered, only identical or similar versions of the likeness would have the potential to infringe. This limits the efficacy of trade marks based on likeness, as 'Often infringement does not involve a trade mark, it's just use of a player's photograph.'[58] Trade marks are beneficial in licensing deals because of their proprietary nature and legal certainty, but they act as a limited deterrent against using persona without permission due to the nature of trade mark law, as discussed in chapter 2.

As for passing off, it acts as the major deterrent to using persona without permission in the piecemeal approach to protection in the UK. However, merchandisers also seek permission because they want high-street stores to stock their products. These stores want assurances that the 'rights have been cleared'.[59]

[53] UK interview 5.
[54] UK interview 17.
[55] UK interview 18.
[56] TMA 1994, s 10(3).
[57] UK interview 18.
[58] UK interview 23.
[59] UK interview 20.

This occurs in the UK even though there is no right of publicity, further demonstrating the power of passing off. The bundle of rights will usually include copyright, trade marks and publicity rights, or 'image rights' as they are termed in the UK. An interviewee in the UK with extensive experience in the merchandising industry gave an example of a photographer who owned the copyright in photographs of a famous model:

> Nobody would buy the material because even if he was in his rights to sell them, anyone of significance would have to fend off legal enquiries from the representatives of the famous model. People do not want the bother, it is too much trouble.[60]

The empirical observations demonstrate that deterrence theory applies in both the US and the UK. In the US, the right of publicity is highly influential in prompting the seeking of permission. In the UK, passing off has strengthened the existing behaviour of seeking permission. Trade marks are considered beneficial in licensing deals, but the presence of a trade mark was not considered to influence merchandisers to seek permission. Rather, they are beneficial to those who would seek permission anyway. Merchandisers in the UK might still seek permission even if not legally required to do so, in order to assuage risk-averse retailers and obtain benefits of collaboration now discussed.

ii. Benefits of Collaboration

The benefits of collaboration encapsulated by contract were observed with equal force in both the US and the UK. In the merchandising industry, collaboration can lead to the creation of better products. This influence holds more weight for modern merchandising than for traditional merchandising, because the latter can simply use a photograph of an individual to achieve the desired effect. It is not difficult to access high-quality photographs, and trade marks need not be used in producing merchandising. Modern merchandising, on the other hand, focuses on a partnership with the individual that involves a wider use of persona for creating and promoting the merchandise.

According to an interviewee, if you enter into a licence to use persona you get 'good quality photography, use of logos and get up for celebrity's names and images, support of the company who owns the intellectual property, potential for an endorsement deal'.[61] Similarly:

> Paying a licence fee gets cooperation and access to materials they [the licensee] might not otherwise have. For example, I did a deal where the family gave access to scrapbooks and memorabilia. [The licensee] found material they did not know existed that they could merchandise. The only way they would get access to this is through a cooperative relationship.[62]

[60] UK interview 16.
[61] UK interview 17.
[62] New York interview 8.

While these benefits are available to both traditional and modern merchandisers, they are vital to modern merchandisers. As one lawyer noted, 'Millennials value authenticity and genuineness and know the difference between someone cashing in and something coming from the right source. The market has become more sophisticated.'[63] The success of collaboration in modern merchandising is evident in the profits generated by fashion lines such as Justin Bieber and Urban Outfitters, and Kanye West and Adidas (prior to the deal's being terminated due to antisemitic statements made by West in 2022). It has also been recognised by the retailing industry:

> Celebrity branded merchandise has also reached new heights, with celebrities such as Rihanna, Justin Bieber, Beyoncé and most notably Kanye West – with their own clothing lines. These celebrities leverage their brand identity with merchandise to create a stronger brand resonance with consumers.[64]

Contract benefits are relevant for all high-street merchandisers, but even more so for high-street modern merchandisers. However, interviewees did not draw a distinction between the importance of collaboration for traditional and for modern merchandise, even though modern merchandise cannot be made without collaboration while traditional merchandise can. As such, the benefits of contracts should be considered as having equal force regardless of the status of the merchandiser, due to interviewee perception. It is the perception, rather than the reality, that influences behaviour.

iii. Social Norms – Signalling

Social norms were also observed in the behaviour of high-street merchandisers seeking permission to use persona. One interviewee speculated that *Fenty*[65] did not change the way entities behave, as permission was generally sought before this case: 'The bigger, better, blue chip brands try to do things the right way. People using image rights in an unauthorised manner tend to be cowboys.'[66] The description of the brands as 'blue chip' and 'cowboy' suggests the presence of signalling theory. This interviewee approves of the brands that seek permission and disapproves of those that do not, which indicates that seeking permission sends a positive signal. The impact of this signal was also evident in a discussion with an interviewee who suggested that the limits of the law are not the only determining factor in the merchandising industry. The interviewee stated:

> Most major retailers are now quite switched on to licensing and the benefits of it. That will not stop them from buying legal products that are not licensed, but they tend to

[63] California interview 14.
[64] Alvarado, J, 'Top five retail trends in celebrity merchandise: Kanye West Case Study' *Linkedin* (12 December 2016) at www.linkedin.com/pulse/5-brand-merchandising-tips-from-marketing-genius-himself-alvarado/ (accessed 30 January 2023).
[65] *Fenty* [2013].
[66] UK interview 24.

> opt for licensed products and have relationship with the major licensing company. Merchandisers might find it difficult to distribute products that are technically legal but not licensed.[67]

The presence of a relationship between retailers and licensors suggests that sending the right signal by securing a licence is important for future cooperation. Failure to secure a licence could limit the channels of distribution for the unauthorised merchandise. This cooperation was further explained by an interviewee who noted that securing a licence provides informational benefits:

> If you buy the licence, you get information on the other companies which have licences for different products, and this information allows you to approach companies for joint marketing initiatives. You are in the club rather than out of the club.[68]

The use of the term 'club' again indicates social norms reasoning, as it suggests an issue of inclusion or exclusion based on the course of action taken. It should be noted that this reasoning is reflective of social norms rather than contract, as the benefits are not linked to the individual but rather to other parties that have also secured a licence to use the individual's persona. The community here indicated by the word 'club' would be the entities that have already secured licences to use the persona. This explains why alternative merchandisers do not seek permission, as discussed in section III – they do not desire to be a part of this community, and thus are not impacted by the influences discussed in chapter 3.

The evidence analysed in this subsection is derived from UK interviews. This does not mean that social norms do not operate in the US, but rather that US interviews did not lend themselves to a social norms analysis. No questions were directly targeted at social norms in either jurisdiction, but the information provided by UK interviewees suggests the presence of the signalling theory of social norms.

iv. Deviation

The deviant behaviour of high-street merchandisers not seeking permission likely occurs in all jurisdictions, the most obvious example in the UK being Topshop in *Fenty*.[69] While there was a lack of clarity as to how passing off would apply to merchandise prior to *Fenty*, the perception that passing off could accommodate a claim against unauthorised merchandise was a deterrent. This deterrent was further entrenched after *Fenty* confirmed the application of passing off. Topshop was not interested in the benefits that could be secured by a licensing deal and did not think of the need to get any assurances beyond the copyright in the photograph, since the company was creating the product itself for sale in its stores. It did not fear litigation apparently, most likely because the firm did not think that

[67] UK interview 16.
[68] UK interview 17.
[69] *Fenty* [2013].

passing off was applicable. Since the facts of that case were unique, it is possible that high-street brands in the UK may continue to create merchandise without seeking the permission of the celebrity but, as noted, the number of brands that might do this should have declined because of the impact of *Fenty*. It is unusual for high-street brands to create merchandise without permission from the celebrity in the US, but it does occur. An interviewee stated 'We're about to go after a huge company right now. We've had demand letters against bigger companies.'[70]

III. Alternative Merchandisers Do Not Seek Permission to Use Persona in Traditional Merchandising

The behaviour discussed in section II distinguished between high-street and alternative merchandisers. This distinction correlates with the second behaviour observed in the merchandising industry in both the US and the UK: alternative merchandisers do not seek permission to use persona in traditional merchandising. In the US, such permission is required under the right of publicity, and would likely also be needed to avoid a false endorsement claim under the Lanham Act. By way of contrast, such permission is not necessarily required under UK law where a trade mark or similar sign is not being used. Additionally, passing off has limited application as it requires a finding of misrepresentation, which may be more difficult in the case of alternative merchandisers due to the channels of distribution used, as will be explained further in what follows. Despite the different legal frameworks, the same non-permission-based behaviour exists in both jurisdictions.

It is interesting to contrast the experiences of interviewees with respect to the high-street and alternative merchandisers. While lawyers felt that high-street merchandisers are more likely to seek permission than in the past, they also felt that there is more infringement by alternative merchandisers. As noted by one lawyer:

> Pre-internet and post-internet is the difference. It's rampant now [using persona without permission]. It happens all over the place. The ease of producing and difficulty of detecting a lot of these things makes the issue proliferate.[71]

Another responded, 'In the last five years, there is more unauthorised use than before.' Similarly, 'In music, it's much easier to sell a counterfeit t-shirt than it used to be and now they can compete on quality. You can get an almost perfect digital image off the internet. You can enhance it.'[72]

[70] California interview 6.
[71] California interview 23.
[72] UK interview 8.

When questioned whether persona is used without permission more frequently in the UK than in the US, an interviewee responded:

> There is not more infringement in the UK, there is tonnes all over. We see a lot in the US. Print presses and digital images are cheap. People are trying a thing. Inventory risk used to be an issue but now everything is print to order. It's low risk to infringe nowadays.[73]

Another noted:

> It happens all the time [using persona without permission]. This morning I woke up to an email saying that unauthorised merchandise was being sold on Amazon. My clients don't want to be associated with substandard product. You'll get unauthorised images [on merchandise] of clients sold on eBay.[74]

As such, the differing legal framework does not appear to have impacted on the operation of this behaviour in either jurisdiction.

A. Alternative Merchandisers Never Seek Permission

Alternative merchandisers do not seek permission to use persona for several reasons. First, some are ignorant of the law: 'People who are doing it do not have access to IP legal counsel.'[75] Second, some are aware of the law but think they will not be detected: 'Because there is so much stuff being pedalled on the internet, there are a lot of companies that put stuff up for sale and think no one will find out.'[76] Third, some merchandisers are indifferent to legal consequences. The ability to create small batches of products means that inventory is not wasted if they must stop production. Furthermore, they can reappear online under a different shop name. The last two reasons indicate that a cost–benefit analysis is undertaken and a decision made to actively disregard the law.

When asked what steps are taken when persona is used without authorisation, the responses varied. In the US, some lawyers said it is not worth pursuing these alternative merchandisers, whereas others said cease-and-desist letters are usually sent. It is rare for litigation to result. A US lawyer noted:

> We've gone to the eve of trial twice and in those cases, it was expensive, protracted litigation over the course of years. Ninety per cent of the time a single email or cease and desist letter will stop it. In the remaining nine per cent a second letter. One per cent of the time you really have to push.[77]

[73] California interview 14.
[74] New York interview 19.
[75] California interview 1.
[76] California interview 23.
[77] California interview 14.

Similarly:

> These things do not normally go to court. As lawyers, we are looking for people to stop it. The smaller ones forever have unauthorised goods. There is a market for these things and whenever we are made aware of a problem, we do what we can to stop it.[78]

Some felt that it was not possible to prevent alternative merchandisers from producing unauthorised products, and would not rely on law because it would not be financially advantageous to do so: 'It is always about suing people with money. It has to be worth it. Suing Topshop was worth it [for Rihanna]. Suing a street trader is not worth it. You cannot stop it [unauthorised merchandise].'[79] Similarly:

> One of the areas that happens a lot is small batch t-shirt creators, street wear companies, various things. They're all really creative, interesting designs that incorporate people's likenesses. Images put on a t-shirt seems to fall clearly into merchandise so all these are actionable. People don't go after them [pursue them legally] because they are relatively small batch.[80]

The impact of the law has not had the effect of eradicating this behaviour of alternative merchandisers using persona without permission. This behaviour was observed in both the UK and US, despite the difference in legal frameworks.

In the US, a cease-and-desist letter may have the desired effect, although this does not prevent unauthorised use from reoccurring. In the UK, on the other hand, there is little avenue for redress. As noted by a California lawyer, 'As soon as I see a link to the website with £'s, it's not worth pursuing. There is no protection to begin with. [And it's] not worth trying to create a law for things that are worth low value.'[81] Passing off is likely to be less enforceable against alternative merchandisers because of the channels of distribution of the products. Alternative merchandisers are probably not seeking high-street stores as their distributors, as interviewees suggested that this merchandise is usually sold online or on market stalls. In other words, the places where this merchandise is sold may make it less susceptible to a claim of passing off in the UK.[82] Thus, Justice Birss placed emphasis on the status of the seller: 'Topshop is not a market stall. It is a leading high street fashion retailer and purchasers would not be surprised to find goods on sale in Topshop which have been endorsed or approved by the celebrity.'[83]

It has yet to be seen whether post-sale confusion, as discussed in the trademark context in *Arsenal Football Club Plc v Matthew Reed*, will apply in the

[78] New York interview 19.
[79] UK interview 15.
[80] California interview 1.
[81] California interview 8.
[82] Although see *Arsenal Football Club Plc v Matthew Reed* [2003] EWCA Civ 96, where trade-mark infringement was found based on the sale of unlicensed merchandise outside Arsenal stadium.
[83] *Fenty* [2013] [55].

merchandising context of persona-based passing-off claims.[84] In terms of the approach to trade marks, an action of trade-mark infringement can only be brought if a sign identical or similar to a registered trade mark is used on the merchandise. Even then, the use must satisfy the criteria for infringement set out in the TMA 1994. In contrast to the UK legal framework's limitations with regard to pursuing alternative merchandisers, the strict-liability right of publicity in the US would apply to alternative merchandisers, yet they are not dissuaded by the legal framework.

IV. Conclusion

This chapter has identified two behaviours concerning the use of persona in the merchandising industry. The behaviours were explained by reference to the status of the merchandiser as well as the type of merchandise. High-street merchandisers seek permission to use persona for both modern and traditional merchandise, whereas alternative merchandisers do not seek permission to use persona on traditional merchandise. High-street merchandisers are those that sell in high-street stores and tend to have access to legal advice. Alternative merchandisers are more likely to sell via online marketplaces and street stalls. While both merchandisers make traditional merchandise, only high-street merchandisers make modern merchandise.

The deterrence theory of law and the desire to collaborate influence the permission-based behaviours. The benefits of collaboration as espoused by contract operate with equal strength in both jurisdictions. The deterrence of law is influential in the US, where the right of publicity is subject to strict liability. Deterrence theory also operates in the UK, due to the perceived impact of passing off as well as the need to secure assurances for high-street retailers. While passing off is limited in scope, *Fenty*[85] has impacted this industry by making risk-averse merchandisers more cautious when using persona. Trade marks, while a valuable asset to licence for the creation of merchandise, have more of more limited impact due to the requirements of registration and the circumstances in which infringement can be found. Social norms also operate in the UK, as merchandisers want to send the right signal in order to ensure future cooperation. This social norm has been directly impacted by the perception of what is required by law, even though it is arguable that traditional merchandise would not fall foul of passing off.

The non-permission-based behaviour of alternative merchandisers creating traditional merchandising without permission also exists in both jurisdictions,

[84] *Arsenal Football Club plc v Matthew Reed* [2003].
[85] *Fenty* [2013].

despite the legal framework. Alternative merchandisers use persona without permission because they disregard or ignore the law. In the UK, not much can be done to address this, whereas in the US, the right of publicity can be used. However, it is not considered a useful tool to deploy against alternative merchandisers as it is not financially viable. This is an instance where there is a notable divergence between the relevant legal frameworks. Yet the same behaviour occurs in the US as in the UK, because alternative merchandisers disregard or are ignorant of the law in the US, while the law is of limited applicability in the UK.

7

Film and Television Industry

Introduction

The film and television production industry (in this chapter referred to as 'the film industry') uses persona by portraying the life of an individual. Unlike the advertising and merchandising industries, which use aspects of persona on goods or for the sale of products or services, film and television production focuses on conveying information about an individual. While the aspects of persona such as name, voice and likeness may be used in the portrayal, the experiences of the individual and her role in society are central to using persona in the film industry.

The nature of use of persona in the film industry distinguishes this industry from the advertising and merchandising industries. While the right of publicity can address uses of persona in advertising and merchandising, the boundaries of the right of publicity do not extend a person's 'life story'. The term 'life story' is used to mean biographical information pertaining to an individual. For the most part, in the US, claims based on the right of publicity against use of 'life story' have been dismissed, as films and television programmes are First Amendment-protected expressive works, as affirmed in *De Havilland v FX Networks*.[1] However, decisions in New York have indicated that a claim might succeed under the State's privacy statute if there were 'knowing fictionalisation'.[2] It is important to clarify that while sections 50 and 51 of the New York Civil Rights Law provide publicity protection, these provisions are couched in terms of privacy, which can indeed be deployed against the use of information pertaining to an individual. Similarly, copyright,[3]

[1] *De Havilland v FX Networks LLC* 21 Cal App 5th 845 (2018): 'Authors write books. Filmmakers make films. Playwrights craft plays … The First Amendment protects these expressive works and the free speech rights of their creators. Some of these works are fiction. Some are factual. And some are a combination of fact and fiction. That these creative works generate income for their creators does not diminish their constitutional protection. The First Amendment does not require authors, filmmakers, playwrights, and television producers to provide their creations to the public at no charge.'

[2] *Binns v Vitagraph Co of Am* 103 NE 1108 (NY 1913); *Redmond v Columbia Pictures* 14 NE 2d 636 (NY 1938); *Spahn v Julian Messner* 21 NY 2d 124 (1967) [127]–[129]; Lentzner, M, 'My Life, My Story, Right – Fashioning Life Story Rights in the Motion Picture Industry' (1989) 12 *Hastings Comm & Ent LJ* 627, 630.

[3] Vandegrift, T, 'Why the New David Bowie Biopic "Stardust" Won't Feature His Music' *Showbiz CheatSheet* (29 August 2019) at www.cheatsheet.com/entertainment/why-the-new-david-bowie-biopic-stardust-wont-feature-his-music.html/ (accessed 6 February 2020).

misuse of confidential information,[4] defamation[5] and false-light privacy[6] may restrict access and use of information about a person. False-light privacy is similar to defamation, but the statement need not be defamatory.[7] Rather, the statement must be false and highly offensive.[8]

While the right of publicity is an unsuitable tool for regulating life story, fieldwork demonstrates that it has impacted upon the behaviours identified in the film industry. This is due to the risk of litigation in the US, where claims have been brought under the right of publicity.[9] However, the right of publicity is just one cause of action out of the several identified above that may be brought against a film or television producer. As such, while the right of publicity influences the behaviours examined in this chapter to an extent, it is difficult to isolate this influence from other potential causes of action. Since this book focuses on the right of publicity, analysis in this chapter examines the influence of that right, while acknowledging other potential causes of action. Notably, copyright can play a major role in securing permission from the individual or estate featured, if a biopic is about a musician or a band. This will be considered further in section II.A.ii.

The findings in this chapter are based on interviews with lawyers who had experience with major film and television producers. These producers tend to have large budgets and create works for global distribution. It is important to emphasise that the behaviours identified in this chapter regulate these large-scale producers, who can afford legal advice from expensive international law firms. Lawyers were unable to provide information on smaller-scale producers, such as YouTube content producers or film festival producers. As such, the behaviours identified in this chapter may not be reflective of producers with more limited resources.

Nineteen lawyers who had experience of the film production industry were interviewed. The most relevant were interviewees who were based in California.

[4] Walsh, C, 'Are personality rights finally on the UK agenda?' (2013) 35 *EIPR* 253, 257–59.

[5] Albrecht, S et al, 'Recent Developments in Media, Privacy, and Defamation Law' (2011) 47 *Tort Trial & Ins Prac LJ* 359, 361–63.

[6] Restatement (Second) of Torts § 652E; Albrecht et al (2011) 365–67.

[7] Zimmerman, D, 'False Light Invasion of Privacy: The Light that Failed' (1989) 64 *NYU L Rev* 364, fn 19: 'Invasion of privacy by placing an individual in false light occurs when something materially false about the plaintiff – whether or not defamatory – is given broad publicity.' For more on the distinction between defamation and false-light privacy, see Digital Media Law Project, 'False Light' (10 September 2022) at www.dmlp.org/legal-guide/false-light (accessed 8 October 2018).

[8] False-light privacy is not discussed in ch 2 as right of publicity is the focus of the book. Restatement (Second) of Torts, § 652E Publicity Placing Person in False Light, states 'One who gives publicity to a matter concerning another that places the other before the public in a false light is subject to liability to the other for invasion of his privacy, if (a) the false light in which the other was placed would be highly offensive to a reasonable person, and (b) the actor had knowledge of or acted in reckless disregard as to the falsity of the publicized matter and the false light in which the other would be placed.'

[9] *De Havilland v FX* (2018); *Porco v Lifetime Entertainment Services* (2017) NY Slip Op 01421; *Sarver v Chartier* 813 F 3d 891 (9th Cir 2016).

Those 9 interviewees worked either for studios or for individuals whose lives had been portrayed on screen. In New York and the UK, three and seven interviewees had experience in the film industry respectively, but they were less informed about the functioning of this industry as it was not their area of expertise. The California lawyers were the most knowledgeable, while the New York lawyers had limited experience. The UK lawyers were able to shed light on the situation in this jurisdiction, but to a lesser extent than the California lawyers in that State. Nonetheless, they provided valuable information on the behaviours that regulate persona in this industry.

This chapter is divided into four sections. Section I explains how persona is used in the film industry. Section II examines the behaviour of seeking permission to portray an individual in a film or television programme where it is likely to be given. Section III examines the behaviour of not seeking permission where it is unlikely to be given. Section IV discusses life-story rights as an extra-legal norm.

I. Use of Persona in the Film and Television Industry

Films and television programmes often use persona as part of their story line. When the life of an individual is the central theme, these programmes are dubbed 'biopics'. According to Custen,

> a biographical film is one that depicts the life of a historical person, past or present … Historical films, or rather re-creation of real events from the past, almost certainly were among the earliest genres of the cinema.[10]

Examples of historical films indicated by Custen include *The Execution of Mary Queen of Scots*, a film produced in 1895, and *Queen Elizabeth* produced in 1912.[11] Biopics have continued to be a popular genre, despite the initial rejection of this term by filmmakers.[12]

Films such as *The Social Network*, based on Mark Zuckerberg's creation of Facebook, *Mandela: Long Walk to Freedom*, recounting Nelson Mandela's role in ending apartheid in South Africa, and *American Crime Story: The People vs OJ Simpson* have told the stories of well-known individuals. Television programmes such as, *Unsolved*, which investigates the murders of rappers Tupac Shakur and Biggie Smalls, and *Narcos*, which tracks the rise of notorious drug dealer Pablo Escobar, have attracted many viewers who want a window into the lives and deaths of these famous individuals.

[10] Custen, GF, *Bio/Pics: How Hollywood Constructed Public History* (Rutgers University Press 1992) 5.
[11] ibid.
[12] This term was thought to be a pejorative since it is difficult to capture the complexity of an individual's life in one film. 'Biopic' has since gained acceptance. Bingham, D, *Whose Lives Are They Anyway?* (Rutgers University Press 2010) 11–14.

A category of biopics that has gained popularity in recent years includes those that explore the life of musicians and bands. Examples include *Bohemian Rhapsody*, depicting the band Queen, and the Elton John-inspired *Rocketman*. While persona is depicted, the producers of these films also ideally need to get permission to use original music to enhance the depiction. As a result, copyright is an avenue of control that may encourage permission to be sought. If the relevant copyright licence is not secured, the film will not be able to use the music in question, as this would inevitably result in a breach of copyright claim.[13] While the necessity for copyright permission is clear, the role of the right of publicity should be more limited. However, the way in which biopics are created has resulted in right of publicity claims.

Biopics generally focus on a key event in someone's life, rather than providing an accurate timeline of the individual's lifespan. They are often characterised by melodrama,[14] as the process of fictionalisation distorts the facts of an individual's life to make the film or television programme more interesting to viewers. This inaccuracy is not unique to biopics, as Custen notes that even written history is 'a text that freezes the narrative in a particular, invested form'.[15] However, the potential for inaccuracy in film production has contributed to the behaviours observed in this chapter, as individuals object to how they are portrayed through the court system in the US, even though the right of publicity is an unsuitable vehicle for addressing inaccurate representations.

Where permission has not been sought to tell an individual's life story, the portrayal may be contested under the right of publicity. This is despite the fact that permission is not required to create a film in any jurisdiction examined. In the US, films are protected under the First Amendment as an expressive work. There have been cases against films that are based on the life of an individual, but these cases usually fail as studios are able to avail themselves of the First Amendment defence or an anti-strategic lawsuit against public participation motion (anti-SLAPP).[16] An anti-SLAPP motion is used to strike out a cause of action that attempts to chill freedom of speech. The failure of right of publicity claims against film producers has not stopped more claims from arising.[17]

In the UK, there have not been any cases against film and television producers, potentially because there is no equivalent right of publicity. Defamation and misuse of confidential information would be more relevant, although they would apply in limited circumstances. Alternatively, the absence of cases in the UK could be due to the fact that films are often distributed worldwide. A claimant

[13] Desta, Y, 'New David Bowie Biopic Probably Won't Have Any David Bowie Music' *Vanity Fair* (1 February 2019) at www.vanityfair.com/hollywood/2019/02/david-bowie-biopic-duncan-jones-music-rights (accessed 6 February 2020).

[14] Baker, A, 'Sports Films, History, and Identity' (1998) 25(2) *Journal of Sport History* 217, 218.

[15] Custen (1992) 9.

[16] Example: First Amendment: *Dora v Frontline Video Inc* 15 Cal App 4th 536 (1993); Anti-SLAPP: *Sarver v Hurt Locker LLC* 813 F 3d 891 (2017).

[17] California Code of Civil Procedure § 425.16.

would probably prefer to sue in a jurisdiction that is more hospitable towards celebrity claimants,[18] such as California. The litigation attempts surrounding films in the US have inevitably impacted UK studios because of the global nature of distribution. This has led to two behaviours regarding the use of persona in the film industry, which will now be discussed in turn. The first behaviour is that permission is sought to portray persona where it is likely to be given, and the second behaviour is that permission is not sought to portray persona where it is unlikely to be given.

II. Permission is Sought to Portray Persona Where it is Likely to be Given

The first behaviour observed in the film industry is that permission is sought to portray persona where it is likely to be given. According to a California lawyer who represents a production studio, 'We regularly deal with right of publicity at the onset of projects; docu-series, docu-dramas, about real-life individuals. They want a life rights agreement.'[19] Another who represents famous individuals noted 'Generally they [studios] lock up the life rights to be safe.'[20] 'Life story' or 'life rights' are the terms used to refer to contracts that consent to the portrayal of an individual in a film or television programme. As noted by a lawyer, 'The basic form of the agreement is almost always characterised as life story … it includes a specific grant of rights relating to privacy and publicity. The individual waives claims that any production violates their rights.'[21] Life-rights agreements are common in the film industry: 'It's a standard operating procedure in the entertainment industry to get publicity rights and pay for them even though you don't need them.'[22] Another noted 'We're pretty good at securing the necessary rights. We don't get sued for right of publicity very often.'[23]

While the above responses were from US lawyers, a similar view prevailed in the UK. However, UK lawyers did not generally use the 'life rights' terminology. The one UK lawyer who used this term referred to it as the 'US concept of life rights',[24] which could indicate that the US law has had an impact on UK behaviours. When asked whether permission would be sought for portraying the life of an individual in a film, one UK lawyer responded 'In practice,

[18] Welkowitz, D and Ochoa, T, 'The Terminator as Eraser: How Arnold Schwarzenegger Used the Right of Publicity to Terminate Non-Defamatory Political Speech' (2005) 45 *Santa Clara L Rev* 651, 659–60.

[19] California interview 2.

[20] California interview 12.

[21] California interview 19.

[22] California interview 21.

[23] California interview 25.

[24] UK interview 13.

we would get permission, even if not actually required.'[25] Another advised 'Yes, should seek permission to avoid a threat of legal action [for portraying life story].'[26] Similarly, 'You should get permission from the person. You err on the side of caution.'[27] While UK lawyers felt that permission is not required by law, deterrence theory was observed, as the potential litigation risk resulted in a consensus that permission is sought where it is likely to be given. In referring to the film *Bend it like Beckham*, a lawyer speculated that 'In practice, they probably got his permission, even if it was not actually required.' David Beckham's life was not central to the plot of the film, but a secondary source confirmed that permission was sought:

> Beckham gave permission for his name to be used in the title, and once Chadha had finished the film, she … showed it to him at a private screening to which he brought along some Manchester United team-mates.[28]

The responses of the lawyers in both jurisdictions indicate that 'life rights' entail both grants and waivers. Grants provide permission to use persona, whereas waivers are used to avoid potential claims. It is important to note that these grants and waivers were engaged in the permission-based behaviour. Lawyers indicated that flattering portrayals were more likely to result in the giving of permission, whereas portrayals of notorious individuals such as criminals would not lend themselves to obtaining permission.[29]

A. Why Seek Permission?

i. The Influence of Law – Avoid the Risk of Litigation

a. United States

The deterrence theory prompts film and television producers to seek permission to use persona to avoid the risk of litigation. Lawyers in the US noted that if permission is not sought, there is a risk that the individual portrayed will sue for infringement of the right of publicity, or rely on another cause of action such as defamation or false-light privacy. A studio lawyer noted 'We regularly respond to claims threatened by people who say their right has been violated in films and TV shows.'[30] Similarly, another lawyer noted 'We've been involved in cases … where

[25] UK interview 5.
[26] UK interview 10.
[27] UK interview 12.
[28] Gritten, D, 'A whole new ball game' *The Telegraph* (2 April 2002) at www.telegraph.co.uk/culture/film/3575466/A-whole-new-ball-game.html accessed 8 October 2018.
[29] California interviews 2, 3, 9, 17, 25.
[30] California interview 2.

studios have depicted real people and those real people don't like the way they are portrayed.'[31] Additionally:

> Maybe the person has a privacy claim based on false light [if you] made outrageous and false accusations about a person's behaviour. You presented something as true to the public but you created something that is fictional and highly damaging.[32]

In considering potential causes of action against a film or television producer, one lawyer opined, 'the right of privacy, defamation … can have a huge impact'.[33] This is particularly so when fictionalisation occurs: 'The further away you get from the facts, [the more] you open yourself up to a potential defamation or false light claim.'[34]

While several causes of action pose a risk, such as copyright (discussed in chapter 2), and can thus influence behaviour, lawyers were questioned on their experience with right of publicity litigation against films and television programmes. They recognised that the right of publicity is an inappropriate avenue for protecting against the portrayal of an individual in a film: 'A work of fiction based on real people is protectable and the real people don't have a right to object to it.'[35] Similarly, 'If you're doing a film about a person, the film is usually protected. People still get permission but you really don't need to when you're making a First Amendment creative work.'[36] Despite the inapplicability of the right of publicity, claims are still brought in the US. As observed by a lawyer:

> There has been a spate of cases recently against films where people are being portrayed based on real stories. Hurt Locker, War Dogs … there was a claim made by the manager of the rap group in Straight Outta Compton. You hear about those claims because they get a lot of press when it involves the film industry. Those are usually claims based on the right of publicity which have failed miserably.[37]

Lawyers were questioned on why people continue to bring claims of infringement of the right of publicity despite the fact that these cases usually fail. It could be suggested that the right of publicity is more favourable to celebrity claimants than defamation in the US, the latter carrying an 'actual malice' standard for public figures.[38] As noted by Welkowitz and Ochoa:

> [P]ublic figures often turn to rights of publicity to avoid the New York Times standard.[39] Although such suits are not always successful, courts are often more sympathetic to right of publicity claims than to defamation claims.[40]

[31] California interview 3.
[32] California interview 9.
[33] California interview 19.
[34] California interview 25.
[35] California interview 9.
[36] California interview 25.
[37] New York interview 2.
[38] Welkowitz and Ochoa (2005).
[39] ibid. The standard of actual malice was introduced in the case of *New York Times Co v Sullivan* 376 US 254 (1964).
[40] Welkowitz and Ochoa (2005) 653.

It is this knowledge that courts are more receptive to the right of publicity that emboldens potential claimants. According to a lawyer, 'People still bring these cases because they often will get a settlement. People are trying to squeeze some money out of the production company.'[41] This is despite the fact that anti-SLAPP is a useful tool for studios against claims brought in California.[42] Sometimes studios prefer to resolve the issue with a settlement than go through filing the motion. A lawyer noted 'The only good thing is, in almost all cases against motion pictures the court ends up finding in favour of the motion picture producer, but it's still annoying and expensive.'[43]

The aforementioned lawyer gave an example of a case concerning a film based on the life of a deceased individual. The individual's daughter sued for an infringement of her father's right of publicity because the studio did not secure permission to use his persona and/or a waiver against liability. This lawsuit caused unnecessary burden:

> We won at the district court level in [names State] and state court, and now we're at the Court of Appeal after spending $200,000. It's a big pain. It's been going on for eighteen months. They tried an injunction against the film which was unsuccessful but it's still stressful and expensive to respond to.[44]

The right of publicity thus has the potential to be used as a money-gouging tool by claimants. This further explains why US lawyers advise seeking permission to use persona. Even though the right of publicity should not be applicable, litigation based on this right can incur unnecessary expense that studios wish to avoid. The materialisation of this risk in recent cases[45] has contributed to the force with which deterrence theory prompts compliance with this permission-based behaviour. However, it is important to reiterate that there are other causes of action against which television and film producers may want to guard. The importance of seeking permission to obtain insurance will be discussed in section II.A.ii, after examining the influence of deterrence theory in the UK.

b. United Kingdom

Deterrence theory can also be observed in the UK due to perceived litigation risk but, unlike in the US, the risk has not materialised in the form of actual litigation. Lawyers in the UK felt that permission should be sought to use persona where

[41] California interview 2.
[42] California interview 25.
[43] California interview 2.
[44] California interview 2. Fee-shifting (or cost-shifting in the UK) is a procedure where the party that loses the case must pay for the legal fees of the successful party. Fee-shifting is not normal procedure in the US. The California Civil Code, s 3344 allows for fee-shifting, but this claim was brought in a different State.
[45] *De Havilland v FX* (2018); *Porco v Lifetime Entertainment Services* 150 NYS 3d 380 (2021); *Sarver v Chartier* 813 F 3d 891 (9th Cir 2016) [905].

it is likely to be given to avoid litigation risk, but recognised the limitations of the existing legal framework in controlling a portrayal of an individual in a film or television programme. Some felt that permission should be sought to prevent claims of defamation:

> Seek permission because it [the portrayal] is so personal. [You] can imagine what people might have said to the producer that may or may not be true. From the producer's point of view, you can face all sorts of action such as defamation.[46]

Others thought passing off could pose a risk, but noted that film producers cannot necessarily be prevented from making films based on someone's life:

> Yes, [you should] get permission from person. Why? Could they actually stop you? There is always the risk if you make a film [there] might be a risk of false endorsement.[47]

Another UK lawyer noted the limitations of the existing framework: 'Are there going to be potential claims of misrepresentation and defamation? If you want to make a story and it is true, I'm not sure anyone can stop it.'[48] This response highlights the limitations of the existing legal framework. While there is potential for litigation, satisfying the misrepresentation element in passing off could prove difficult, and passing off has not yet been tested against a film or television programme. A portrayal of which the individual does not approve may not satisfy the 'serious harm' criteria for defamation.[49] Furthermore, the defences of truth,[50] honest opinion[51] and/or publication on a matter of public interest[52] may shield the film or television programme. Nonetheless, the responses examined thus far reveal that defamation may influence permission to be sought to portray persona.

While defamation poses a risk, there is no cause of action that controls 'life story'. This was referred to by two UK lawyers: '[There is] no need to seek permission to make a film on someone's life.'[53] Another said 'I think they should [seek permission] but I don't think they have to.'[54] A few UK lawyers noted the threat of litigation posed by US law: 'Yes, should seek permission. [There is a] threat of legal action because [the] film will be visible not just in the UK but everywhere.'[55] Similarly, 'US law might come in [for consideration] for distribution.'[56] The impact of the US law is particularly relevant to the film industry since films may be distributed in the US.

[46] UK interview 9.
[47] UK interview 12.
[48] UK interview 24.
[49] Defamation Act 2013, s 1.
[50] Defamation Act 2013, s 2.
[51] Defamation Act 2013, s.3.
[52] Defamation Act 2013, s.4.
[53] UK interview 11.
[54] UK interview 23.
[55] UK interview 10.
[56] UK interview 13.

In contrast to California interviewees, no UK interviewee was able to provide an example of being sued for failing to secure a life-rights agreement. Nor could they provide any evidence that complaints had been made.[57] As such, litigation risk is merely a risk in the UK, whereas the risk has resulted in claims in the US. Thus, deterrence theory arguably applies with greater force in the US than the UK with regard to litigation risk. However, the next subsection will explain that insurance requirements bolster deterrence theory in both jurisdictions.

ii. *Insurance Industry Requirements*

Since litigation risks are present in both jurisdictions, it is important to obtain errors and omissions insurance to defend against potential legal claims.[58] According to the California lawyers interviewed, insurance companies may require a waiver from the individual portrayed as a condition of obtaining insurance: 'Insurance company will send [the] licensee a questionnaire which will cover copyright uses, publicity issues … [It asks] what have you done to address them?' Securing a 'life rights' deal addresses the risk posed by the right of publicity and other potential claims. However, life-right deals are not a legal requirement: 'As long as you don't defame [the individual], you can make a film without having a life rights deal.'[59]

Despite the lack of legal underpinning, life-rights deals have become an established practice in California and are requested by insurance companies. Failure to acquire life rights will result in higher premiums to obtain errors and omissions insurance: 'If a studio is unable to get the rights, they are more cautious when proceeding. Insurance companies will charge higher deductibles to their clients to make these projects without consent.'[60] As a result, producers pay for rights that are not legally required to obtain a favourable insurance rate.

One studio lawyer in California lamented the popularity of life-rights deals:

> They are a legal fiction. No one owns the rights to the facts about his or her life, so I try to encourage clients not to call them life rights agreements and instead call them consulting agreements in which you get a basket of rights.[61]

Similarly, another lawyer noted:

> People get rights all the time when they don't need to. It's a standard operating procedure to pay for publicity rights even though you don't need them. But who wants to

[57] This could be due to the fact that lawyers in the UK had less experience with film and television production. Even in New York, lawyers interviewed did not specialise in film and television production, whereas some of the lawyers interviewed in California dealt exclusively in this area.

[58] New York interview 8; Tarantino, B, 'You're getting sued for what? An E&O Odyssey (Pt 13)' *Entertainment & Media Law Signal* (29 July 2014) at www.entertainmentmedialawsignal.com/category/errors-and-omissions-insurance (accessed 12 April 2018).

[59] California interview 2.

[60] California interview 2.

[61] California interview 2.

> go through the litigation? We're always asked, 'Do I need these rights?'. We say no, but they get them anyway. There's a First Amendment defence but no one wants to test out litigation.[62]

A third interviewee noted:

> The business people always say we need the life story rights. But there's no such thing as life story rights. It's a term that has been created and they think it has legal significance, but it really doesn't.[63]

While studio lawyers objected to the concept of life-rights deals, despite recognising their commonality, lawyers who represent famous individuals did not share the same frustrations. The experiences of these lawyers further establish the prevalence of this behaviour. One lawyer noted that he 'just did the life rights deal with Universal Studios for a famous athlete'.[64] Similarly, a lawyer who represents celebrities stated 'In the film industry we do deals for life rights. Hollywood wants to make a film about [client's] life. They [the studio] come and say they want to option life rights.'[65]

The extent of permeation of life-rights agreements in the UK is unclear, and it is possible that this behaviour has more footing in the US. One UK lawyer noted 'I've done a few life rights deals. You are trying to put in a contractual framework by using image rights agreements and licensors.'[66] A limitation of the fieldwork is that it prevents a balanced comparison, as more studio lawyers were interviewed in the US. This was not intentional; rather, California remains the hub of the television and film production industry.[67] Once a film is distributed in the US the litigation risk exists, so the US law has significant potential impact on UK behaviour.

Errors and omission insurance coverage was examined in both the US and the UK to determine whether there were any differences in policies that could indicate the influence of the right of publicity in the development of this behaviour with regard to insurance requirements. La Playa Media & Digital offers coverage of 'infringement of intellectual property rights' in both the US and UK, but does not specify the right of publicity in either jurisdiction.[68] Film Emporium, licensed to sell insurance in New York and California, covers 'improper use of celebrity's name or likeness',[69] but does not explicitly mention the right of publicity.

[62] California interview 21.
[63] California interview 25.
[64] California interview 10.
[65] California interview 23.
[66] UK interview 13.
[67] Contreras, J and Fagundes, D, 'Solving the Life Story Puzzle: Docudramas, Modularity and Hollywood Private Order' (2023) 14(2) *Harvard Sports & Entertainment LJ* (forthcoming).
[68] La Playa, 'Film Errors and Omission Insurance' *La Playa Insurance* at www.laplayapartners.com/media-digital-2/film-errors-and-omissions/ (accessed 1 October 2018).
[69] Film Emporium, 'Errors & Omissions (E&O) Insurance' *Film Emporium* at http://filmemporium.com/errors--omissions/ (accessed 1 October 2018).

IMS Film and Media Insurance, based in the UK, protects against 'violations of the privilege as to one's own image', but also does not mention the right of publicity.[70] The British Film Commission advises that 'All film productions in the UK must be insured.'[71] They advise that errors and omissions insurance should cover 'libel, slander, breach of copyright, invasion of privacy, unauthorised use of trade marks and slogans'.[72] The breadth of the insurance policy thus extends to other potential causes of action that might be used against a film or television producer.

Front Row insurance, in a blog post entitled 'The Delicate Art of Making a Bio Pic w/o Getting Permission', notes that the right of publicity cannot be used to protect one's life story. However, the blog post goes on to state that a consequence of not seeking permission to depict the individual is a

> much higher deductible for cases where the individual or estate of the individual decides to start a lawsuit. In some cases your deductible could jump from around $10,000 to as high as $250,000 for that one item … So in order to protect yourself and your project when making a docudrama about a celebrity, getting his or her permission may still be the best choice …[73]

By the 1980s, the practice of acquiring life-story rights became entrenched and required by insurance studios.[74] Considering that films are generally shielded from the right of publicity by the First Amendment, and there is no right of publicity in the UK, the impact of the law should be limited. However, errors and omissions insurance also guards against defamation,[75] copyright infringement and a host of other causes of action.[76] This makes it difficult to ascertain how influential the right of publicity was in shaping the behaviour of seeking permission, because it is only one release of liability in a bundle of other rights. As such, the behaviour of seeking permission to use persona in the film industry can be attributed to developments in the insurance industry that require waivers to be sought. More recently, the right of publicity has bolstered this behaviour, as cases in the US indicate an increased litigation risk, but this is unlikely to be the only source of law influencing permission to be sought.[77]

[70] IMS, 'Errors & Omissions Insurance' *IMS Film & Media Insurance* at https://filminsurance.co.uk/film-product-range/errors-omissions-insurance/ (accessed 1 October 2018).

[71] 'Film Insurance' at http://dev.britishfilmcommission.org.uk/tv-production/entering-the-uk/film-insurance/ (accessed 1 October 2018).

[72] ibid.

[73] Young, J and Elmeweihi, T, 'The Delicate Art of Making a Bio Pic w/o Getting Permission' *Front Row Insurance Brokers* (25 June 2015) at www.frontrowinsurance.com/articles/the-social-network-without-getting-permission-from-mark-zuckerberg-part-3 (accessed 1 October.2018).

[74] Contreras and Fagundes (2023).

[75] Fish, M, 'Life Story Rights in the United Kingdom' (9 September 2013) *Fieldfisher* at www.fieldfisher.com/publications/2013/09/life-story-rights-in-the-united-kingdom (accessed 1 October 2018).

[76] Simensky, M and Osterberg, E, 'Insurance and Management of Intellectual Property Risks' (1999) 17(2) *Cardozo Arts & Ent LJ* 321, 326.

[77] *De Havilland v FX* (2018).

iii. Contracting for Collaboration, Exclusivity and Waivers

The preceding sections have explained that life-story deals are sought to avoid litigation risk and to comply with insurance requirements. While these motivations are about protecting the producer, there are also benefits of seeking permission to gain access to information that can be used to produce a better film or television series, sometimes on an exclusive basis. While UK lawyers did not express these benefits during fieldwork due to limited experience in the film industry, such benefits exist independently of the legal framework, and thus are likely to be relevant in the UK. A life-rights deal with an individual may involve

> getting them to do interviews, getting them to show you their diaries, writings, works of art, introductions for interviews with friends and family, helping write the film, or at least not disparaging it when it's about to be released. That's kind of the basket of benefits our clients are looking for rather than the legal right to tell someone's story because that right doesn't exist.[78]

Collaborating with an individual, or an individual's estate, can provide materials that would not otherwise be accessible:

> There is also a sense of getting access to people to get information, to get diaries, have them call their friends, sign releases and get interviewed … Often, but not always, you get more materials. I have done deals where that was absolutely the key. There was a story that happened in the 1930s where all the people who were involved were dead so from a legal point of view it was all in the public domain. No privacy or defamation issues, no right of publicity because it is a historical issue, but one of the principal characters had written a diary of the catalogue of events and we thought the diary would be a roadmap. It was unpublished and the family guarded it carefully so we could only get access by making a deal. More often, it might be papers or photographs to help get the look right.[79]

Collaborating can be advantageous, because the producers may be able to acquire information that is not publicly available. This can lead to a better film or television series. But this would depend on the nature of the film being made and the centrality of the individual to the script. If the individual is a secondary character, it may not be considered beneficial to enter into a life-rights deal. Life-rights deals can also have negative consequences: 'It's not necessarily better to get the consent of the person. There are a lot of downsides – they will want approval right, right to review the script, and that's not acceptable for many of my clients.'[80] Production companies may be hindered in their portrayal, which is problematic if the person is interesting because of the controversial or unsavoury details of their lives.

Despite the difficulties created by life-rights deals, they may be considered valuable if exclusivity is desired. A producer may want to be able to say to a studio

[78] California interview 2.
[79] California interview 19.
[80] California interview 2.

'I have exclusive rights so you have to deal with me, and you don't have to worry about competition.'[81] This can make the film or series more valuable to financiers. A lawyer noted:

> There are practical reasons why you would want to get permission. You can get access to the person you're making the film about and have them consult and be part of the process which might result in a better product. There's also value if you're the 'authorized' biography versus unauthorized from a marketing standpoint.[82]

Claiming a film or television series is 'authorised', that is, one the person has consented to being made, can be an attractive marketing strategy because viewers feel they will be getting intimate information. Furthermore, in contrast to advertising, exclusive deals[83] are not necessarily respected in this realm, so having the featured celebrity's approval can support the marketing of the film. A lawyer commented:

> Let's say that Disney reaches an agreement with Kim Kardashian to do the Kim Kardashian story. They're going to have exclusive rights to merchandising, advertising with her image, clothing, t-shirts, everything. Netflix decides it wants to do a Kim Kardashian story. Assuming that they're not interfering with the contract, they're not creating liability between themselves and Disney.[84]

The right of publicity cannot be legally enforced against content producers since it does not confer a proprietary 'life story' right.[85] This allows the story of individual lives to be told from different perspectives, although this has not stopped individuals from trying to manipulate the right of publicity to maintain exclusivity. A New York lawyer whose clients are content producers in the UK gave the example of a dispute she advised on. The clients wanted to make a documentary on the life of a deceased celebrity, so they contacted the estate in the hopes of gaining access to information. Their request was denied, and they were also told they could not use the name of the celebrity. The lawyer advised the producers that they could in fact proceed, but the broadcaster they were working with was hesitant in light of the response of the estate.

As the benefits of exclusivity are limited, since such exclusivity cannot be fully enforced, the benefits offered by contract are more strongly rooted in access to information gained by working with an individual or her estate. The influence of the desire to collaborate via contract then hinges on whether such collaboration is actually desirable in given circumstances. Where there is no need to collaborate, deterrence theory is more influential in prompting film producers to seek permission to use persona where it is likely to be given to obtain waivers of liability.

[81] California interview 19.
[82] California interview 25.
[83] See ch 5, section III.
[84] California interview 7.
[85] The scenario described involves a third party creating a film without the permission of the individual featured. As such, the tort of inducement of breach of contract would not be applicable in these circumstances.

III. Permission Not Sought Where Considered Unnecessary or is Unlikely to be Given

Not all producers seek life-rights deals, even where they are likely to be granted. As noted, life-rights deals are not a legal requirement, so producers are free to proceed without them. If the producer does not consider the access to information to be valuable, or is willing to pay the higher deductibles charged by the insurance company for failure to get a waiver and run the risk of litigation, it will not pursue a life-rights deal. None of the interviewees were able to give examples of productions they had personally worked on where a life-rights deal was not sought if it was likely to be forthcoming, but they noted it does occur.[86]

Where permission is unlikely to be given, it is not sought. Lawyers were able to provide examples of films and television programmes produced without a life-rights deal: 'Our company is doing one on notorious criminals. That poses some challenges because you're not going to get the permission of them.'[87] A pair of lawyers noted that their client complained about being featured in a television programme without permission: 'We're consulting on a case where somebody's relative was killed. The show talked about members of the family and didn't ask to portray them.'[88]

Lawyers also gave examples of films and television programmes they were aware had been produced without permission. For example, the founder of Facebook was portrayed in a 2010 film that chronicled his experiences leading up to the development of the platform: 'Mark Zuckerberg would never have agreed to them making the Social Network.'[89] Films may also feature deceased individuals without securing permission from the estate: 'There was recently an unauthorised biopic done on Michael Jackson on Lifetime [television network].'[90] Others referred to productions which featured criminals: 'The Menendez brothers have biopics based on them. They have not given consent, nor will they.'[91] One lawyer noted that in the New York case of *Porco v Lifetime*,[92] the plaintiff, 'from prison, wrote a complaint saying that his right of publicity had been violated because no one got permission to create this film'.[93] It should be noted that the claim in *Porco* actually proceeded under the guise of privacy.

There are many situations where life-rights deals will not be granted so that it would be futile to pursue one. No UK lawyer provided any examples of films or television programmes, but producers of programmes such as *The Crown*, which

[86] California interviews 2, 3, 9, 17, 21, 25; UK interviews 5, 11, 21.
[87] California interview 25.
[88] California interview 17.
[89] California interview 2.
[90] California interview 25.
[91] California interview 9.
[92] *Porco v Lifetime* (2017).
[93] New York interview 10.

features the lives of the British Royal Family, are unlikely to have secured permission for the portrayals. The absence of applicable law/limitations of existing causes of action explained in the Introduction to this chapter allows studios to progress production without seeking permission of the individual featured. However, when asked if studios would be more cautious with proceeding if they were unable to get the rights, a lawyer stated 'Yes, they are. If a studio is unable to get the rights, they are more cautious when proceeding. Insurance companies would charge higher deductibles to their clients to make these projects without consent.'[94] An example where life-rights would not be agreed is films and televisions programmes that portray criminals. During fieldwork, *Law and Order: True Crime* was heavily advertising its mini-series on the Menendez brothers, who were convicted of murdering their parents. A lawyer confirmed that permission was not sought to portray the Menendez brothers in this series.[95] When making productions where life rights are not likely to be given, producers undertake a cost–benefit analysis, assessing whether it is worth proceeding despite the litigation risk posed by several causes of action.[96]

The risk of litigation for biopics has potentially increased due to a decision of the New York Supreme Court, Appellate Division, Third Department, which was being debated among lawyers during fieldwork. In the case of *Porco*, Lifetime Entertainment Services made a television film about a murderer but fictionalised some aspects of the account.[97] This is not an unusual practice when creating these types of films. However, the murderer sued from jail on the basis of breach of privacy under sections 50 and s 51 of the New York Civil Rights Law. The Appellate Division, in the procedural stage, reversing a motion to dismiss, interpreted the case law in New York as disallowing 'substantially fictitious biography', as it considered that this constituted using persona for trade in a way that cannot benefit from the newsworthiness exception. The Appellate Court cited *Messenger*,[98] which held 'a work may be so infected with fiction, dramatization or embellishment that it cannot be said to fulfil the purpose of the newsworthiness exception.'[99]

Porco was eventually dismissed in favour of the producer, Lifetime, but as the case was in progress at the time interviews were conducted, lawyers were asked their opinions on the impact of the decision. One lawyer stated, 'In light of *Porco*, you have to be factually accurate or at least have good sources to support the

[94] California interview 2.
[95] California interview 25.
[96] California interview 25.
[97] *Porco v Lifetime* (2017).
[98] *Messenger v Gruner and Jahr Printing and Publishing* 93 NY 2d 948 (1999). The complaint concerned a minor whose photograph had been used to illustrate an advice column with the title, 'I got trashed and had sex with three guys.' Defamation was not successful in this case, but the right of publicity was. Knowing fictionalisations have also resulted in claimants' being successful in *Spahn v Julian Messner* [1967] and *Binns v Vitagraph* [1913].
[99] *Porco v Lifetime* (2017) [1254]–[1255], citing *Messenger* (1999) [466].

factual portrayal.'[100] The lawyer also expressed the opinion that the progression of the *Porco* case could be because the 'New York statute does not have an expansive protection of the First Amendment. Once you start fictionalising too far, the newsworthy exception no longer applies.'[101] *Porco* is not the first case of this nature, but it caused a stir because of the reasoning applied. Lawyers correctly speculated that the producers would likely prevail in *Porco*, so they were not considering changing their practices.[102] However, this case further demonstrates that breach of privacy is another cause of action against which producers need to guard.

IV. Life-Story Rights: An Extra-Legal Social Norm

Contreras and Fagundes, in their article, 'Solving the Life Story Puzzle: Docudramas, Modularity and Hollywood Private Ordering', come to similar findings about the existence of life-story rights as those advanced by this chapter.[103] From their empirical work, which consisted of interviews with 13 entertainment industry professionals, they conclude that life-story rights have become entrenched as a social norm. This bundle of rights is not legally required but has become normalised. This normalisation can be traced to the history of New York privacy law, with permission being sought from the early 1900s. However, this practice became popular for films only in the 1950s, and for television series from the 1970s onwards. The authors summarise the elements of a life-story deal as 'a putative conveyance of rights; a waiver of liability; an exclusivity provision; and an agreement to grant access or cooperate'.[104] Obtaining a life-story deal also sends several signals: the agreement of the individual featured can result in positive public reception, and competitors are warned and must work around exclusivity.[105]

Despite these benefits, it may be difficult or unfeasible to secure life-story rights because the subject does not want to surrender artistic control, objects to any fictionalisation or asks for an unreasonable sum of money. Life-story rights deals often attract sums around $35,000–$75,000, much smaller than many anticipate. Only in rare instances will the deal attract a large payment, and those instances are reserved for the very famous. When non-famous people are featured, the costs awarded at trial for any infringement of rights is likely to be low, hence the payment is proportionate to the risk that is being guarded against. In some instances, producers may proceed without the life-story rights, but they may have to pay higher insurance premiums, as discussed in section II.A.ii.

[100] California interview 25.
[101] California interview 25.
[102] New York interviews 10, 16; California interviews 2, 7, 22, 25.
[103] Contreras and Fagundes (2023).
[104] ibid.
[105] ibid.

The prevalence of securing life-story deals has resulted in the entrenchment of this practice as a social norm. Contreras and Fagundes suggest that the entertainment industry can be considered a close-knit group due to its members' common interest, similar to roller-derby participants,[106] diamond merchants[107] and cotton traders.[108] This close-knit characterisation is based on the common interest shared by the preceding groups, as well as the geographical proximity originally outlined by Ellickson, as the entertainment industry remains concentrated in Los Angeles. This concentration was reflected in the fieldwork for this book, where most lawyers with experience in film and television were based in that city.

In terms of norms regarding dispute resolution, the findings advanced earlier in this book are reflective of the practices of this industry. In Contreras and Fagundes' study, they found that 'interview subjects could not recall a single instance of a subject flouting them [life-story agreements] or a claim of breach by either side'.[109] This is in alignment with the proposition that individuals in a contractual relationship are unlikely to sue their counterpart as they want to maintain the relationship and/or avoid the reputational harm that could result from litigation. In addition, the hesitancy towards adopting legal recourse evidences that the relationships operate on a norms basis. In fact, the authors found that some of their interviewees willingly entered into life-rights deals because they had internalised the practice and felt that sanctions in the form of reputational harm could result if they flouted this norm.

The solidification of this practice as a social norm illustrates the role that law can play in developing norms. As explained in chapter 3, social norms are often considered to be outside of the law. While this is true to an extent, the boundaries between law and social norms are porous. Even if there is no valid claim, the threat of litigation has resulted in a practice to guard against liability. As stated by UK interviewee 13, 'I've done a few life rights deals … It's best practice. Getting someone to say yes makes it less likely that they will sue.' This potential for litigation has gone beyond precautionary contracting to internalisation in some instances. California interviewee 19 said 'There is equally a sense that people … have some sort of property right in their person and if I am going to make a movie I should go and acquire that.' This interviewee also remarked that the right of publicity generally is not sufficiently clear and that, 'with the law, you want to create guides for action for people. That goes back to market and efficient allocation …' Yet in the absence of law, norms intervene to achieve these goals, and that is what has seemingly occurred in the realm of life-story rights. This does not mean the situation is ideal, as freedom-of-speech concerns could be raised in relation to the hesitation to proceed without a deal. But the practice arose to create efficiency by minimising the risk posed by the threat of legal actions.

[106] ibid.
[107] ibid.
[108] ibid.
[109] ibid.

V. Conclusion

The right of publicity has had an impact on the regulation of persona in the film and television production industry, despite the inapplicability of this right to protecting life stories. However, it is difficult to isolate this cause of action from other potential causes of action that may be deployed. The presence of deterrence theory is observable through litigation risk caused by various potential causes of action, including defamation and breach of privacy. While the risk of a right of publicity claim has materialised in the US,[110] it is but one cause of action that influences the seeking of permission. Right of publicity is subsumed by the web of potential claims that must be addressed to satisfy insurance requirements.

The desire to secure the benefits of permission through contracting also influences producers to seek permission when portraying an individual in a film or television programme. The benefits of collaboration are mainly access to information that can be used to produce a better film or television programme. Exclusivity may also be considered beneficial, but this exclusivity relates to the access rather than the right to portray the individual, as there is no proprietary life-story right. That being said, the individual's agreement to a portrayal can assist with commercial success, by having the individual agree not to provide information to competitors. The second behaviour observed in this industry is that permission is not sought where it is unlikely to be given. This behaviour is influenced by futility as well as absence of applicable law.

This chapter has demonstrated the strength of influence of the deterrence theory of law. In neither jurisdiction is there a right that protects 'life stories', yet the risk of litigation posed by several causes of action influences the permission to be sought. While the benefits of collaboration exist independently of the law, collaboration will not always be necessary and is not always beneficial, as it will require ceding some control of the depiction to the individual whose permission is being obtained. Nonetheless, these influences have not prevented films and television programmes from being made without permission in accordance with the second behaviour discussed in section III.

The inapplicability of the right of publicity to life-story deals, combined with the limited likelihood of success of other claims that are guarded against, makes this industry unique when compared to the others focused on in this book. The film and television industry is comparatively the most protected in terms of products, due to freedom-of-speech protections afforded to expressive works. Yet a practice has emerged to guard against the risk of liability and to secure the benefits of collaboration. This practice is aptly described as a social norm, but one that is operating as an extra-legal behaviour as a result of legal considerations. Thus, the porous nature of law and social norms, and the perception of law rather than the substantive application of the law, has resulted in the quasi-legal recognition of life-story rights.

[110] *De Havilland v FX* (2018); *Porco v Lifetime* (2017); *Sarver v Chartier* (2016) [905].

8

Reality Sports Video Games

Introduction

This chapter examines how law, contract and social norms influence the commercialisation of persona in reality sports video games. 'Reality sports video games'[1] are defined for the purpose of this book as video games that create life-like avatars of athletes and allow the player of the video game to control the avatar in a simulation of the relevant sport. In recent US litigation, athletes claimed their right of publicity had been infringed by being portrayed as avatars in video games.[2] In 2011, the US Supreme Court had confirmed that video games are expressive works, subject to First Amendment protection.[3] As such, the transformative use test is used by US courts to determine whether producers of video games have a defence against right of publicity infringement. The test, developed in the 2001 case of *Comedy III v Saderup*,[4] applies five factors[5] to determine whether the work in question has 'transformed' the persona to an extent that the use should be 'immunized from liability for right of publicity infringement'.[6] The transformative

[1] This term should not be confused with 'virtual reality sports'. In virtual reality sports, players experience 'a virtual or simulated three-dimensional environment that is generated by a computer. It is typically experienced through a helmet or headset with a built-in screen, which deliver audio and visual stimuli to the user.' See 'Virtual Reality in Sports' *Sports Business Journal* (24 August 2017) at www.sportsbusinessjournal.com/Daily/Issues/2017/08/24/Technology/virtual-reality-sports.aspx (accessed 3 October 2018).

[2] *Davis v Electronic Arts* 775 F 3d 1172 (2015); *In re NCAA Student-Athlete Name & Likeness Licensing Litigation* 724 F 3d 1268 (9th Cir Cal 2013); *Hart v Electronic Arts* 717 F 3d 141 (2013); *Keller v Electronic Arts* (not reported) 2010 WL 530108.

[3] Like the protected books, plays and movies that preceded them, video games communicate ideas – and even social messages – through many familiar literary devices (such as characters, dialogue, plot and music) and through features distinctive to the medium (such as the player's interaction with the virtual world). That suffices to confer First Amendment protection – *Brown v Entertainment Merchants Association* 564 US 786 (2011) [790].

[4] *Comedy III Productions Inc v Gary Saderup Inc* 25 Cal 4th 387 (2001).

[5] There are five factors used by the court to determine whether a use is transformative: (i) Literal depictions are unlikely to be transformative. Conventional artistic choices are not enough. (ii) If the celebrity image is 'the very sum and substance' of the work rather than the 'raw materials from which an original work is synthesized', it is unlikely to be transformative. (iii) Work that is 'primarily the defendant's own expression rather than the celebrity's likeness' is likely to be transformative. (iv) It needs to be considered whether the elements that dominate the work are literal and imitative or creative, based on quantitative assessment. (v) If the marketability of the work is primarily a result of the celebrity depicted, it is unlikely to satisfy the test.

[6] McCarthy, T and Schechter, R, *Rights of Publicity and Privacy* (Thomson Reuters 2022) § 8:72.

use test has been applied to the use of persona in video games with varying degrees of success. Reality sports video games[7] often fail this test, as the use of persona in these types of video games is found to be an accurate representation rather than a transformative use.

There has been no similar litigation on the portrayal of individuals in video games in the UK, possibly because of the absence of the right of publicity on which to base a claim.[8] Video-game developers create games that are distributed globally.[9] This means that developments in US law are likely to impact the UK reality sports video game industry. However, this chapter will demonstrate that the recent US legal developments, while influential, have not drastically changed the way in which persona is used in this industry, as the common behaviour has always been to seek permission from leading athletes. This behaviour existed prior to US litigation and was influenced by the benefits of collaboration. The recent litigation has centred around a deviation from this behaviour.

The legal regulation of persona in reality sports video games is a niche field, with few specialist lawyers. Lawyers in California had the most experience in this area: six California lawyers were able to provide information on the use of persona in video games; four UK lawyers also had experience, as they represented athletes whose personas have been licensed for use in video games; and three New York lawyers demonstrated an awareness of issues surrounding reality sports video games but were not directly involved in this industry. Due to the limited number of lawyers in this field, the data collected are supported by secondary sources to confirm their veracity and to shed more light on the experiences of interviewees.

It is important to recognise the significance of the role of the right of publicity in this niche field. Advertising and merchandising have been the main uses of persona in right-of-publicity and passing-off cases. Films and television programmes are often shielded from the right of publicity due to First Amendment protection (although it is difficult to isolate the right of publicity from other claims in the area). Video games are also subject to First Amendment protection, but they have been revealed to be susceptible to right-of-publicity

[7] There are sports video games that do not make use of avatars of real-life individuals. The term 'reality sports video games' has been chosen to differentiate these types of games. The games being considered in this section are made by producers such as Electronic Arts, Take-Two Interactive, Big Ant, Activision, 2K Games and Ubisoft.

[8] Lee suggests that trade marks and passing off may provide viable avenues for protecting likeness in video games: Lee, Y, 'Putting a face to the game: the intellectual property implications of using celebrity likenesses in videogames' (2018) 13(2) *JIPLP* 143.

[9] This book focuses on the US and the UK, but it should be noted that Japan is also a major centre for video-game development. Interviewees did not provide data on the impact of the Japanese market – 'The 50 Top Video Game Design Companies' *GameDesigning* at www.gamedesigning.org/game-development-studios/ (accessed 1 November 2018).

claims due to the failure to satisfy the transformative use test. Video games are not just used at home; rather, eSports (video game competitions)[10] attract millions of viewers and, in turn, sponsorship, media coverage and investment. Deloitte and *The eSports Observer* estimated that $4.5 billion were invested in the eSports industry in 2018.[11] While not all eSports feature persona, there are indeed competitions for reality sports video games, for example the FIFA eClub World Cup.[12] The susceptibly of reality sports video games to the right of publicity has far-reaching consequences, which may potentially stretch beyond the parameters of the actual games in question.

This chapter is divided into two main sections. Section I examines how persona is used in video games. Section II identifies the behaviour of seeking permission to use persona in video games, and looks at recent developments in the legal field that have strengthened this behaviour through an analysis of the relevant influences. For the sake of clarity, the individuals who purchase and play video games are referred to as 'players', and the personas featured in these video games are referred to as 'athletes'.

I. Use of Persona in Video Games

The first video game was created in 1958,[13] but the video-game-development industry was not established until the 1970s.[14] Electronic Arts (EA) was the pioneer in this field of reality sports video games. Its first sports video game, based on basketball, *Dr J and Larry Bird Go One-on-One* was produced in 1983.[15] This game

> brought professional athletes into the video-game realm for the first time … There had been games like MLB Baseball for Intellivision that slapped the logo on a box, but there had never been a video game that allowed people to play as the athletes they watched.[16]

[10] For the development of eSports, see Willingham, AJ, 'What is eSports? A look at an explosive billion-dollar industry' *CNN* (27 August 2018) at https://edition.cnn.com/2018/08/27/us/esports-what-is-video-game-professional-league-madden-trnd/index.html (accessed 6 February 2020).

[11] Deloitte, eSports Observer, *The rise of esports investments – A deep dive with Deloitte Corporate Finance LLC and The Esports Observer* (April 2019).

[12] FIFA, 'FIFA eWorld Cup 2020' *FIFA* at www.fifa.com/fifaeworldcup/fifa-eclub-world-cup/ (accessed 6 February 2020).

[13] APS News, 'This Month in Physics History – October 1958: Physicist Invents First Video Game' (2008) 19(9) *APS News* 2.

[14] Kent, S, *The Ultimate History of Video Games* (Prima Life 2001).

[15] ibid.

[16] Sauer, P, 'How Dr J and Larry Bird helped build a video game empire' *Vice* (25 May 2017) at https://sports.vice.com/en_us/article/wje9kq/how-dr-j-and-larry-bird-helped-build-a-video-game-empire (accessed 3 April 2018).

In addition to allowing players to control avatars of athletes, this game was also ground-breaking because it was made on licence from the featured athletes:

> It was the first time a computer game company had licensed an athlete's name. Though earlier games had been made based on movies such as Tron, Krull and Star Wars, and Mattel had acquired licenses from the NFL and the NBA, no one had ever approached an individual sports star.[17]

Subsequently, EA created a baseball game having consulted Earl Weaver, former baseballer and then manager of the Baltimore Orioles baseball team. The game was entitled *Earl Weaver Baseball.*[18]

The success of these games led EA to develop *Madden NFL*, released in 1988, which went on to become one of the most successful reality sports video games in history.[19] Hawkins, founder of EA, established the behaviour of seeking permission to use persona in *Dr J and Larry Bird*, which was adapted by other video-game developers. Reality sports video games became firmly established as a popular type of video game in the early 2000s. Many games continue to be created on licence from the athletes, such as *Tony Hawk's Pro Skater* and *Major League Baseball featuring Ken Griffery Jr.*[20]

Playing a reality sports video game allows the player to control animated avatars of the featured athletes in an interactive medium. Players are tasked with making strategic decisions, and are able to move their players using the console controller. Players can also select features such as weather conditions, time of day and stadium setting. The evolution of technology has led to enhanced graphics and more sophisticated gameplay. Athletes are represented in a life-like manner, and biographical information, such as weight and height and performance statistics, are incorporated into the games. The appeal of reality sports video games is captured in the *FIFA 19 Champions Rise* Official Launch trailer, where a player states 'They all want to meet Neymar. But me, I am Neymar. I'm De Bruyne and Dybala.'[21] These games are crafted so that the player can control the most realistic versions of the athlete's avatar. Face scans are used to capture different expressions[22] and the range of movements are made as realistic as possible by use of motion-capture technology.[23] These features combine to create a game that is appealing to players.

[17] Kent (2001).

[18] Nachman, C, 'The Evolution of Sports Video Games' *Business Insider* (25 August 2011) at www.businessinsider.com/sports-video-games-history2011?IR=T (accessed 3 October 2018).

[19] 'Madden NFL is one of the most successful video game series ever' *Madden Store* (1 November 2017) at www.madden-store.com/news/madden-nfl-is-one-of-the-most-successful-video-game-series-ever (accessed 3 October 2018).

[20] Nachman (2011).

[21] FIFA, 'FIFA 19 l Champions Rise l Official Launch Trailer' *YouTube* at www.youtube.com/watch?v=OumZxTdMq_c (accessed 8 October 2018).

[22] ibid.

[23] 'Incredible l Motion capture for FIFA 18 ft Dele Alli & Akinfenwa' *F2Freestylers – Ultimate Soccer Skills Channel* (3 October 2017) at www.youtube.com/watch?v=xb3H465Oil4 (accessed 8 October 2018).

II. Seek Permission to Use Persona in Reality Sports Video Games

Lawyers were questioned on whether they would advise permission to be sought when using persona in video games. In addressing this question, it became apparent that expertise was limited to reality sports video games. As such, the behaviour of seeking permission was observed in this specific category of video game. However, an online search revealed the celebrities have been used in other types of video games, and that they agreed to the portrayals.[24] It is important to note that permission is sought for the elements of persona such as name, voice, likeness and signature. Lawyers did not indicate that permission is sought for other information, such as statistics or biographical information.

A. United Kingdom

The UK lawyers believed that permission should be sought when using persona in reality sports video games, and that permission is usually obtained. As noted by one lawyer, 'Yes, I would advise them to get clearance [to use persona]. On a whole, they do get permission.'[25] Similarly, 'You would obtain a commercial waiver confirming the individual would not object to use of image [in the video game].'[26] A third lawyer, who had experience with English football teams and footballers, advised 'you need to negotiate between the individual and the team to secure the rights [to persona].'[27] One lawyer suggested 'Go to the Premier League first to ascertain who has rights to teams and their kits. Then go to the team to find out who owns the rights to the athletes. Big athletes might own their own rights.'[28] Another with similar experience noted that video-game developers need to secure a 'FIFPro licence [which] gives rights around particular players'.[29] A FIFPro licence can be obtained from the International Federation of Professional Footballers, and it 'gives the game developers the rights to use real player names and likenesses'.[30]

[24] '33 Hollywood Actors Who Appear in Video Games' *GameSpot* (6 April 2020) at www.gamespot.com/gallery/33-hollywood-actors-who-appear-in-video-games/2900-31/#7 (accessed 13 December 2022); 'Glu Mobile Scaling Back on Celebrity Games' *Licensing International* (17 March 2017) at https://licensinginternational.org/news/glu-mobile-scaling-back-on-celebrity-games/ (accessed 13 December 2022).
[25] UK interview 23.
[26] UK interview 20.
[27] UK interview 9.
[28] UK interview 9.
[29] UK interview 24.
[30] Davidson, N, 'Behind the scenes, worldwide licensing team works on FIFA soccer video game' *City News* (7 October 2013) at https://toronto.citynews.ca/2013/10/07/behind-the-scenes-worldwide-licensing-team-works-on-fifa-soccer-video-game/ (accessed 3 October 2018).

The UK lawyers mainly focused on the FIFA video game, produced by EA. As noted, FIFPro may administer licences for use of athletes' persona. The FIFPro legal department is tasked with 'asserting the interests of players in relation to commercial aspects of football (such as image rights)'.[31] In the 'Agreement regarding the minimum requirements for standard player contracts in the professional football sector in the European Union and in the rest of the UEFA territory', Article 8 on Image Rights states:

> 8.1 The Club and the Player have to agree how the Players' image rights are exploited.
> 8.2 As a recommendation and principle the individual player may exploit his rights by himself (if not conflicting with Clubs' sponsors/partners) whilst the Club may exploit the Players' image right as part of the whole squad.[32]

Football associations that are members of FIFPro may elect to take part in collective bargaining for players' persona with regard to video games.[33] As such, reality sports video-game producers might be required to approach this organisation to secure the appropriate licence.

B. United States

California lawyers recounted that permission is sought from key athletes, but it would not be feasible to seek permission from all athletes featured in a video game.[34] However, permission could be sought from a governing body where relevant: 'NFL (National Football League), NBA (National Basketball Association) – there is some type of collective bargaining for those rights.'[35] Another responded that games may not be made if the licences cannot be obtained: 'They [video game developers] are trying to avoid a liability situation and avoid a situation that is going to trigger legal fees.'[36] If the appropriate licence agreement is not secured, 'the magic … is killed if rather than playing as Manchester United, you're actually controlling Man Red – playing in black'.[37]

While permission is sought to use persona in reality sports video games, California lawyers felt that permission should not be legally required, as video

[31] FIFPRO, 'FIFPro Legal Department' *FIFPRO* at https://fifpro.org/en/players/legal/about-fifpro-legal-department (accessed 1 November 2018).

[32] 'Agreement regarding the minimum requirements for standard player contracts in the professional football sector in the European Union and in the rest of the UEFA territory' *FIFPro* at www.uefa.com/MultimediaFiles/Download/uefaorg/EuropeanUnion/02/63/58/66/2635866_DOWNLOAD.pdf (accessed 1 November 2018).

[33] Downie, A, 'Rights mess keeps Brazil clubs out of best-selling game' *Reuters* (10 October 2014) at www.reuters.com/article/us-soccer-brazil-fifa15/rights-mess-keeps-brazil-clubs-out-of-best-selling-game-idUSKCN0HZ1MN20141010 accessed (1 November 2018).

[34] California interview 1.

[35] California interview 7.

[36] California interview 1.

[37] Dayus, O, 'A game of two halves' *GameSpot* (15 September 2017) at www.gamespot.com/reviews/pes-2018-review/1900-6416757/ (accessed 9 April 2018).

games should be shielded from the right of publicity since they constitute an expressive work.[38] The treatment of video games by the courts will be considered further in section II.C.i in discussing deterrence theory, but it has arguably influenced this behaviour. According to one lawyer, 'Companies making video games are much more careful about making licensing decisions [now].'[39] Unlike the film industry, where other causes of action have to be considered and have informed the behaviour of seeking permission, the right of publicity is the main cause of action in relation to the use of persona that influenced this behaviour, and this is a recent development that has resulted from the *NCAA* litigation.[40]

When video-game developers do not secure the licence, they usually do not make use of persona in either jurisdiction.[41] An example of this can be seen in the popular FIFA games as compared to Pro Evolution Soccer (PES). FIFA has robust licensing arrangements with many athletes, whereas PES has historically had less authenticity due to licensing difficulties.[42] A PES fan noted in his review of *PES 2018*:

> Playing as 'Gregs' rather than Ryan Giggs was funny when I was 10 years old, and even this year, looking at PES 2018's teams did spark a fun game of guessing who 'West Glamorgan City', 'East Dorsetshire', and 'ST Yellow' were in real life.[43]

As one interviewee noted:

> Take FIFA done by EA. The basic core rights to put those games on are done through leagues, not individuals. When individuals play the league, their image might be used. Leagues will have pre-clearance to allow them to do deals with video game companies.[44]

A UK lawyer confirmed that 'unofficial' games, not made on licence, can be created: 'If you want the official game, you need all the rights. If you want an interactive game where it's not official, you can do it. For example Red Lakes simulated to be Liverpool.'[45] However, to make the game as realistic as possible, video-game developers must secure licence agreements. There is a potential correlation between licensing persona and video game sales: FIFA17 sold

[38] California interviews 1, 2, 3, 7, 16, 22.
[39] New York interview 6.
[40] *In re NCAA* (2013).
[41] The exclusion of persona where licences are not secured can be observed in other jurisdictions as well. *FIFA 2015* excluded Brazilian football clubs because EA was unable to secure licences for athletes' personas: Downie (2014).
[42] Stubbsy, M, 'Konami's Adam Bhatti talks taking on EA and securing partnerships with Liverpool, Dortmund and more' *Red Bull* (5 September 2016) at www.redbull.com/gb-en/how-pes-is-staking-a-claim-in-the-licensing-war (accessed 10 April 2018) – 'But there has always been one area that PES has struggled with ever since its first outings: licensing. FIFA has almost every licensed team you could ever want, along with many of the top competitions from around the globe.'
[43] Dayus (2017).
[44] UK interview 20.
[45] UK interview 24.

1.1 million copies within the first week of release, whereas PES sold 50,000 copies in a similar timeframe.[46]

C. Theories of Compliance

i. Law – Deterrence Theory

The deterrence theory was observed in fieldwork due to the litigation risk that results if permission to use persona is not sought. Since video games are distributed globally, they face the same issue as films: regardless of whether publicity rights exist in the jurisdiction of production, a litigation risk is present because of the distribution schedule. This was noted by a UK interviewee, who remarked 'Normally, you go and clear those rights because you are exploiting the game internationally and personality rights would exist in some jurisdiction.'[47]

The litigation risk has heightened with the developments in graphics,[48] as game developers can represent athletes graphically even if their names are not used. The litigation risk for using persona without permission in video games is arguably relatively recent, as the first claim brought against a video-game producer was in the 2006 case of *Kirby v Sega of America*,[49] where a singer claimed that an alien avatar infringed her right of publicity because the avatar used similar expressions and had similar facial features and manner of dress. Her claim was unsuccessful as the use of persona was assessed as transformative, so was defended against the right of publicity.[50]

As an expressive work, video games can be defended against the right of publicity if the use of persona is transformative. The issue with reality sports video games is that they strive to be as accurate as possible. This means there is a serious litigation risk if licences are not acquired. In 2014, WIPO published guidance for video-game developers and recognised that licences are needed to create video games that use persona:

> Publicity rights are important in the game context in a few instances. First, using a person in a game … usually requires that person's permission. The same is true for using a person's voice or other recognisable characteristic. Failing to obtain the person's permission could result in a court granting an injunction halting sales of the game and/or ordering damages to the person whose image was used without consent.

[46] O'Connor, R, 'How FIFA Crushed PES to Become the Undisputed King of Football Video Games' *Bleacher Report* (29 September 2017) at https://bleacherreport.com/articles/2735656-how-fifa-crushed-pes-to-become-the-undisputed-king-of-football-video-games (accessed 1 November 2018).

[47] UK interview 20.

[48] Blanke, JM, 'No Doubt about It – You've got to Have Hart: Simulation Video Games May Redefine the Balance between and among the Right of Publicity, the First Amendment, and Copyright Law' (2013) 19 *BU J Sci & Tech L* 26, 32.

[49] *Kirby v Sega of America Inc* 144 Cal App 4th 47 (Cal App 2006).

[50] ibid [60]–[61].

> These damages will likely have a punitive characteristic on top of the court derived fair market value for licensing the person's right of publicity.[51]

The litigation risk became significant in the US in 2009, when the first claim of infringement of the right of publicity in a reality sports video game was lodged. Prior to this litigation, the benefits of collaboration overshadowed deterrence as a theory for compliance. Now, the risk has materialised and is significant. According to a New York lawyer:

> There has been quite a spate of cases against video games. [Athletes'] avatars appear in those games because they are based on real life [athletes]. Those are big money cases. Big money cases get brought. Most rights of publicity cases are generally [resolved by] demand letters.[52]

It is worth examining the history of reality sports video-game cases to understand how this risk has developed. Claims have been brought by four individual American footballers: Ryan Hart, Samuel Keller, Ed O'Bannon and Tony Davis. The first three claims related to college footballers, whereas the last claim related to retired footballers. The first claim was brought by Ryan Hart in 2009 in New Jersey.[53] The New Jersey District Court granted summary judgment in favour of EA, finding that the use of Hart's persona was transformative. However, in 2013,[54] the 3rd Circuit reversed the District Court's ruling and found that Hart's right of publicity had been infringed.

Samuel Keller also brought a claim in 2009, in California. The motion to dismiss by EA was denied by the District Court, as it was held that the use of persona was not transformative.[55] As noted by Reinckens and Ganas, 'Prior to the Third Circuit's opinion in *Hart*, the two lower court decisions were viewed as inconsistent, and arguably irreconcilable, given the near factual identity of the right of publicity claims asserted.'[56] Keller's claim was subsequently consolidated with a claim brought by Ed O'Bannon, in *Re NCAA Student-Athlete Name and Likeness Licensing Litigation*.[57] O'Bannon's claim was against the National Collegiate Athletic Association (NCAA) and Collegiate Licensing Company (CLC) for an illegal restraint of trade, whereby amateur players were prevented from receiving compensation for commercialisation of their persona. Keller's claim was against EA for misappropriation of persona, as well as against the NCAA and CLC for

[51] WIPO, *Mastering the Game: Business and Legal Issues for Video Game Developers* (2014) para 3.1.5.

[52] New York interview 2.

[53] 'In 2009, Appellant Ryan Hart brought suit against Electronic Arts Inc for allegedly violating his right of publicity as recognized under New Jersey law.' *Hart v Electronic Arts* (2013) [145].

[54] The development of the case is outlined ibid [146]–[147].

[55] *Keller v Electronic Arts* (not reported) 2010 WL 530108.

[56] Reinckens, M and Ganas, M, 'The right of publicity in college sports' *Law in Sport* (18 September 2013) at www.lawinsport.com/blogs/dla-piper/item/the-right-of-publicity-in-college-sports (accessed 4 October 2018).

[57] *In re NCAA* (2013).

allowing this misappropriation. This case was settled in 2015 for $60 million, to be distributed among 24,000 former college athletes.[58]

Tony Davis claimed that EA had infringed the right of publicity by using avatars of retired football players in *Madden NFL* in 2014. In 2015, the 9th Circuit denied First Amendment protection.[59] On remand in 2017, a California District Court granted partial summary judgment in favour of EA on the statutory right of publicity claim, as the retired players were not 'readily identifiable' from the avatars and thus could not satisfy a statutory claim.[60] However, a subsequent motion was lodged to dismiss the remaining claims, including the common law right of publicity and copyright pre-emption.[61] In discussing the application for summary judgment, Judge Seeborg stated:

> [The] reasonable inference is that EA was trying to have it both ways: it wanted its customers to believe they could have genuine re-enactments of games with representations of the actual players, while simultaneously hoping to remove enough identifying features that the former players could not claim a license was legally required. Although a fact-finder may very well conclude that avatars are not sufficiently identifiable to support plaintiffs' claims, the present record does not allow for such a finding to be made as a matter of law.[62]

In 2018, an application for a class action suit was denied.[63] The last development in the case was in September 2018, when Davis was denied leave to seek reconsideration of the order denying a second motion for class action.[64]

Lawyers in California were questioned about how this spate of litigation has affected the way in which video-game developers use persona. All the lawyers felt that the treatment of these cases by the courts had stifled creativity, and that the right of publicity had been misconstrued in its application to video games as expressive works. On the desire to avoid litigation, one lawyer stated:

> When the designers and producers of the game have ideas, and run them by lawyers, the lawyers are very aware of how aggressively [the] right of publicity can be used in the video game world and steer clear of things they think potentially attract a claim.[65]

[58] '$60 Million Settlement Approved in NCAA Video Game Lawsuit' *New York Times* (17 July 2015).

[59] *Davis v Electronic Arts* 775 F 3d 1172 (2015).

[60] *Davis v Electronic Arts* Case No 10-cv-03328-RS Order Granting Motion for Partial Summary Judgment.

[61] *Davis v Electronic Arts* (2018) Case No 10-cv-03328-RS Order Denying Motion for Summary Judgment. The court determined that the likeness of the player was not 'fixed' as required by copyright, so the contested subject matter did not fall wholly within the scope of copyright protection, thus excluding it from copyright pre-emption. See Ryan, F and Ganas, M, 'Athletes' Right of Publicity Claims Directed to Sports Video Games Not Pre-empted by Copyright Act' *Lexology* (23 January 2018) at www.lexology.com/library/detail.aspx?g=fcadf6f8-798a-43e7-84bd-414579eda2d8 (accessed 4 October 2018).

[62] *Davis v Electronic Arts* (2018) Case No 10-cv-03328-RS Order Denying Motion for Summary Judgment at para 3.

[63] *Davis v Electronic Arts* (2018) Case No 10-cv-03328-RS Order Denying Class Certification.

[64] *Davis v Electronic Arts* (2018) Case No 10-cv-03328-RS Order Denying Leave to seek Reconsideration.

[65] California interview 1.

Another noted:

> The Supreme Court has held clearly that video games are protected speech, so they are entitled to the full breadth of the First Amendment. And yet, courts have allowed plaintiffs in several cases to pursue right of publicity claims because avatars of players were depicted.[66]

Similarly, in response to questioning on the outcome of the cases discussed above, 'I do think they have come out incorrectly. It is interesting because you're gaining through including the name and likeness of another but it is in a protected work. Video games are protected speech.'[67] Another felt that judges did not understand the concept of a video game, which had resulted in these rulings:

> The games have expressive elements that create this highly expressive world. In every case, they [EA] offered to send a technician from EA to do a simulation of the game for the judges … only one judge took up the offer. [EA] also sent a gaming set, the controller, the game itself, so that they [judges] could experience it. It is surprising that more of the judges didn't take advantage. They see video games as merchandise as opposed to films or television which they see as expressive works.[68]

A similar view was expressed:

> I have to think they [judges] didn't fully appreciate – they were focused on the game aspect and the commercial aspect … you're picking your team and carrying out a fantasy. I think it was a lack of creativity and appreciation of how creative that technology is. Video games are some of the most creative works that you can have but I think they thought of it as a product.[69]

It is beyond the scope of this book to assess whether the approach to the right of publicity and video games is correct, but the implications have bolstered the behaviour of seeking permission to use persona due to the fear of litigation risk. It is also interesting to note that US lawyers, despite generally supporting the right of publicity in accordance with morality theory, agreed that video games should be exempted from such protection. But since the right can indeed apply, reality sports video-game developers 'need to work out who owns what'.[70] The desire to avoid litigation was emphasised by a UK lawyer, who stated:

> What you do not want is … someone trying to sue depending on the rights. That's quite a motivating factor. People have to give warranties therefore they want to make sure they have cleared the rights so they can give them upfront, but [that's] not always the case.[71]

[66] California interview 3.
[67] California interview 7.
[68] California interview 2.
[69] California interview 22.
[70] UK interview 9.
[71] UK interview 20.

ii. The Desire to Contract

There are two benefits of seeking permission to use persona for the video-game developer. The first is that it helps the game be more realistic. The second is that the athlete can be employed for marketing the game in which she is featured. This latter motivation is similar to the role of celebrities in co-branded merchandise: the creation of the product is followed by a strategic marketing plan. In both industries, the persona is endorsing the product, thus it may be noted that endorsement-style advertisements may relate to products with which celebrities are directly involved.

Video-game developers work with athletes to make the video game lifelike and to market the game, contributing to the success of the game. A host of video games secure licences from athletes. Examples include *Madden NFL*, *Bradman Cricke*t, *NBA Live*, *FIFA* and *Steep: Road to the Olympics*. In 2019, Apple released *Ultimate Rivals*, described as 'a new sports game franchise that brings together athletes across hockey, basketball, football, baseball and soccer into a single officially licensed video game, a first in sports and gaming'.[72] It is important to recognise the benefits of working with the athletes to create these games, as prior to 2009, when the first reality sports video-game claim was lodged, this influence was more significant than deterrence theory.

The benefits of collaboration have been important to the reality sports video-game industry since inception, but they have increased in relevance as the technology has developed. Technological developments have enhanced the ability of video-game developers to create life-like simulations:

> The producers use a motion capture system to create the movements of the athletes. In a studio, professional athletes or former college players are outfitted in spandex neoprene suits, and light sensors are positioned throughout their torso on every joint. Athletes perform a variety of shots and skill moves, and the captured body movements become the basis for those of the players in the game. Adjustments to mimic specific athletes' individual skills are then made by a design team with input from scouts, former players and coaches.[73]

Improvements in graphics[74] have allowed developers to capture the facial features and physique of athletes in a way that would have been unimaginable

[72] 'Apple launches "Ultimate Rivals" from Bit Fry Game Studios, an all-new sports games franchise available today exclusively on Apple Arcade' *Apple Newsroom* (12 December 2019) at www.apple.com/newsroom/2019/12/apple-launches-new-ultimate-rivals-sports-game-franchise-on-apple-arcade/ (accessed 13 December 2022).

[73] Brescia, J, 'For Pro Athletes, Practice That's All in the Thumbs' *New York Times* (2 April 2010).

[74] For an explanation on how developments have allowed games to be more life-like, see this advertisement for *Forza Motorsport 7* where game developers explain how they have enhanced the gaming experience: Xbox, 'Forza Motorsport 7: Built for Xbox One X' *YouTube* (7 November 2017) at www.youtube.com/watch?v=H38yNXIhV7I (accessed 10 April 2018).

when reality sports video games were first developed in 1983.[75] The developers also try to make the games authentic by including personal touches. For example, *FIFA* includes footballers' signature celebration moves.[76] Collaborating with key athletes allows the game developers to make the most accurate representations possible, which fans enjoy.[77] Players expressed satisfaction on a *FIFA* forum on the announcement of Italian team licences: 'EA have acquired the licence to have the Serie A, Serie B and Coppa Italia for FIFA 19. Tears in my eyes. Finally Serie B, after all those years of FIFA. My body is ready.'[78] Another responded on this forum in response to a comment that more athletes' faces will be used:

> I find face scans pretty important tbh [to be honest]. When I score a goal with a player I like and then see faceless Mr Thingy celebrating, I feel annoyed. It's part of the game we are paying for so EA must do it properly. Full stop.[79]

Ted Lasso, an American football coach who moved to London to manage AFC Richmond, was included in *FIFA 23* as an option under career mode.[80] This installation of the game, which features the 2022 Qatar Men's World Cup and the 2023 Australia and New Zealand Women's World Cup, boasts of HyperMotion2 Technology, which utilises bodysuits to capture movements from real-life matches.[81]

In addition to working with athletes to make a life-like game, collaborating with athletes can assist in marketing the game, as they may appear in advertisements.[82] Cristiano Ronaldo has endorsed *FIFA 18*. In addition to participating in motion capture,[83] he appeared in advertisements and on the cover of

[75] For an idea of how graphics have evolved, compare *One on One – Dr J vs Larry Bird* with *NBA 2k18* on *YouTube*: Floppy Deep Dive, 'One on One – Dr J vs Larry Bird' *YouTube* (21 November 2022) at www.youtube.com/watch?v=XXjIZIelTM8 (accessed 16 March 2023); Full Court, 'NBA 2k18 – 2 Best MyTeam Money Plays' *YouTube* (28 September 2017) at www.youtube.com/watch?v=Q2J0AX4wtTE (accessed 10 April 2018).

[76] Murphy, R, 'FIFA 18 celebrations: How to do Pogba's dab, Dybala's mask & more on Xbox One and PS4' *Goal* (28 September 2017) at www.goal.com/en-gb/news/fifa-18-celebrations-how-to-do-pogbas-dab-dybalas-mask-more/4yn9zvszquin1mqhu9q25cafn (accessed 10 April 2018).

[77] Parkin, S, 'FIFA: the video game that changed football' *The Guardian* (21 December 2016).

[78] FIFA, 'Italian License Finally Here!' *FIFA Forums* (7 June 2018) at https://fifaforums.easports.com/en/discussion/396407/italian-licenses-finally-here (accessed 8 October 2018).

[79] ibid.

[80] 'AFC Richmond are in the Game' *FIFA 23* at www.ea.com/en-gb/games/fifa/fifa-23/news/fifa-23-ted-lasso-afc-richmond? (accessed 13 December 2022).

[81] EA Sports, 'FIFA23 Reveal Trailer| The World's Game' *YouTube* (20 July 2022) at www.youtube.com/watch?v=o3V-GvvzjE4 (accessed 13 December 2022).

[82] Examples of advertisements can be viewed at: EA Sports FIFA, 'FIFA 17 – The Golden Controller – ft Reus, Hazard, Martial, James' *YouTube* (24 November 2016) at www.youtube.com/watch?v=y2njbeoClrw (accessed 1- April 2018); EA Sports, 'Madden NFL 17 – Start Me ft Von Miller' *YouTube* (8 August 2016) at www.youtube.com/watch?v=-pV7PFY_7n8 (accessed 10 April 2018); Xbox, 'Tony Hawk's Pro Skater 5 – Launch Trailer' *YouTube* (29 September 2015) at www.youtube.com/watch?v=05x2gGngJac (accessed 10 April 2018).

[83] Swan, R, 'What Cristiano Ronaldo did to stun EA Sports staff during FIFA 18 motion capture shoot' *Give Me Sport* (11 June 2017) at www.givemesport.com/1075030-what-cristiano-ronaldo-did-to-stun-ea-sports-staff-during-fifa-18-motion-capture-shoot (accessed 10 April 2018).

the game case.[84] Several wrestlers appeared in the promotional video for *AEW Fight Forever*, 'the first video game officially licensed by All Elite Wrestling'.[85] Collaborating with athletes has advantages for game development as well as the marketing of the game, regardless of any legal requirements.

When licences are not secured, developers include a feature that allows users to create these likenesses and upload them to a central system, which other users can then access. There is a possibility that a claim could be brought for contributory infringement, but no claim has been brought against this feature to date. This gives developers some leeway, as they do not have to take licences from all athletes but just the popular ones. This can be a cost-reducing strategy for developers that want to limit their spending on licences. Players are most likely to care about popular athletes when considering how realistic the game is. These athletes are also likely to be the most influential in marketing the games. As such, licences may not be sought from less famous athletes, at least not on an individual basis.

iii. Deviation

Electronic Arts deviated from the behaviour it had established when it started making college athlete video games. It proceeded without securing rights of publicity from the athletes because the NCAA did not grant licences for using the athletes, and college athletes as amateurs are not meant to be paid,[86] so EA could not approach them directly. The first instalment of this game was produced in 1998, but claims for infringement of the right of publicity were not brought until 2009. The game was discontinued by EA in 2013 as a result of litigation.[87] However, the game is being revived for 2023. It is not clear yet whether real athletes will be featured, but in 2021, as a result of a Supreme Court ruling in *NCAA v Alston* concerning violation of antitrust law,[88] the NCAA policy was changed to allow athletes to be paid, opening the possibility of licensing college-athlete personas.

No other examples of defectors from the reality sports video-games behaviour of seeking permission were noted in fieldwork, although, as noted, licences may not be sought from less famous athletes. In *Champion v Take Two Interactive*, a basketballer who goes by the name 'Hot Sizzle' claimed infringement of his right

[84] Collaborating for advertising purposes can have negative implications if the athlete brings himself into disrepute. FIFA changed their Twitter banner, which featured Ronaldo, after rape allegations were made against the cover star. Yin-Poole, W, 'EA "closely monitoring" situation following "concerning" rape claim against FIFA 19 cover star Cristiano Ronaldo' *EuroGamer* (4 October 2018) at www.eurogamer.net/articles/2018-10-04-ea-closely-monitoring-situation-following-rape-allegations-against-fifa-19-cover-star-cristiano-ronaldo (accessed 8 October 2018).

[85] 'AEW Fight Forever' *ThQNordic* at https://aew.thqnordic.com/ (accessed 13 December 2022).

[86] NCAA, *2011-12 NCAA Division I Manual*, s 12.02.2: 'Pay is the receipt of funds, awards or benefits not permitted by the governing legislation of the Association for participation in athletics.'

[87] Weber, C, 'Update on College Football' *EA* (26 September 2013) at www.ea.com/news/update-on-college-football (accessed 10 April 2018).

[88] *NCAA v Alston* 141 St C 2141 (2021).

of publicity by inclusion of a non-playable character that allegedly resembled him and used his number 1 and the similar name 'Hot Sizzles' on its basketball tank top.[89] The court dismissed the claim as the avatar was not recognisable as the plaintiff and insufficient evidence was provided to support the assertion that he was 'ubiquitously known' as 'Hot Sizzle'. In fact, the court referenced *Gravano*[90] and *Lohan*[91] and opined that those plaintiffs had stronger claims factually yet they were still insufficient to be successful.

There have been instances of use of persona without permission in other jurisdictions. For example, *FIFA World Cup 2002* was banned in Germany after it was found that that Oliver Kahn's likeness was used without permission: EA had obtained a FIFPro licence and a licence from the German Bundesleague, but Kahn was not a member of these organisations.[92] *EA Sports MMA 2014* did not secure a licence from Ultimate Fighting Championship (UFC), which already had an exclusive licence with rival video-game producer (THQ) at the time.[93] Thus, EA entered deals with non-UFC fighters. The game featured a 'Create-a-Fighter' feature, but the game disabled sharing content because of difficulties: '[T]here's a whole grey area where our game allows users to make a Rocky character that's the intellectual property of somebody else, it causes a ton of problems.'[94] This statement by creative director Brian Hayes could refer to copyright in the movie *Rocky*, but there were likely also right-of-publicity concerns regarding the creation by fans of UFC fighters that were not featured, given that litigation had commenced against EA for unauthorised use of Keller in 2009.

III. Conclusion

Prior to litigation, the benefits of collaboration as espoused were the driving force for compliance in seeking permission to use persona for reality sports video games. Athletes benefitted by being paid for the use of their persona, and video-game developers benefitted by making the games as realistic as possible and from their subsequent marketing efforts. The benefits have increased in recent years due to advancements in technology, which allow for motion capture and face scans to make the avatars a realistic representation of the athlete.

[89] *Phillip Champion v Take Two Interactive Software Development* 64 Misc 3d 530 (2019).

[90] *Lohan v Take-Two Interactive Software Inc* 31 NY3d 111 (2018).

[91] *Gravano v Take-Two Interactive Software, Inc* 142 AD 3d 776 [1st Dept 2016].

[92] Pinsent Masons, 'Football game banned over player's image rights' *Out-Law* (30 April 2003) at www.out-law.com/page-3520 (accessed 1 November 2018).

[93] Deleon, N, 'Conspiracy theory: Is EA setting up EA Sports MMA to flop in order to secure the UFC license later on? *TechCrunch* (10 December 2009) at https://techcrunch.com/2009/12/10/conspiracy-theory-is-ea-setting-up-ea-sports-mma-to-flop-in-order-to-secure-the-ufc-license-later-on/ (accessed 13 December 2022).

[94] Sarkar, S, 'EA Sports UFC won't let you share created fights due to copyright concerns' *Polygon* (23 March 2013) at www.polygon.com/2014/3/28/5558518/ea-sports-ufc-no-fighter-share-copyright-concerns (accessed 13 December 2022).

While there was an underlying risk of litigation posed by the right of publicity, this risk was arguably minimal until 2009 when the first claims were brought. Following the claims in *Keller* and *Hart*, the risk has materialised and is significant. This litigation has elevated the force of deterrence theory, making it as influential as the desire to collaborate. The developments in US case law were opposed by California lawyers, who felt that video games should be immunised from the right of publicity as First Amendment works. While the balancing exercise between the right of publicity and the use of persona in video games is still in its infancy, it is important to underscore the impact that the cases discussed in this chapter have had on the regulation of persona. They have not only strengthened the pre-existing behaviour of seeking permission, which developed in tandem with the reality sports video-game industry, they have also made video-game developers more cautious about defecting. In other words, video-game makers are likely to think twice before they make a game without securing a licence.

9

Conclusion

I. The Role of Law in Each Industry

The difference in legal regulation of persona in the US, in the form of the right of publicity, as compared to the UK's approach, which concentrates on passing off, has a greater impact on the dispute resolution sphere than the transactional sphere. In the dispute resolution sphere, the differences become apparent, as settlement and litigation are more likely to occur in the US under the strict-liability right of publicity as compared to the UK, where the deception-based tort of passing off has been successfully used to protect persona only since 2003. The false endorsement action under passing off is relatively young compared to the right of publicity, which has been in existence for 70 years at this point, but 20 years is still a long period of time during which actions could occur. Yet until *Fenty*,[1] the only other case in which false endorsement was recognised was *Irvine*.[2] This lack of case law in the UK can be attributed to the law itself, but also to the divergence in the legal systems. While both the US and UK operate a common law legal system, the UK, which operates under parliamentary sovereignty, is less likely to introduce a new right and would rather leave such development to the legislative ability of Parliament. The hesitancy to expand the law was made clear in both *Irvine* and *Fenty*, where the courts explicitly denied the existence of an 'image right'. In contrast, the US appears to have embraced the common law tradition very strongly, as the introduction of a tort of privacy was followed by the right of publicity, and subsequent developments have been complemented and/or codified by statutory intervention.

This final chapter looks at the role of law in each industry and considers the other influences on persona: the desire to collaborate via contract and social norms.

A. Deterrence

The deterrence theory was observed in both jurisdictions. There was a common observation that passing off could expand in the UK, and thus permission should

[1] *Fenty and others v Arcadia Group Brands Ltd (trading as Topshop) and another* [2013] EWHC 2310 (Ch).
[2] *Irvine and another v Talksport Ltd* [2002] EWHC 367 (Ch).

be sought before using persona in both the advertising and the merchandising industries. This observation is diametrically opposed to the numerous responses that suggested it is hard to bring a claim under passing off because of the strength of evidence required to succeed, and the unique circumstances of the *Fenty*[3] and *Irvine*[4] cases. Passing-off claims were mainly discussed in the advertising and merchandising industries. Passing off was seen as a tenuous cause of action for the movie and television industry, but one that nonetheless should be considered. For the sports video-game industry, the US right of publicity is a greater concern than passing off. Both the film and television industry and the sports video game industry operate on a global basis. Therefore, the law of the countries of distribution must be considered, which means the right of publicity and other US laws must be considered even if a product is made in the UK.

In the advertising industry, the deterrence theory in the UK only extended to situations where there was a likelihood of passing off. The possible expansion already mentioned is most relevant to the illustrative-style advertisements. While endorsement-style advertisements would often constitute a clear case of passing off, the illustrative-style advertisements occupy a grey area. On the one hand, they depict a celebrity using the product or service in question. On the other hand, they do not go so far as to suggest that the celebrity promotes the product or service. This means that there is a risk that the misrepresentation element might not be made out. As discussed in chapter 2, misrepresentation requires more than mere confusion, it requires deception. Since illustrative advertisements straddle the boundary between deception and mere confusion, lawyers generally advise against taking a risk. Permission is therefore usually sought. However, evocative and topical advertisements are made without permission in the UK. These types of advertisements are not generally made in the US, and should not be, as this would constitute an infringement of the right of publicity.

In the UK, the misrepresentation element of passing off is again the most relevant when considering evocative and topical advertisements. Due to the way in which these advertisements are made, there is little chance of a successful passing-off action because these advertisements only allude to celebrities, or even if they refer to them explicitly, they do so in relation to a current event. The Advertising Codes could be deployed against these styles of advertisements and have been,[5] but brands weigh the risk and run the advertisements for a short period of time. The consequence of this is that limiting persona protection in the UK to passing off as opposed to a right of publicity leaves room for freedom of expression to prevail in the form of evocative and topical advertisements. In contrast, commercial speech in the US, which receives lesser protection than

[3] *Fenty* [2013].
[4] *Irvine* [2002].
[5] See ch 2.

other categories of speech,[6] is generally trumped by the right of publicity if a celebrity is featured. It was made clear in early case law that identity could be broadly construed. Where there is no common law right, a plaintiff would be limited to the statutory protection of persona. In those instances, topical and evocative advertisements would only be permitted if they drew reference to the individual without use of a protected element of persona.

The advertising industry is the only industry where the difference in legal frameworks resulted in different behaviours. This is interesting, because the products made by the other industries are arguably less likely to be susceptible to passing-off claims. The law plays a role in encouraging permission to be sought, even though there is tenuous basis for strong passing-off claims, as expressed in chapter 4. However, it should also be noted that the advertising industry is more likely to be localised, as compared to the film and television industry and the sports video-game industry. These global industries must account for variances in persona protection to avoid litigation in any country of distribution. This globalisation is impactful, yet the merchandising industry, which is also likely to be localised, operates in the same way in both the US and UK.

An interviewee who worked in UK merchandising for over 35 years argued that *Fenty*[7] was an outlier, as permission is routinely sought from celebrities before featuring them.[8] This permission-based norm therefore pre-dated *Irvine*.[9] It is not clear when permission seeking became the norm, as the interviewee knew this to be established practice when he started working in the industry. However, it should be noted that this interviewee works for a body that is in the business of licensing. He noted that some unauthorised products are still made, particularly calendars. Other interviewees stated that permission is generally sought because retailers will want to know that the rights have been cleared. Arguably, there is a lower likelihood of a successful passing-off claim in the merchandising industry, because products can be made by using a photograph of the individual. It is only modern merchandising that actually requires collaboration for the product to be made. Yet retailers do not want any risk, and thus act in a similar manner to insurance agents in the film and television industry, who require waivers of rights to mitigate against litigation. Similar to the film and television insurance, which looks to a basket of rights, only one of which is the right of publicity, retailers will also want to ensure that copyright and trade-mark rights have been secured. Therefore, it is difficult to separate the risk of passing off in relation to the retailers.

[6] Shiner, R, *Freedom of Commercial Expression* (Oxford University Press 2007); Rothman, JE, 'Commercial Speech, Commercial Use, and the Intellectual Property Quagmire' (2015) 101 *Va L Rev* 1929; Garon, JM, 'Beyond the First Amendment: Shaping the Contours of Commercial Speech in Video Games, Virtual Worlds, and Social Media' (2012) 2012 *Utah L Rev* 607.

[7] *Fenty* [2013].

[8] UK interviewee 16.

[9] *Irvine* [2002].

While the retailers' need for clearance plays a part, the impact of *Fenty* was to solidify the already established practice of seeking permission. Interviewees felt that *Irvine* was a warning signal, but since it dealt with an advertisement, it was not directly related to merchandise. However, *Fenty* centred on a t-shirt. While the evidence in the case was unique, and the past relationship between Rihanna and Topshop was a focal point, interviewees generally thought that *Fenty* underscored that there is a realisable risk of litigation when creating unauthorised merchandise. This is despite the fact that it was an unlikely thought that the risk would result in a successful claim. Merchandisers rather avoid the risk than fight a case. However, it must be recalled that this deterrence is only relevant for traditional merchandisers, as modern merchandise that uses co-branding cannot be made without collaborating with the celebrity in any event. In addition, the creation of counterfeit merchandise is rife, indicating that the law has limits to its effectiveness.

The video-game industry is an interesting one, because while permission is often sought, the deterrence theory was operating with less force than in the two aforementioned industries given the existence of the games that featured college athletes without their permission.[10] While interviewees advised that a risk has always been present, the decision of EA, a major video-game developer, to produce the college-athlete games indicated that the risk was not considered as substantial as in the industries noted previously: EA could not legally enter into licences with the college athletes, due to the rules surrounding their amateur status and remuneration, but this does not mean that the risk of infringement of the right of publicity was not present. Arguably, the situation was unclear, as video games are protected as free speech. Hence, the courts used the transformative test for this expressive work.

Video-game developers may not have considered this risk to be significant before the NCAA litigation, and the motivation behind seeking permission could be due to the history of sports video games, which have always worked with athletes. The developments in technology necessitate collaboration for the best product. Yet it is worth noting that PES does not usually include athletes since it has not secured the licences. One reason for this could be because PES does not want to breach any exclusive licences with competitors. While this could be on the basis of social norms similar to those in the advertising industry, where exclusive deals are respected, there is a possibility that this action also indicates the recognition of a proprietary right that has been secured via the licence. Thus, using an athlete without permission would open the video-game developer not only to liability to the athlete, but also to liability to the exclusive licensee competitor.

[10] *Davis v Electronic Arts* 775 F 3d 1172 (2015); *In re NCAA Student-Athlete Name & Likeness Licensing Litigation* 724 F 3d 1268 (9th Cir Cal 2013); *Hart v Electronic Arts* 717 F 3d 141 (2013); *Keller v Electronic Arts* (not reported) 2010 WL 530108.

It is now clear that depicting an individual in a video game in the US will require permission in order to avoid infringement of the right of publicity. While there is no equivalent right in the UK, the global distribution of video games necessitates that this risk be accounted for. So far, all the industries examined have varying degrees of risk, which results in observation of the deterrence theory in mitigation practices. The film and television industry is an outlier compared to other industries, as neither the right of publicity nor passing off could be deployed against the portrayal of an individual. And yet the spate of right-of-publicity cases in the last decade may prompt studios to secure waivers of rights to avoid the hassle of groundless claims. This industry is the one that is most susceptible to the expansion of the law in the US courts. The progression of the *Porco* case,[11] with reference to *Messenger*,[12] opened the door to liability in New York where there has been 'substantial fictionalization'. While Lifetime ultimately succeeded in *Porco*, as did FX Networks in *De Havilland*,[13] the progression of these cases during the interview period had lawyers on high alert, and fearful that there could be more claims of this nature.

Even though the right of publicity has not succeeded against a film portrayal, there are also other causes of action that have to be accounted for. Defamation, where the information conveys damage to the reputation of the individual; breach of privacy, where information is revealed that would otherwise be considered private; and copyright infringement, if the proper licences are not acquired, all need to be mitigated against. Copyright infringement would be most relevant for biopics that feature bands or artistes, as use of the music would be necessary to tell the fullest story. Despite the higher standards that celebrities face in bringing defamation[14] and privacy claims,[15] interviewees reported that failure to get waivers of rights will result in more costly errors and omissions insurance policies. A parallel can be drawn here with the merchandising industry, where retailers in the UK prefer rights to be cleared even if there is little chance of a successful claim. Except that the right of publicity can definitely be deployed against a US retailer, and passing off, while more difficult, has arguably been bolstered by *Fenty*.[16] Unlike the UK merchandising industry, which has not been subjected to a barrage of claims of passing off, there has been a host of claims against movies in the US, despite the fact that movies are generally immunised against these claims under the First Amendment. The annoyance that these claims cause prompts permission to be sought if it is likely to be given, but this does not mean that movies will not be made if permission is not secured. Rather, mitigation tactics are deployed where they are likely to work. The global distribution of movies necessitates that

[11] *Porco v Lifetime Entertainment Services* 150 NYS 3d 380 (2021).
[12] *Messenger v Gruner and Jahr Printing and Publishing* 93 NY 2d 948 (1999).
[13] *De Havilland v FX Networks LLC* 21 Cal App 5th 845 (2018).
[14] *New York Times Co. v Sullivan* 84 SCt 710 (1964).
[15] *Carlisle v Fawcett Publications Inc* 201 Cal App 2d 733 (5th Dist 1962).
[16] *Fenty* [2013].

all potential causes of action be accounted for, even if the cause of action is less relevant in the UK than in the US. And apparently, even though the right of publicity should not impact movie production in the US, the presence of past claims spurs on risk-averse behaviour.

B. Persona as Property

The deterrence theory operates in both the US and the UK, but it is arguably stronger in the US due to the more expansive right of publicity. However, it is the perception of the law rather than the law itself that results in deterrence. In the US, there is a realistic chance of expansion, whereas the UK takes a more conservative approach, but the risk of litigation is still perceived as significant enough to avoid in many instances. Hence, the behaviours across jurisdictions were the same with the exceptional behaviours in the advertising industry. As will be discussed in section II and section III, though, the similarities in behaviours cannot just be attributed to the deterrence theory; the desire to collaborate and the presence of social norms have also resulted in these similarities. This is notwithstanding the divergence in the way interviewees in the US viewed persona as opposed to those in the UK. Despite the fact that not all US interviewees were cognisant of the proprietary nature of the right of publicity, which allows exclusive licensees to pursue litigation for infringement, nearly all interviewees felt that persona should be treated as property reflecting morality theory. The views on the limits of this property right differed, as some felt that exceptions should be made for video games and movies, but there was consensus that individuals should not be subject to commercialisation via advertising or merchandising without their authorisation. This book does not look at the theories for persona protection, but it seems that the Hegelian personality theory, and Locke's labour theory, could be mapped to the responses of interviewees. In contrast, incentive and reward theory had little traction. Allocative efficiency was evident in the response of only some interviewees.

In the US, where the right of publicity is proprietary, it is apparent that lawyers embrace the ability for individuals to be in control of commercialisation of their persona. In contrast, in the UK, where there is no equivalent proprietary right, lawyers were generally not in favour of introducing legislation that would give this level of control to an individual. One reason that can be deduced from the findings is that no additional protection is necessary because unauthorised use by reputable entities is rare, and unauthorised use by non-reputable entities is common regardless of the law. Therefore, the entities that individuals would be most keen to pursue legally are the ones least likely to use persona without authorisation. Another reason that can be advanced for this difference in views is the difference in the legal frameworks. The right of publicity in the US has been established and developed for over seven decades, which means that all lawyers interviewed were accustomed to it. In accordance with morality theory, law can inform what is considered as 'right' versus wrong. Hence, the mere existence of the law has coloured the views of US lawyers, whereas the hesitancy of UK courts to acknowledge such a right has informed the views of UK lawyers. This is why the morality theory of compliance with law was observed only in the US. Even though UK lawyers generally agreed with the outcome of *Fenty*,[17] there was nothing to suggest that this agreement was based on morality; rather, they agreed with the analysis of the fact-specific evidence assessed by the court.

C. Limits of the Law

Despite the strength of deterrence theory in both jurisdictions, and the addition of morality theory in the US, the law can only do so much. In the UK, the law is limited to its current form with a fear of expansion that is arguably unfounded. In the US, the law has been unconstrained in its development, which leads to a justified fear of expansion. But even with the expansive approach in the US, unauthorised use still occurs in the advertising and merchandising industries. There was unauthorised use in sports video games in the *NCAA* litigation, but this was exceptional and not reflective of the general practice whereby permission is sought from featured athletes. Arguably, the one area where the law requires limits is film and television production, to preserve freedom of speech/expression. However, as discussed in chapter 7, the right of publicity is just one right in a bundle of rights that need to be cleared for insurance purposes. While unfounded claims have proved an unnecessary hassle, such claims generally do not succeed. But insurance companies will still prefer a waiver of various rights, including the right of publicity, to avoid these claims altogether.

The fact that unauthorised use occurs in the US in the advertising and merchandising industries even when permission would clearly be required under the right of publicity, shows that the law can only do so much. The law is more likely to influence entities that have access to legal advice and are selling their products in mainstream market places, whether distributing to a store or via an online seller. In the UK, there are avenues of redress available for advertising under the Advertising Codes, despite the fact that interviewees did not find the Codes to be particularly useful due to their non-legal force and the absence of damages.

In battling unauthorised merchandise, celebrities are free to register their names as trade marks. In January 2023, Harry Styles filed a claim in the Chicago Federal Court against online sellers. But rather than targeting the individual counterfeiters, a strategy often futile according to interviewees, Styles had instead targeted market places:

> Online marketplace platforms such as eBay, AliExpress, Alibaba, Amazon, Wish, Walmart, Etsy, and DHgate shall disable and cease displaying any advertisements used

[17] ibid.

> by or associated with defendants in connection with the sale of counterfeit and infringing goods using the Harry Styles trademarks.[18]

It is acknowledged that a photograph is more likely to be used than just a name, so this is a lacuna in the law in the UK. Unauthorised merchandise is rife in both jurisdictions, but those in the US are more likely to have a valid claim under the right of publicity, despite the limited benefits of actually bringing a claim.

II. The Desire to Collaborate: Fans and Access

The influence of law on persona commercialisation is significant, but it is not the only reason why entities will seek permission to use persona. In fact, it is clear that this permission would be sought regardless of whether the law requires it, because of the reason that spurs on use of persona in the first place: appealing to the fans. Celebrities are commercialised to tap into their fan base and sell the fans products. While fans do buy fake merchandise, as indicated by the Harry Styles claim, reputable entities that want the benefit of the celebrity will pay for that benefit to capitalise on the existing para-social relationships. Additionally, changes in technology necessitate collaboration in order to achieve the best product.

A. Appealing to Fan Base

As noted by Hackley and Hackley, 'the economic uses of celebrity have been evident to marketers with a flair for communication ever since print enabled the picture-led story'.[19] The desire to collaborate with celebrities is evident across all the industries examined. Apart from the need to mitigate legal risk, working with a celebrity allows for access to materials and information that would not otherwise be possible. For the advertising industry, an endorsement by a celebrity would only be effective if fans think it is genuine. Endorsements can be photoshopped in the way the brochure was photoshopped with a picture of Eddie Irvine listening to TalkSport in *Irvine*,[20] but in the era of social media, endorsements are usually more advanced than this. Brands might want the celebrity to post on their accounts, pose with the product and make public appearances. It would be difficult to achieve the desired effect without collaborating with the celebrity. Therefore, even in the absence of legal risk, the potential gain from a celebrity

[18] *Harry Styles v The Partnerships and Unincorporated Associations Identified on Schedule A*, Case no 1:2022cv07117 (2022).

[19] Hackley, C and Hackley, RA, 'The iconicity of celebrity and the spiritual impulse' (2016) 19 *Consumption Markets & Culture* 269, 275.

[20] *Irvine* [2002].

in the advertising sphere spurs permission to be sought. Some recent endorsements include White Lotus stars Simona Tabasco and Beatrice Grannó for Skims' 2023 Valentine's Day campaign,[21] Emily Ratajkowski for Viktor & Rolf's Flowerbomb,[22] Jimin of BTS as a global brand ambassador for Dior,[23] and Rosé of BLACKPINK as the global brand ambassador for Tiffany & Co.[24] In addition to posing for photographs for the aforementioned endorsements, the celebrities have undertaken other activities, including modelling in videos, attending events for the brands and making public comments.

The power of celebrity endorsements has been recognised by both the FTC in the US[25] and the UK Advertising Standards Commission.[26] The FTC reaffirmed its position requiring disclosure of endorsement deals after the notorious Fyre Fest disaster of 2017. The festival was meant to take place in the Bahamas, but instead ended up being a calamitous event where attendees were left hungry, thirsty and without proper accommodation. Several popular celebrities had endorsed the festival, including Kendall Jenner, Hailey Bieber and Bella Hadid.[27] None of these celebrities disclosed that they had received payment. While the FTC did not take action, the endorsement guide, issued in 2009, states:

> When there exists a connection between the endorser and the seller of the advertised product that might materially affect the weight or credibility of the endorsement (ie, the connection is not reasonably expected by the audience), such connection must be fully disclosed.[28]

While compliance with the guides is voluntary, similar to the ASA Codes, the FTC can choose to take legal action under section 5 of the Federal Trade Commission Act, which prohibits unfair or deceptive acts or practices.[29] The more common

[21] Strater, Z, '"White Lotus" Actresses Beatrice Grannò and Simona Tabasco Star in SKIMS Valentine's Day Campaign' *People Magazine* (23 January 2023). SKIMS is owned by Kim Kardashian.

[22] Phillips, H, 'Emily Ratajkowski joins Viktor & Rolf as Face of Flowerbomb – Reveals her favourite scent on a man' *People Magazine* (18 January 2023).

[23] Richford, R, 'BTS' Park Jimin Steal the Show at Dior' *WWD* (20 January 2023).

[24] Tiffany & Co, 'Tiffany Collections' at www.tiffany.com/collections/ (accessed 26 January 2023).

[25] FTC, 'Disclosures 101 for Social Media Influences' *FTC* at www.ftc.gov/business-guidance/resources/disclosures-101-social-media-influencers (accessed 26 January 2023).

[26] ASA, 'Celebrities' (29 July 2017) at www.asa.org.uk/advice-online/celebrities.html (accessed 26 January 2023).

[27] 'Fyre Festival Failure and the Strength of Celebrity Endorsements' *Networks* (19 November 2019) at https://blogs.cornell.edu/info2040/2019/11/19/fyre-festival-failure-and-the-strength-of-celebrity-endorsements/#:~:text=The%20festival%20was%20endorsed%20by,being%20paid%20for%20their%20endorsements (accessed 24 January 2023).

[28] Federal Trade Commission 16 CFR pt 255, s 255.5: Guides Concerning the Use of Endorsements and Testimonials in Advertising at www.ftc.gov/sites/default/files/attachments/press-releases/ftc-publishes-final-guides-governing-endorsements-testimonials/091005revisedendorsementguides.pdf (accessed 23 January 2023).

[29] Federal Trade Commission Act of 1914; FTC, 'Federal Trade Commission Act Section 5: Unfair or Deception Acts or Practices' at www.federalreserve.gov/boarddocs/supmanual/cch/200806/ftca.pdf (accessed 24 January 2023).

course of action is to send a warning letter. The FTC has sued influencers only once, and this claim was settled.[30] More recently, the FTC has sued companies that use influencers, including Lord & Taylor in 2016[31] and Teami in 2020,[32] but continue the practice of sending warning letters to the influencers.[33]

In 2022, the FTC reached a settlement with Google for breach of 'truth in advertising' by hiring radio personalities to make on-air testimonials about Google phones without ever having used the phones, but no consequences were meeted out to the personalities.[34] The Securities Exchange Commission (SEC), however, sued Kim Kardashian in 2021 for failing to disclose an endorsement of a crypto-currency company. She included the #ad, but the SEC said this was insufficient to meet the requirements of the securities laws, which require the amount paid for the endorsement to also be disclosed.[35] The FTC called for comments in 2022 in order to update the endorsement guide, in light of 'increased knowledge of how consumers view endorsements'.[36]

In the UK, the ASA provided advice in 2017 on the issue of celebrity endorsements:

> However, if a celebrity is being paid to endorse a product on social media, it needs to be clear that the communication is an ad. Essentially, that means making it easy for the average consumer to be able to judge whether or not they are looking at an ad. If you're getting a celebrity to endorse your brand, then they too have to adhere to this rule.[37]

In 2012, a complaint was lodged against Nike when Wayne Rooney and Jack Wilshere posted statements on Twitter accompanied by links to Nike's website. The complaint, which was upheld, alleged that the posts were not 'obviously identifiable' as marketing communications. ASA ruled that the ads were to be removed.[38]

[30] FTC, 'CSGO Lotto Owners Settle FTC's First-Ever Complaint Against Individual Social Media Influencers' *FTC* (7 September 2012) at www.ftc.gov/news-events/news/press-releases/2017/09/csgo-lotto-owners-settle-ftcs-first-ever-complaint-against-individual-social-media-influencers (accessed 23 January 2023).

[31] FTC, 'Lord & Taylor Settles FTC Charges It Deceived Consumers Through Paid Article in an Online Fashion Magazine and Paid Instagram Posts by 50 "Fashion Influencers"' (15 March 2022) at www.ftc.gov/news-events/news/press-releases/2016/03/lord-taylor-settles-ftc-charges-it-deceived-consumers-through-paid-article-online-fashion-magazine (accessed 24 January 2023).

[32] Fair, L, 'FTC's Teami case: Spilling the tea about influencers and advertisers' *FTC* (6 March 2020) at www.ftc.gov/business-guidance/blog/2020/03/ftcs-teami-case-spilling-tea-about-influencers-and-advertisers (accessed 23 January 2023).

[33] ibid.

[34] *Google LLC and iHeart Midea, Inc*, FTC Matter/File Number: 2023092 (2022).

[35] SEC, 'SEC Charges Kim Kardashian for Unlawfully Touting Crypto Security' (3 October 2022) at www.sec.gov/news/press-release/2022-183 (accessed 23 January 2023).

[36] FTC, 'Guides Concerning the Use of Endorsements and Testimonials in Advertising: Federal Trade Commission 16 CFR pt 255' at www.ftc.gov/system/files/ftc_gov/pdf/P204500%20Guides%20Concerning%20Endors%20and%20Testimonials.pdf (accessed 24 January 2023).

[37] ASA (2017).

[38] ASA Adjudication on Nike (UK) (2012).

More recently, in 2022, ASA provided updated guidance as a result of ASA research on labelling influencing marketing,[39] conducted in 2019:

> In contrast to the posts on a brand's own social media page, when an influencer talks about a particular brand it isn't self-evident whether they are expressing an independent opinion or whether they have been incentivised to do so by the brand. This is why it's important for influencer ads to be clearly and obviously distinguished from other posts.[40]

The interventions by both the US FTC and the UK ASA make it clear that celebrities are being used in advertisements, and that fans are attracted to these advertisements. Therefore, regardless of the law, there is an obvious draw to celebrities for advertising, which has only increased in the age of social media marketing.

In contrast to advertising, the assessment of the role of fans is less clear-cut with regard to the merchandising industry, at least for traditional merchandising. It is apparent that fans will buy fake merchandising, so it is difficult to say that permission is sought for this reason. However, the desire to support a celebrity could lead a fan to choose an authorised product over an unauthorised one. The real pull in the merchandising industry, though, is evident in co-branded products. This type of product gained momentum in the late 2000s and is now a normal feature in high-street stores. Co-branded lines include Morphe Cosmetics and make-up influencer Abby Roberts,[41] Reebok and rapper Cardi B,[42] and Adidas and Ivy Park (owned by Beyoncé).[43] Crocs footwear is a perfect example, as the brand has had multiple celebrity co-branded collaborations, including Justin Bieber, Ruby Rose, Jimmy Kimmel, Luke Combs, Drew Barrymore and Sza.[44]

In the video-game industry, fans like to play as their favourite athletes. It is now clear that permission is legally required, but subsequent advertising will not be achieved without initial collaboration. The role of technology was arguably the most influential force until the legal requirement for seeking permission was clarified. As for movies, the situation is less clear. Fans will appreciate a biopic movie approved by the celebrity featured, but of greater relevance is the access to information and materials that can be used when making the film. It is the content that determines the movie's success. Therefore, appealing to fans does not require

[39] ASA, 'Labelling of influencer advertising' (5 September 2019) at www.asa.org.uk/resource/labelling-of-influencer-advertising.html (accessed 25 January 2023).

[40] ASA, 'Recognising ads: Social media and influencers marketing' (29 December 2022) at www.asa.org.uk/advice-online/recognising-ads-social-media.html (accessed 26 January 2023).

[41] 'Morphe x Gabby Roberts' at https://eu.morphe.com/collections/morphe-x-abby-roberts-the-artcasts (accessed 26 January 2023).

[42] 'Reebok x Cardi B' at www.reebok.com/us/cardi_b (accessed 26 January 2023).

[43] 'Adidas X Ivy Park Dreams of Ivytopia, A collection that inspires an escape to your personal nirvana this summer!' (8 July 2022) at https://news.adidas.com/originals/adidas-x-ivy-park-dreams-of-ivytopia--a-collection-that-inspires-an-escape-to-your-personal-nirvana-/s/72d05226-b86e-4e56-81e9-9b80ff3517df (accessed 26 January 2023).

[44] 'Crocs Collaborations' at www.crocs.com/collaborations.html (accessed 26 January 2023).

approval of the celebrity per se; but if a collaboration is entered into, the access granted will result in a more appealing production.

B. Collaboration Spurred by Technological Developments

The difference that technology has made in the way in which persona is commercialised is vast. Traditional print and television advertising and mass-produced merchandise still exist, but the increase in endorsements and co-branded products has necessitated collaboration with celebrities. Social media provides a platform for consuming celebrity products, but technology has not necessarily had a major impact on the products or advertisements themselves. Rather, it is the methods of sale that have changed due to technology, and, consequentially, the way in which advertisements and modern merchandise are made has changed to suit. According to *The Economist*, 'The proliferation of social media means there are many new ways of attracting consumers' eyeballs. Young shoppers never knew a world without smartphones.'[45]

An area in which technology has resulted in a change in the actual product is the video-game industry. The representation of players is much more realistic than the original games, which used rudimentary figures to depict athletes. Now, EA uses 3D scans of athletes' faces. Since athletes have hectic schedules, they employ a moveable rig that uses 17 cameras. 'By capturing the athlete's face from every angle, EA can digitise the face and use it as the foundation for its animators to create the face of the character in the video game.'[46] The athlete does, however, have to go to a set location for motion capture. Athletes are kitted out with motion sensors and recorded by 153 cameras to replicate the most realistic movements in the game.[47] Games can be made without this level of detail, and there are several unlicensed sports video games on the market.[48] However, even games with such details do not necessarily license every athlete featured on an individual basis. In fact, many footballers came forward in 2021 to say that they did not consent to FIFA's use of their name and likeness after it was revealed that David Beckham was paid $40 million to appear as an icon in the game.[49] The developer, EA Sports, responded that this issue was between the footballers and FIFPro, which had

[45] 'How the young spend their money' *The Economist* (16 January 2023).

[46] 'How EA quickly captures 3D scans of athletes' faces for its sports games' *Venture Beat* (20 Janaury 2019) at https://venturebeat.com/business/how-ea-quickly-captures-3d-scans-of-athletes-faces-for-its-sports-games/ (accessed 26 January 2023).

[47] ibid.

[48] Pursey, J, '10 Great Unlicensed Sports Games' *GameRant* (20 December 2020) at https://gamerant.com/sports-games-best-unlicensed/#super-stickman-golf-3 (accessed 26 January 2023).

[49] Stroud J, 'FIFA 21: 300 players back Zlatan Ibrahimovic in image rights feud v EA Sports, says Mino Raiola' *GiveMeSport* (27 November 2020) at www.givemesport.com/1622309-fifa-21-300-players-back-zlatan-ibrahimovic-in-image-rights-feud-v-ea-sports-says-mino-raiola (accessed 26 January 2023).

granted EA the relevant name and image licences.[50] Some of the footballers who made comments on social media had actually appeared in the marketing material for *FIFA 21 Global*,[51] which indicates that they knew they were in the game. Despite the controversies surrounding the depiction of players, it remains clear that the collaboration to make the best product has been a major factor. Now, the deterrence theory is likely to surpass this desire to collaborate, due to the confirmation of the need to secure a licence for the right of publicity.

In contrast to the aforementioned industries, the film industry is the one that has been least affected by technological developments. The platform to consume movies has changed to include streaming services, but movies themselves have not undergone any changes that alter the way in which celebrities are portrayed. So far, there are no technologically related advantages that necessitate working with a celebrity, but only time will tell whether the use of holograms might require working with the estate.[52] The introduction of the New York post-mortem right foresees this possibility and explicitly addresses digital replicas of celebrities.[53]

III. Social Norms: Less Than, More Than and Equal to the Law

Social norms were observed in the dispute resolution sphere, and in the transactional sphere in the advertising, merchandising and film industries. In all instances, social norms shared a relationship with the law, but to varying extents. Since brands work with celebrities to leverage the para-social relationships for advertising and merchandising, they hesitate to sue even if the celebrity is in breach. They do not want to face a backlash from fans, nor do they want to be perceived as negative to work with. Sending the right signal often involves pleasing the celebrity. This means not exercising legal entitlements in order to maintain a relationship.

Reflecting the law in the US is the practice of respecting exclusive advertising deals. Most interviewees were not aware that an exclusive licensee could litigate against a third party who infringes the right of publicity of the celebrity who is the exclusive licensor. And yet it was considered bad practice to undermine these deals, as brands should respect one another. The same sentiment was observed in

[50] Badenhausen, K, 'EA Sports Responds to Zlatan Ibrahimovic and Mino Raiola criticism of FIFA video game' *Forbes* (25 November 2020) at www.forbes.com/sites/kurtbadenhausen/2020/11/25/exclusive-ea-responds-to-zlatan-ibrahimovic-and-mino-raiola-criticism-on-fifa-video-game/?sh=1d1e44bc17b9 (accessed 26 January 2023).

[51] ibid.

[52] See generally Greer, C, 'International Personality Rights and Holographic Portrayals' (2017) 27 *Ind Int'l & Comp L Rev* 247; Jougleux, P and Synodinou, TE, 'Holograms and Intellectual Property Law: A Multidimensional Issue' (2016) 38(8) *EIPR* 492.

[53] New York Civil Code, s 50(f).

the UK, where passing off would be less clear-cut depending on how persona is used. Undermining such deals would be considered discourteous and would send a negative signal regarding the status of the brand.

Going beyond the law is the practice of 'life-story rights' deals. While it is difficult to separate the right of publicity from the other rights for which insurers require waivers, 'life-story rights' are often linked to the right of publicity. Getting a waiver for this right in particular goes beyond what is legally required, and is a point of frustration for lawyers who represent studios. Similarly, obtaining a licence for traditional merchandise in the UK, while impacted by the law, goes beyond what is likely to be required, but was generally accepted and not a point of contention. In fact, such licences were being obtained even before *Irvine*,[54] indicating the legal developments bolstered this existing social norm. Obtaining a licence is considered 'the proper' way of doing things and thus, in order to send the right signal, a licence would be needed regardless of legal requirements.

IV. Persona Commercialisation: A Web of Influential Factors

Analysing the legal framework in isolation cannot provide a full picture of industry practices. This book has revealed that the law is just one influence in persona commercialisation, and that the influences of social norms that are impacted by law to varying extents, and the desire to collaborate, spurred on by technological changes and the consumption of persona via social media, have resulted in distinct practices across various industries. It is difficult to isolate these influences because they all work in tandem, but it can be said that the desire to collaborate with celebrities to benefit from para-social relationships is the strongest driving factor for more modern products: endorsement advertisements, modern merchandise, sports video games and, in some instances, biopics. Outside of these categories, where the desire to collaborate is not as strong, for example, for traditional merchandising and illustrative advertisements, the law is the determining factor. This is an interesting observation, because the more recent products are arguably less impacted by the law, which is more fully developed than ever before.

Social norms also impact practices, as licences have been obtained for traditional merchandise even where the legal risk was arguably lower in the UK than it is presently. And in both jurisdictions, exclusive licensing deals in advertising are respected regardless of the law because it is considered improper to breach them. Yet the same cannot be said for the film industry, where multiple biopics may be

[54] *Irvine* [2002].

made of the same person regardless of any exclusive deals. This is regardless of the fact that deals are often sought out while not being legally required.

Where there is no risk of law, no desire to collaborate and no social norm, persona will be used without permission. However, even in the UK, with a more conservative approach to persona regulation, this only results in a narrow category of evocative and topical advertisements made by reputable advertisers. In the US, these are not made by reputable advertisers. But in both jurisdictions, the law is only effective against reputable entities anyway.

Even in the dispute resolution sphere, where the law arguably plays a more eminent role than in the transactional sphere, the desire to maintain a relationship and the role of social norms are evident. The presence of these factors stacks the advantage in the celebrity's favour as, if the celebrity breaches a contract, the contractor might hesitate to sue because it does not want to be negatively perceived by fans, or by other celebrities, fearing sanctions in the form of reputational harm. This is not to say that this never happens: Jay-Z was sued by Parlux for failing to promote a perfume bearing his name;[55] he counterclaimed for breach of contract. Both sides lost their claims. Sarah Jessica Parker settled out of court after being sued for breach of contract for failing to promote a collaborative jewellery line.[56] Kendall Jenner was sued for failing to appear for a photoshoot for an Italian fashion house.[57] These types of claims are most likely to be brought where the celebrity is central to the product in question and has blatantly failed to fulfil obligations relating to the sought-after value creation.

More often than not, disputes involving a celebrity breach will be handled out of court. But if the contractor is in breach, the celebrity is more inclined to sue. Such breaches on the part of the contractor do not appear to be common but they do occur. For example, Flo Rida was awarded $82.6 million in January 2023 for breach of an endorsement agreement with Celsius energy drinks. The company failed to transfer stock to him that was owed under the agreement. While both the contractor and the celebrity could sue for breach of contract, the social norms often dissuade contractors while empowering celebrities. Contractors could face sanctions if they send the signal that they are litigious, whereas celebrities do not seem to be adversely affected by sending the same signal.

The empirical analysis presented in this book concludes that law is just one influence in persona commercialisation. While it is the most relevant influence in the dispute resolution sphere, even then, social norms can be observed that

[55] Degregory, P, 'Jay-Z doesn't have to pay up in perfume company's $68M breach of contract suit' *New York Post* (10 November 2021).

[56] Associated Press, 'Jeweller, Sarah Jessica Parker settle breach-of-contract suit' *Page Six* (24 April 2019).

[57] Heller, C, 'Kendall Jenner Sued for $1.8 Million for Breach of Modelling Contract' *E News* (4 August 2021) at www.eonline.com/news/1296264/kendall-jenner-sued-for-s1-8-million-for-breach-of-modeling-contract (accessed 26 January 2023).

dictate the course of action taken. These norms are often influenced by the law in the relevant jurisdiction, hence the reserved approach in the UK as opposed to the litigious culture of the US. In the transactional sphere, the need to collaborate spurred on by developments in social media and technology, as well as social norms that inform fan reactions and future collaborations, all contribute to the industry practices.

BIBLIOGRAPHY

Books

Adler, J and Van der Broek, M, *Right of Publicity Claims in a Digital Age* (American Bar Association 39th Annual Forum on Franchising 2016)

Anon, *Understanding Media and Culture: An Introduction to Mass Communication* (University of Minnesota Libraries Publishing 2010)

Aplin, T, 'Commercialising Privacy and Privatising the Commercial: The Difficulties Arising from the Protection of Privacy via Breach of Confidence' in Kur, A et al (eds), *Intellectual Property, Unfair Competition and Publicity - Convergence and Development* (Edward Elgar 2014) 189–215

Atiyah, PS, *The Rise and Fall of Freedom of Contract* (Clarendon Press 1985)

Baillie, I, 'Merchandising: an historical survey' in Adams, J, Hickey, J and Tritton, G (eds), *Merchandising Intellectual Property* (Butterworths Law 1987) xxv–xxvii

Barbour, R and Schostak J, 'Interviewing and focus groups' in Somekh, B and Lewin, C (eds), *Research Methods in the Social Sciences* (SAGE Publications 2004) 41–48

Battersby, G and Grimes, C, *2016 Licensing Update* (Wolters Kluwer 2016)

Beverley-Smith, H, *Commercial Appropriation of Personality* (Cambridge University Press 2002)

Bingham, D, *Whose Lives Are They Anyway?* (Rutgers University Press 2010)

Black, G, *Publicity Rights and Image: Exploitation and Legal Control* (Hart Publishing 2011)

Blumstein, A, Cohen, J and Nagin, D, *Deterrence and Incapacitation: Estimating the Effects of Criminal Sanctions on Crime Rates* (National Academy of Sciences 1978)

Bowrey, K and Handler, M, *Law and Creativity in the Age of the Entertainment Franchise* (Cambridge University Press 2014)

Collins, H, *The Law of Contract* (4th edn, Cambridge University Press 2003)

Creswell, T, *Research Design: Qualitative, Quantitative and Mixed Methods Approaches* (4th edn, Sage 2014)

Custen, GF, *Bio/Pics: How Hollywood Constructed Public History* (Rutgers University Press 1992)

Dahl, S, *Social Media Marketing: Theories and Applications* (2nd edn, SAGE Publications 2018)

Ellickson, R, *Order without Law* (Harvard University Press 1994)

Escalas, JE and Bettman, J, 'Managing Brand Meaning through Celebrity Endorsement' in Macinnis, D and Park, CW (eds), *Brand Meaning Management* (Emerald Group Publishing Limited 2015) 29–52

Fried, C, *Contract as Promise: A Theory of Contractual Obligation* (Oxford University Press 2015)

Hesselink, MW and de Vries, GJP, *Principles of European Contract Law* (Kluwer 2001)

Ibbeston, D, *A Historical Introduction to the Law of Obligations* (Oxford University Press 2001)

Jones, M, Dugdale, A and Simpson, M (eds), *Clerk and Lindsell on Torts* (21st edn, Sweet & Maxwell 2016)

Kagan, R, 'On the Visibility of Income Tax Law Violations' in Roth, J and Scholz, J (eds), *Taxpayer Compliance*, vol 2 (University of Pennsylvania Press 1989) 76–125

Kent, S, *The Ultimate History of Video Games* (Prima Life 2001)

Kronman, A and Posner, R, *Economics of Contract Law* (Little Brown & Co Law & Business 1979)

Large, J, *Criminality, Consumption and the Counterfeiting of Fashion Items* (PhD Thesis, Leeds University 2011)

LexisNexis, *Encyclopaedia of Forms and Precedents, Entertainment and Media*, vol 15(3)(C), pt 2: 'Merchandising, Product Endorsement and Sponsorship' (LexisNexis 2015)

Lindey, A, *Lindey on Entertainment, Publishing and the Arts* (3rd edn, Thomson Reuters 2018)
Litman, J, *Digital Copyright* (2nd edn, Prometheus Books 2006)
May, T, *Social Research: Issues, methods and process* (Open University Press 2010)
McCarthy, T and Schechter, R, *Rights of Publicity and Privacy* (Thomson Reuters 2022)
Mellor, J et al, *Kerly's Law of Trade Marks and Trade Names* (16th edn, Sweet & Maxwell 2017)
NCAA, *2011–12 NCAA Division I Manual* (NCAA 2011)
Nichols, CA, *Nichols Cyclopedia of Legal Forms Annotated* (Thomson Reuters 2017)
Perot, E, 'Post-mortem rights of publicity – A comparison of New York and California' in Rosati, E and Bosher, H (eds), *Developments and Directions in Intellectual Property Law: 20 Years of the IPKat* (Oxford University Press 2023) 348–366
Ponser, E, *Economic Analysis of Law* (9th edn, Wolters Kluwer 1992)
——, *Law and Social Norms* (Harvard University Press 2000)
Rothman, J, *The Right of Publicity: Privacy Reimagined for a Public World* (Harvard University Press 2018)
Shiner, R, *Freedom of Commercial Expression* (Oxford University Press 2007)
Smith, S, *Contract Theory* (Oxford University Press 2004)
Sundara Rajan, MT, *Moral Rights: Principles, Practice and New Technology* (Oxford University Press 2011)
Tan, D, *The Commercial Appropriation of Fame: A Cultural Analysis of the Right of Publicity and Passing Off* (Cambridge University Press 2017)
Tuten, T, *Advertising 2.0 – Social Media Marketing in a Web 2.0 World* (Greenwood Publishing Group 2008)
Tyler, T, *Why People Obey the Law* (Princeton University Press 1990)
Wadlow, C, *The Law of Passing-Off: Unfair Competition by Misrepresentation* (Sweet & Maxwell 2016)
Raphael, J, 'Paul Walker: The Facts and the Fiction' in Lam, C, Raphael, J and Weber, M (eds), *Disassembling the Celebrity Figure: Credibility and the Incredible* (Brill Rodopi 2018) 149–170

Journal Articles

Adkins, BA, 'Crying out for Uniformity: Eliminating State Inconsistencies in Right of Publicity Protection through a Uniform Right of Publicity Act' (2009) 40 *Cumb L Rev* 499
Albrecht S et al, 'Recent Developments in Media, Privacy, and Defamation Law' (2011) 47 *Tort Trial & Ins Prac LJ* 359
Aplin, T, 'The Future of Breach of Confidence and the Protection of Privacy' (2007) 7 *Oxford U Commw LJ* 137
APS News, 'This Month in Physics History – October 1958: Physicist Invents First Video Game' (2008) 19(9) *APS News* 2
Ayres, I, 'Fair Driving: Gender and Race Discrimination in Retail Car Negotiations' (1991) 104 *Harv L Rev* 817
Bachman, R, Paternoster, R and Ward, S, 'The Rationality of Sexual Offending: Testing a Deterrence/Rational Choice Conception of Sexual Assault' (1992) 26 *Law & Socy Rev* 343
Bains, S, 'Personality rights: should the UK grant celebrities a proprietary right in their personality? Part 3' (2007) 18(7) *Ent L Rev* 237
——, 'Personality rights: should the UK grant celebrities a proprietary right in their personality? Part 2' (2007) 18(6) *Ent L Rev* 205
——, 'Personality rights: should the UK grant celebrities a proprietary right in their personality? Parts 1–3' (2007) 18(5) *Ent L Rev* 164
Baker, A, 'Sports Films, History, and Identity' (1998) 25(2) *Journal of Sport History* 217
Barajas, ADL, 'Personality rights in the United States and the United Kingdom – is Vanna too much? Is Irvine not enough?' (2009) 20 *Ent L Rev* 253

Barnett, R, 'A Consent Theory of Contract' (1986) 86 *Colum L Rev* 269
Baumer, D and Marschall, P, 'Wilful Breach of Contract for the Sale of Goods: Can the Bane of Business Be an Economic Bonanza?' (1992) 65 *Temp L Rev* 159
Beach, S, 'Fact & Fiction: Amending Right of Publicity Statutes to Include Life Story and Fictional Characters Rights' (2017) 42(1) *Seton Hall Legis J* 131
Beale, H and Dugdale, T, 'Contracts between businessmen: Planning and the use of contractual remedies' (1975) 2 *Brit J Law & Society* 45
Bellamore, T, 'Is Vanna White Really So Dangerous – An Empirical Assessment of the Impact of *White v Samsung Electronics* on Parody and Advertising' (2003) 11 *U Miami Bus L Rev* 53
Bendor, J and Swistak, P, 'The evolution of norms' (2001) 106(6) *Amer J Sociology* 1493
Benson, P, 'Contract as a Transfer of Ownership' (2007) 48 *Wm & Mary L Rev* 1673
Bernstein, L, 'The Questionable Empirical Basis of Article 2's Incorporation Strategy: A Preliminary Study' (1999) 66 *U Chi L Rev* 710
——, 'Merchant Law in a Merchant Court – Rethinking the Code's Search for Immanent Business Norms' (1996) 144 *U Pa L Rev* 1765
——, 'Opting out of the legal system – Extralegal Contractual Relations in the Diamond Industry' (1992) 21 *J Legal Stud* 115
Bix, B, 'The Promise and Problems of Universal, General Theories of Contract Law' (2017) 30 *Ratio Juris* 395
Blackshaw, I, 'Protecting Sports Image Rights in Europe' (2005) 6 *Bus L Intl* 270
Blanke, JM, 'No Doubt about It – You've got to Have Hart: Simulation Video Games May Redefine the Balance between and among the Right of Publicity, the First Amendment, and Copyright Law' (2013) 19 *BU J Sci & Tech L* 26
Bowal, P and Kirsch, A, 'The World's Legal Systems' (2010–2011) 35 *LawNow* 23
Boyd, S, 'Does English law recognise the concept of an image or personality right?' (2001) 13 *Ent L Rev* 1
Boyd, S, 'Image wrongs: Causes of action for misappropriation – Part 2' (2006) 14 *SATLJ* 4
Buccafusco, C and Masur, J, 'Innovation and Incarceration: An Economic Analysis of Criminal Intellectual Property Law' (2014) 87 *Southern California L Rev* 275
Buccafusco, CJ, 'On the legal consequences of sauces: Should Thomas Keller's Recipe be per se copyrightable?' (2006) 24 *Cardozo Arts & Ent LJ* 1121
Burke, J, 'Contract as a Commodity: A Nonfiction Approach' (2000) 285 *Seton Hall Legis J* 291
Burleson, K, 'Learning from Copyright's Failure to Build Its Future' (2014) 89 *Ind LJ* 1299
Byrne, A, Whitehead, M and Breen, S, 'The baked truth of celebrity endorsement' (2003) 105 (4/5) *British Food Journal* 288
Carlson, J, 'Recycling Norms' (2001) 89 *Cal L Rev* 1231
Carroll, B, 'Celebrity Adjudication: Comparative Analysis of United States Verdict Rates for Celebrity Defendants' (2013) 11 *ESLJ* 1
Carty H, 'Advertising, publicity rights and English law' (2004) 3 *IPQ* 209
Catanzariti, T, 'Swimmers, surfers and Sue Smith – personality rights in Australia' (2002) 13 *Ent L Rev* 135
Choi, S and Rifon, N, 'Who is the Celebrity in Advertising? Understanding Dimensions of Celebrity Images' (2007) 40(2) *The Journal of Popular Culture* 304
Cohen, M, 'The Basis of Contract' (1933) 46 *Harv L Rev* 553
Contreras, J and Fagundes, D, 'Solving the Life Story Puzzle: Docudramas, Modularity and Hollywood Private Order' (2023) 14(2) *Harv J Sports & Ent L* (forthcoming)
Coombe, RJ, 'Author/izing the Celebrity: Publicity Rights, Postmodern Politics, and Unauthorized Genders' (1991) 10 *Cardozo Arts & Ent LJ* 365
Cooter R, 'Three Effects of Social Norms on Law: Expression, Deterrence and Internalization' (2000) 79 *Or L Rev* 1
——, 'Expressive Law and Economics' (1998) 27 *J Leg Stud* 585
Czarnota, P, 'The right of publicity in New York and California: A critical analysis' (2012) 19 *Jeffrey S Moorad Sports LJ* 481

Davies, G, 'Celebrity and Trade Marks: The Next Instalment' (2004) 1 *SCRIPTed* 230
Davis, J, 'Why the United Kingdom should have a law against misappropriation' (2010) 69 *Cambridge LJ* 561
Deazley, R, 'Introducing Publicity Rights – Breach of Confidence, the Photograph and Commodifying the Image' (2003) 54 *NILQ* 99
Dogan, S and Lemley, M, 'What the right of publicity can learn from trade mark law' (2006) 58 *Stan L Rev* 1161
Druzin, B, 'Law, Selfishness, and Signals: An Expansion of Posner's Signalling Theory of Social Norms' (2011) 24 *Can J L & Jurisprudence* 5
Eagle, L and Dahl, S, 'Product Placement in Old and New Media: Examining the Evidence for Concern' (2018) 147 *Journal of Business Ethics* 605
Epstein, L, 'Unconscionability: A Critical Reappraisal' (1975) 18 *J Law & Econ* 293
Fagundes, D, 'Talk Derby to me: Emergent intellectual property norms governing roller derby pseudonyms' (2010) 90 *Texas L Rev* 1093
Farber, D and Mattheson, J, 'Beyond Promissory Estoppel: Contract Law and the "Invisible Handshake"' (1985) 52 *Chi L Rev* 903
Fauchart, E and von Hippel, E, 'Norms-Based Intellectual Property Systems: The case of French chefs' (2008) 19 *Organization Science* 187
Feinman, J, 'The Significance of Contract Theory' (1989) 58 *U Cin L Rev* 1283
Feldman, Y, 'The development and enforcement of group norms' (1984) 9(1) *Acad Manangement Rev* 47
Fernando, O, 'Conceptual Differences between the Civil Law System and the Common Law System' (1990) 19 *Sw U L Rev* 1161
Fletcher, S et al, 'Court of Appeal found no love for Topshop tank: the image right that dare not speak its name' (2015) 37 *EIPR* 394
Ford, JB, 'What Do We Know About Celebrity Endorsement in Advertising?' (2018) 58 *Journal of Advertising Research* 1
Fuller, L and Perdue, W, 'The Reliance Interest on Contract Damages' (1936) 46 *Yale LJ* 52
Gallagher, W, 'Trade Mark and Copyright Enforcement in the Shadow of IP Law' (2011) 28 *Santa Clara Computer & High Tech LJ* 453
Garbharran, A and Thatcher, A, 'A Case for Using a Social Cognitive Model to Explain Intention to Pirate Software' (2009) 7 *eHealth Tech & Application* 87
Garon, JM, 'Beyond the First Amendment: Shaping the Contours of Commercial Speech in Video Games, Virtual Worlds, and Social Media' (2012) 2012 *Utah L Rev* 607
Gibbs, JP, 'Norms: The problem of definition and classification' (1965) 70(5) *Amer J Sociol* 586
Gibson, J, 'Risk Aversion and Rights Accretion in Intellectual Property Law' (2007) 116 *Yale LJ* 882
Goodenough, OR, 'Retheorising privacy and publicity' (1997) 1 *IPQ* 37
Grady, M, 'A positive economic theory of the right of publicity' (1994) 1 *UCLA Ent L Rev* 97
Grasmick, H and Bursik, R, 'Significant Others, and Rational Choice: Extending the Deterrence Model' (1990) 24 *Law & Soc Rev* 837
Grasmick, H and Green, D, 'Legal Punishment, Social Disapproval and Internalization as Inhibitors of Illegal Behaviour' (1980) 71 *Crim L & Criminology* 325
Greenberg, M and Lovitz, M, 'Right of Publicity and the intersection of copyright and trade mark law' (2012) *GGU Law Digital Commons*, Paper No 484
Greer, C, 'International Personality Rights and Holographic Portrayals' (2017) 27 *Ind Int'l & Comp L Rev* 247
Jougleux, P, Synodinou, TE, 'Holograms and Intellectual Property Law: A Multidimensional Issue' (2016) 38(8) *EIPR* 492
Grinvald, L, 'Policing the Cease-and-Desist Letter' (2015) 49 *Usf L Rev* 409
——, 'Shaming Trademark Bullies' (2011) 90 *Wis L Rev* 625
Hackley, C and Hackley, RA, 'The iconicity of celebrity and the spiritual impulse' (2016) 19 *Consumption Markets & Culture* 269
Halpern, S, 'Right of Publicity: Maturation of an Independent Right Protecting the Associative Value of Personality' (1994) 46 *Hastings LJ* 853

Hansen, R, 'Voting Without Law?' (1996) 144 *U Pa L Rev* 2135
Hillman R, 'The Unfulfilled Promise of Promissory Estoppel in the Employment Setting' (1999) 31 *Rutgers LJ* 1
——, 'Questioning the 'New Consensus' on Promissory Estoppel: An Empirical and Theoretical Study' (1998) 98 *Colum L Rev* 680
Horton, D and Richard Wohl, R, 'Mass Communication and Para-Social Interaction' (1956) 19 *Psychiatry* 215
Hortwitz, E and Levi, B, 'Fifty Years of the Lanham Act: A Retrospective of Section 43(a)' (1996) 7(1) *Fordham Intell Prop Media & Ent LJ* 58
Hsieh, H-F and Shannon, S, 'Three approaches to qualitative content analysis' (2005) 15(9) *Qualitative Health Research* 1277
Hylton, J, 'Baseball cards and the birth of the right of publicity: The curious case of Haelan Laboratories v Topps Chewing Gum' (2001) 12(1) *Marq Sports L Rev* 273
Jackson, J et al, 'Why do People Comply with the Law?: Legitimacy and the Influence of Legal Institutions' (2012) 52 *The British Journal of Criminology* 1051
Jensen, C, 'The More Things Change, the More They Stay the Same: Copyright, Digital Technology, and Social Norms Note' (2003) 56 *Stan L Rev* 531
Johnston, J, 'The Statute of Frauds and Business Norms: A Testable Game-Theoretic Model' (1996) 144 *U Pa L Rev* 1859
Jones, W, 'A Theory of Social Norms' (1994) *U Ill L Rev* 545
Kahan, M and Klausner, M, 'Antitakeover Provisions in Bonds: Bondholder Protection or Management Entrenchment?' (1993) 40 *UCLA L Rev* 931
Kahan, M and Klausner, M, 'Standardization and Innovation in Corporate Contracting' (1997) 83 *Va L Rev* 713
Kaikati, JG, 'Celebrity Advertising – A Review and Synthesis' (1987) 6 *International Journal of Advertising* 93
Karrh, JA, McKee, KB and Pardun, CJ, 'Practitioners' Evolving Views on Product Placement Effectiveness' (2003) 43 *Journal of Advertising Research* 138
Keating, D, 'Exploring the Battle of the Forms in Action' (2000) 98 *Mich L Rev* 2678
——, 'Measuring Sales Law Against Sales Practice: A Reality Check' (1997) 17 *JL & Com* 99
Keel, A, Nataraajan R, 'Celebrity Endorsements and Beyond: New Avenues for Celebrity Branding' (2012) 29(9) *Psychology and Marketing* 690
Kim, P, 'Bargaining with Imperfect Information: A Study of Worker Perceptions of Legal Protection in an At-Will World' (1997) 83 *Cornell L Rev* 105
Klink, J, '50 years of publicity rights in the United States and the never-ending hassle with intellectual property and personality rights in Europe' (2003) 4 *IPQ* 363
Kiser, J, 'To Bully or Not to Bully: Understanding the Role of Uncertainty in Trademark Enforcement Decisions' (2013) 37(1) *Col J Law and Arts* 211
Knittel, CR and Stango, V, 'Celebrity Endorsements, Firm Value, and Reputation Risk: Evidence from the Tiger Woods Scandal' (2014) 60 *Management Science* 21
Korobkin R, 'Empirical Scholarship in Contract Law: Possibilities and Pitfalls' [2002] *U Ill L Rev* 1033
——, 'The Status Quo Bias and Contract Default Rules' (1998) 83 *Cornell L Rev* 608
——, 'Inertia and Preference in Contract Negotiation: The Psychological Power of Default Rules and Form Terms' (1998) 51 *Vand L Rev* 1583
Kwall, R, 'Fame' (1997) 73 *Ind LJ* 1
La Belle, M, 'Against Settlement of (Some) Patent Cases (2014) 67 *Vand L Rev* 375
Landes, W, 'An Empirical Analysis of Intellectual Property Litigation: Some Preliminary Results' (2004) 41 *Hous L Rev* 749
Lapter, A and McKenna, M, 'How the Other Half Lives (Revisited): Twenty Years Since Midler v Ford – A Global Perspective on the Right of Publicity' (2006) 15 *Tex Intell Prop LJ* 239
Large, J, 'Get real, don't buy fakes' (2015) 15(2) *Criminology & Criminal Justice* 169
Large J and Wall D, 'Jailhouse Frocks' (2010) 50 *British Journal of Criminology* 1094
Leaffer, M, 'The Right of Publicity: A Comparative Perspective' (2006-2007) 70 *Alb L Rev* 1357

Lee, M, 'Agents of Chaos: Judicial Confusion in Defining the Right of Publicity-Free Speech Interface' (2003) 23 *Loy LA Ent L Rev* 471
Lee, Y, 'Putting a face to the game: the intellectual property implications of using celebrity likenesses in videogames.' (2018) 13(2) *JIPLP* 143
Lemley, M, 'Privacy, Property, and Publicity' (2019) 117 *Mich L Rev* 1153
——, 'Fame, Parody, and Policing in Trademark Law' (2019) 1 *Mich St L Rev* 1
Lentzner, M, 'My Life, My Story, Right – Fashioning Life Story Rights in the Motion Picture Industry' (1989) 12 *Hastings Comm & Ent LJ* 627
Levitt, S, 'The Effect of the Prison Population Size on Crime Rates: Evidence from Prison Overcrowding Litigation' (1996) 111 *Quarterly Journal of Economics* 319
Litman, J, 'The Exclusive Right to Read' (1994) 13 *Cardoza Arts & Ent LR* 29
Loughlan, P, 'You Wouldn't Steal A Car … Intellectual Property and the Language of Theft' (2008) Legal Studies Research Paper No 08/35 at http://ssrn.com/abstract=1120585
Lueck, JA, 'Friend-zone with benefits: The parasocial advertising of Kim Kardashian' (2015) 21 *J of Marketing Comm* 91
Lunceford, B and Lunceford, S, 'Meh. The Irrelevance of Copyright in the Public Mind' (2008) 7 *Nw J Tech & Intell Prop* 33
Macaulay, S, 'An Empirical View of Contract' (1985) 3 *Wis L Rev* 465
——, 'Non-Contractual Relations in Business – A Preliminary Study' (1963) 28 *Am Soc Rev* 55
MacNeil IR, 'Relational Contract Theory: Challenges and Queries' (1999) 94 *NW U L Rev* 877
——, 'Contracts: Adjustment of Long-Term Economic Relations under Classical, Neoclassical, and Relational Contract Law' (1977) 72 *Nw U L Rev* 854
Madow, M, 'Private Ownership of Public Image: Popular Culture and Publicity Rights' (1993) 81 *Cal L Rev* 125
Manesh, M, 'The Immorality of Theft, the Amorality of Infringement' [2006] *Stan Tech L Rev* 5
Manta, I, 'Bearing Down on Trademark Bullies' (2012) 22 *Fordham Intell Prop Media & Ent LJ* 853
McAdams, R, 'An Attitudinal Theory of Expressive Law' (2000) 79 *Oregon L Rev* 339
——, 'Signaling Discount Rates: Law, Norms, and Economic Methodology Book Review' (2000) 110 *Yale LJ* 625
McCarthy, JT, 'The Human Persona as Commercial Property: The Right of Publicity' (1994) 19 *Colum VLA JL & Arts* 129
McChesney, F, 'Tortious Interference with Contract Versus "Efficient" Breach: Theory and Empirical Evidence' (1999) 28 *J Leg Stud* 131
McGeveran, W, 'The Imaginary Trademark Parody Crisis (and the Real One)' (2015) 90(2) *Washington L Rev* 713
Mcghee, T, 'The rise and rise of athlete brand endorsements' (2012) 1(1) *J of Brand Strategy* 79
McKenna, M, 'The right of publicity and autonomous self-definition' (2005) 67 *U Pitt L Rev* 225
Meares, TL, 'Signalling, Legitimacy, and Compliance: A Comment on Posner's Law and Social Norms and Criminal Law Policy Commentary' (2002) 36 *U Rich L Rev* 407
Mnookin, RH and Kornhauser, L, 'Bargaining in the Shadow of the Law: The Case of Divorce' (1979) 88 *Yale LJ* 950
Morgan, J, 'Privacy, Confidence and Horizontal Effect: Hello Trouble' (2003) 62 *Cambridge LJ* 444
Murray, J, 'Contract Theories and the Rise of Neoformalism' (2002) 71 *Fordham L Rev* 869
Nadler, J, 'Flouting the Law' (2005) 83 *Texas L Rev* 1399
Nagin, D and Paternoster, R, 'The preventive effects of the perceived risk of arrest: testing an expanded conception of deterrence' (1991) 29 *Criminology* 561
Nagin, D, 'Criminal Deterrence Research at the Outset of the Twenty-First Century' (1998) 23 *Crime and Justice: A Review of Research* 1
Ng, C, 'The law of passing off – goodwill beyond goods' (2016) 47(7) *IIC* 817
Nimmer, M, 'The Right of Publicity' (1954) 19 *Law & Contemp Probs* 203
O'Flynn, T, 'File Sharing: An Holistic Approach To The Problem' (2006) 17 *Ent L Rev* 218
Oliar, D and Sprigman, C, 'There's no free laugh (anymore): The emergence of intellectual property norms and the transformation of stand-up comedy' (2008) 94(8) *Virginia L Rev* 1789

Paternoster, R, 'The Deterrent Effect of Perceived Certainty and Severity of Punishment: A Review of the Evidence and Issues' (1987) 4 *Just Q* 173
Paternoster, R and Simpson, S, 'Sanction Threats and Appeals to Morality: Testing a Rational Choice Theory of Corporate Crime' (1997) 30 *Law & Society Rev* 549
Petire, N, 'Reforming the Remedy: Getting the Right Remedial Structure to Protect Personal Privacy' (2012) 17 *Deakin L Rev* 121
Phillips, J and Coleman, A, 'Passing off and the common field of activity' (1985) 101 *LQR* 242
Port, K, 'Trademark Extortion: The End of Trademark Law' (2008) 65 *Wash & Lee L Rev* 585
Porter, H, 'Character merchandising: does English law recognise a property right in name and likeness?' (1999) 10 *Ent L Rev* 180
Posner E, 'Law and Social Norms: The Case of Tax Compliance' (2000) 86(8) *Va L Rev* 1781
——, 'Symbols, Signals and Social Norms' (1998) 27 *J Legal Stud* 765
——, 'Standards, Rules and Social Norms' (1997) 21 *Harv J L & Pub Pol'y* 101
——, ' The Right of Privacy' (1978) 393 *GA L Rev* 411
Prosser, W, 'Privacy' (1960) 48 *Cal L Rev* 383
Rachlinski, JJ, 'The Limits of Social Norms Symposium on Law' (1998) 74 *Chi-Kent L Rev* 1537
Robin, A, 'Copyright Infringement and the Internet: An Economic Analysis of Crime' (2005) 11 *BU J of Science & Tech Law* 256
Robinson, P and Darley, J, 'Does Criminal Law Deter? A Behavioural Science Investigation' (2004) 24 *OJLS* 173
Rothman, J, 'The Questionable Use of Custom in Intellectual Property Law' (2007) 93 *Virginia L Rev* 1899
Rothman, JE, 'Commercial Speech, Commercial Use, and the Intellectual Property Quagmire' (2015) 101 *Va L Rev* 1929
Sampson, R and Cohen, J, 'Deterrent Effects of Police on Crime: A Replication and Theoretical Extension' (1998) 22 *Law & Socy Rev* 163
Schultz, M, 'What jambands can teach us about persuading people to obey copyright law' (2006) 21 *Berkeley Tech LJ* 651
Schwab, S, 'A Coasean Experiment on Contract Presumptions' (1988) 17 *J Leg Stud* 237
Scott, J, 'Empirical studies strike back against the force of contract theory' (1997) 4 *UCL Jurisprudence Rev* 256
Seng, M, 'Aspects of the Common Law System in the United States' (2001) 2 *Common L Rev* 6
Sherman, L, 'Police Crackdowns: Initial and Residual Deterrence' (1990) 12 *Crime and Justice* 1
Shipley, D, 'Publicity never dies; it just fades away: The right of publicity and federal pre-emption' (1981) 66 *Cornell L Rev* 673
Simensky, M and Osterberg, E, 'Insurance and Management of Intellectual Property Risks' (1999) 17(2) *Cardozo Arts & Ent LJ* 321
Sims, A, 'Right of Publicity: Survivability Reconsidered' (1981) 49 *Fordham L Rev* 453
Stallard, H, 'The Right of Publicity in the United Kingdom' (1997) 18 *Loy LA Ent LJ* 565
Sugden, P, 'The Power of One! The failure of criminal copyright laws (piracy) to blend into greater cultural consciousness' (2014) 26 *EIPR* 367
Tan, D, 'Fame Monster Reloaded: The Contemporary Celebrity, Cultural Studies and Passing Off' (2010) 32 *Sydney L Rev* 291
——, 'Much Ado about Evocation: A Cultural Analysis of Well-Knownness and the Right of Publicity' (2010) 28 *Cardozo Arts & Ent LJ* 317
Trimble, M, 'Setting Foot on Enemy Ground: Cease and Desist Letters, DMCA Notifications and Personal Jurisdiction in Declaratory Judgment Actions' (2010) 50 *IDEA* 777
Tushnet R, 'Registering Disagreement: Registration in Modern American Trademark Law' (2017) 130 *Harv L Rev* 867
——, 'Raising Walls against Overlapping Rights: Pre-emption and the Right of Publicity' (2016) 92 *Notre Dame L Rev* 1539
——, 'A Mask That Eats into the Face: Images and the Right of Publicity' (2014) 38 *Colum JL & Arts* 157
Tyler T, 'Psychological Perspectives on Legitimacy and Legitimation' (2006) 57 *Annual Rev of Psychology* 375

——, 'Procedural fairness and compliance with the law' (1997) 133 Swiss Journal of Economics and Statistics 219

Tyler, T and Darley, J, 'Taking Public Views about Morality and the Legitimacy of Legal Authorities into Account when Formulating Substantive Law' (2000) 28 *Hofstra L Rev* 707

Tzoumaka, E, Tsiotsou, R and Siomkos, G, 'Delineating the role of endorser's perceived qualities and consumer characteristic in celebrity endorsement effectiveness' (2014) 22(3) *Journal of Marketing Communications* 307

Verkerke, J, 'An Empirical Perspective on Indefinite Term Employment Contracts: Resolving the Just Cause Debate' (1995) 4 *Wis L Rev* 838

Walsh, C, 'Are personality rights finally on the UK agenda?' (2013) 35 *EIPR* 253

——, 'The justifications underlying personality rights' (2012) 24 *Ent LR* 17

Wander, P, 'First Amendment supports uncensored fictionalised stories about celebrities: De Havilland v FX Networks LLC' (2018) 29(8) *Ent L Rev* 25

Wang, S and Liu, MT, 'Celebrity endorsement in marketing from 1960 to 2021: a bibliometric review and future agenda' (2022) 11(8) *Asia Pacific Journal of Marketing and Logistics* 342

Warren, S and Brandeis, D, 'Right to Privacy' (1890) 4 *Harv L Rev* 193

Wei, G, 'Effectively Protecting Private Facts – Privacy and Confidentiality' (2012) 24 *Sac LJ* 223

Weintraub, R, 'A Survey of Contract Practice and Policy' (1992) 1 *Wis L Rev* 1

Welkowitz, D and Ochoa, T, 'The Terminator as Eraser: How Arnold Schwarzenegger Used the Right of Publicity to Terminate Non-Defamatory Political Speech' (2005) 45 *Santa Clara L Rev* 651

West, M, 'Legal Rules and Social Norms in Japan's Secret World of Sumo' (1997) 26 *J Leg Stud* 165

White, J, 'Promise Fulfilled and Principle Betrayed' (1988) 1 *Ann Surv Am L* 7

Whitmore, P, 'A Statistical Analysis of Noncompetition Clauses in Employment Contracts' (1990) 15 *J Corp L* 483

Williams, K and Hawkins, R, 'Perceptual Research on General Deterrence: A Critical Review' (1986) 20 *Law & Socy Rev* 545

Winterich, KP, Gangwar, M and Grewal, R, 'When Celebrities Count: Power Distance Beliefs and Celebrity Endorsements' (2018) 82(3) *Journal of Marketing* 70

Witzleb, N, 'Monetary Remedies for Breach of Confidence in Privacy Cases' (2007) 27 *Legal Studies* 430

Young, P, 'The Evolution of Social Norms' (2014) 7 *Annual Review of Economics* 359

Zerehi, S, 'Valuating a Celebrity's Right of Publicity for Estate Tax Purposes' (2017) 8 *Harv J Sports & Ent L* 125

Zimmerman, D, 'False Light Invasion of Privacy: The Light that Failed' (1989) 64 *NYU L Rev* 364

Newspaper Articles

'$60 Million Settlement Approved in NCAA Video Game Lawsuit' *New York Times* (17 July 2015)

'Eddie Irvine wins £25,000 damages in TalkSPORT appeal' *Campaign* (1 April 2003) at www.campaignlive.co.uk/article/eddie-irvine-wins-25000-damages-talksport appeal/175837?src_site=brandrepublic (accessed 23 July 2017)

'How the young spend their money' *The Economist* (16 January 2023)

'Paddy Power's 10 most controversial adverts' *The Telegraph* (29 August 2012)

'Pop star Rihanna wins image battle' *BBC* (22 January 2015) at www.bbc.co.uk/news/entertainment-arts-30932158 (accessed 13 May 2016)

'Rihanna wins legal battle with Topshop over T-shirt' *The Telegraph* (22 January 2015) at www.telegraph.co.uk/news/celebritynews/11362116/Rihanna-wins-legal-battle-with-Topshop-over-T-shirt.html (accessed 1 February 2017)

'Sarah Jessica Parker sued for not promoting jewellery label' *Harper's Bazaar* (26 April 2018)

'Virtual Reality in Sports' *Sports Business Journal* (24 August 2017) at www.sportsbusinessjournal.com/Daily/Issues/2017/08/24/Technology/virtual-reality-sports.aspx (accessed 3 October 2018)

Associated Press, 'Jeweller, Sarah Jessica Parker settle breach-of-contract suit' *Page Six* (24 April 2019)
Badenhausen, K, 'EA Sports Responds to Zlatan Ibrahimovic and Mino Raiola criticism of FIFA video game' *Forbes* (25 November 2020) at www.forbes.com/sites/kurtbadenhausen/2020/11/25/exclusive-ea-responds-to-zlatan-ibrahimovic-and-mino-raiola-criticism-on-fifa-video-game/?sh=1d1e44bc17b9 (accessed 26 January 2023)
Baird, D, 'Paddy Power's Oscar Pistorius ad named most complained-about of 2014' *The Guardian* (20 February 2015)
Bolton, P, 'Specsavers say sorry to Kevin Pietersen for Hot Spot row' *The Telegraph* (2 October 2013)
Bowcott, O, 'Rihanna wins Topshop T-shirt row' *The Guardian* (22 January 2015) at www.theguardian.com/music/2015/jan/22/rihanna-topshop-tshirt-court (accessed 15 November 2017)
Brescia, J, 'For Pro Athletes, Practice That's All in the Thumbs' *New York Times* (2 April 2010)
Camenkar, J, 'Serena Williams 2022: Net Worth, Salary and Endorsements' *Essentially Sports* (2 September 2022) at www.essentiallysports.com/tag/serena-williams/ (accessed 16 January 2023)
Cozens, C, 'MacKenzie's TalkSport loses £275,000 to Irvine' *The Guardian* (2 April 2003) at www.theguardian.com/media/2003/apr/02/radio.business (accessed 17 October 2016)
Davidson, N, 'Behind the scenes, worldwide licensing team works on FIFA soccer video game' *City News* (7 October 2013) at https://toronto.citynews.ca/2013/10/07/behind-the-scenes-worldwide-licensing-team-works-on-fifa-soccer-video-game/ (accessed 3 October 2018)
Davies, A, 'Formula one ace wins high court battle over 'doctored' ad' *The Guardian* (13 March 2022) at www.theguardian.com/media/2002/mar/13/advertising.formulaone (accessed 10 October 2017)
Day J, 'Beckham asks for EasyJet donation' *The Guardian* (28 August 2003) at www.theguardian.com/media/2003/may/28/marketingandpr.advertising (accessed 24 September 2017)
——, 'EasyJet risks further Beckham wrath' *The Guardian* (16 June 2003)
Degregory, P, 'Jay-Z doesn't have to pay up in perfume company's $68M breach of contract suit' *New York Post* (10 November 2021)
Desta, Y, 'New David Bowie Biopic Probably Won't Have Any David Bowie Music' *Vanity Fair* (1 February 2019) at www.vanityfair.com/hollywood/2019/02/david-bowie-biopic-duncan-jones-music-rights (accessed 6 February 2020)
Downie, A, 'Rights mess keeps Brazil clubs out of best-selling game' *Reuters* (10 October 2014) at www.reuters.com/article/us-soccer-brazil-fifa15/rights-mess-keeps-brazil-clubs-out-of-best-selling-game-idUSKCN0HZ1MN20141010 (accessed 1 November 2018)
Ell, K, 'Sarah Jessica Parker and Kat Florence reach preliminary settlement' *Women's Wear Daily* (4 February 2019)
Evans, M, 'Holly Willoughby dragged into weight loss scam as company uses her to advertise "Keto pills"' *Metro* (8 May 2019) at https://metro.co.uk/2019/05/08/holly-willoughby-dragged-weight-loss-scam-company-uses-advertise-keto-pills-9448202/ (accessed 12 June 2019)
Freeman, A, 'Top-Earning TikToker-ers 2022: Charli and Dixie D'Amelio and Addison Rae Expand Fame – And Paydays' *Forbes* (7 January 2022) at www.forbes.com/sites/abrambrown/2022/01/07/top-earning-tiktokers-charli-dixie-damelio-addison-rae-bella-poarch-josh-richards/?sh=7c88a8963afa (accessed 16 January 2023)
Gardner, E, 'Fox Sued for Using Muhammad Ali in Super Bowl Advertisement' *Hollywood Reporter* (10 October 2017)
——, 'No Doubt, Activision Settle Lawsuit Over Avatars in "Band Hero"' *The Hollywood Reporter* (3 October 2012) at www.hollywoodreporter.com/thr-esq/no-doubt-activision-lawsuit-band-hero-376217 (accessed 8 November 2018)
Gritten, D, 'A whole new ball game' *The Telegraph* (2 April 2002) at www.telegraph.co.uk/culture/film/3575466/A-whole-new-ball-game.html (accessed 8 October 2019)
Heller, C, 'Kendall Jenner Sued for $1.8 Million for Breach of Modelling Contract' *E News* (4 August 2021) at www.eonline.com/news/1296264/kendall-jenner-sued-for-s1-8-million-for-breach-of-modeling-contract (accessed 26 January 2023)

Hooton, C, 'Luis Suarez bites again: Nando's, Snickers, McDonald's and other brands sink their teeth in on Twitter' *The Independent* (26 June 2014) at www.independent.co.uk/sport/football/international/luis-suarez-bites-again-nandos-snickers-mcdonalds-and-other-brands-weigh-in-with-twitter-memes-9561637.html (accessed 11 September 2018)

Kain, E, 'Court tosses out Lindsay Lohan's "Grand Theft Auto V" lawsuit' *Forbes* (2 September 2016) at www.forbes.com/forbes/welcome/?/sites/erikkain/2016/09/02/court-tosses-out-lindsay-lohans-grand-theft-auto-v lawsuit/&toURL=http://www.forbes.com/sites/erikkain/2016/09/02/court-tosses-out-lindsay-lohans-grand-theft-auto-v-lawsuit/&refURL=&referrer=#7fc66c7e6f2c (accessed 29 July 2019)

Khalil, M, 'Adidas celebrate 20-year partnership with footballing icon avid Beckham' *Esquire* (9 November 2017) at www.esquireme.com/content/24703-adidas-celebrate-20-year-partnership-with-footballing-icon-david-beckham (accessed 29.07.19)

Kleinman, M, 'Beckham agents threaten EasyJet over image use' *Campaign* (28 May 2003) at www.campaignlive.co.uk/article/beckham-agents-threaten-easyjet-image-use/181185 (accessed 29 July 2019)

Love, F, 'Lindsay Lohan sues "Grand Theft Auto V" makers for allegedly using her likeness in video game' *Newsday* (2 July 2014) at www.newsday.com/entertainment/celebrities/lindsay-lohan-sues-grand-theft-auto-v-makers-for-allegedly-using-her-likeness-in-video-game-1.8641134 (accessed 29 July 2019)

Mellor, S, 'Kanye Wet is keeping quiet after reportedly losing his coveted billionaire status. Here's the money he's lost' *Fortune* (26 October 2022) at https://fortune.com/2022/10/26/kanye-west-keeping-quiet-losing-billionaire-status-money-he-lost/ (accessed 16 January 2023)

Nachman, C, 'The Evolution of Sports Video Games' *Business Insider* (25 August 2011) at www.businessinsider.com/sports-video-games-history2011?IR=T (accessed 3 October 2018)

O'Connor, R, 'How FIFA Crushed PES to Become the Undisputed King of Football Video Games' *Bleacher Report* (29 September 2017) at https://bleacherreport.com/articles/2735656-how-fifa-crushed-pes-to-become-the-undisputed-king-of-football-video-games (accessed 1 November 2018)

Parkin, S, 'FIFA: the video game that changed football ' *The Guardian* (21 December 2016)

Phillips, H, 'Emily Ratajkowski joins Viktor & Rolf as Face of Flowerbomb – Reveals her favourite scent on a man' *People Magazine* (18 January 2023)

Richford, R, 'BTS' Park Jimin Steal the Show at Dior' *WWD* (20 January 2023)

Sarkar, S, 'EA Sports UFC won't let you share created fights due to copyright concerns' *Polygon* (23 March 2013) at www.polygon.com/2014/3/28/5558518/ea-sports-ufc-no-fighter-share-copyright-concerns (accessed 13 December 2022)

Sauer, P, 'How Dr J and Larry Bird helped build a video game empire' *Vice* (25 May 2017) at https://sports.vice.com/en_us/article/wje9kq/how-dr-j-and-larry-bird-helped-build-a-video-game-empire (accessed 3 April 2018)

Strater, Z, '"White Lotus" Actresses Beatrice Grannò and Simona Tabasco Star in SKIMS Valentine's Day Campaign' *People Magazine* (20 January 2023)

Voytko, L, 'The Highest-Paid Entertainers 2022' *Forbes* (9 February 2022) at www.forbes.com/sites/lisettevoytko/2022/02/09/the-highest-paid-entertainers-2022/?sh=603b320c331a (accessed 16 January 2023)

Ward, F, 'Ruth Langsford forced to address slimming endorsement claims' *Hello!* (23 March 2019) at www.hellomagazine.com/healthandbeauty/health-and-fitness/2019032371209/ruth-langsford-addresses-health-slimming-claims/ (accessed 29 July 2019)

Ware, H, 'Taco you very much, 50 cent wins suit' *New York Post* (24 November 2009) at http://nypost.com/2009/11/24/taco-you-very-much-50-cent-wins-suit/ (accessed 10 September 2019)

Wash, S and Benitez, G, 'BBB: Deceptive "free trial" offers and fake celebrity endorsements are a billion dollar problem' *GMA* (12 December 2018) at www.goodmorningamerica.com/culture/story/bbb-deceptive-free-trial-offers-fake-celebrity-endorsements-59754945 (accessed 19 January 2020)

Whitehead, J, 'David Beckham unwitting star of another EasyJet ad' *Campaign* (23 July 2003) at www.campaignlive.co.uk/article/david-beckham-unwitting-star-easyjet-ad/183582 (accessed 24 September 2017)

Wie, W, 'Tiger Woods lost $22 Million in Endorsements in 2010' *Sports Illustrated* (21 July 2010)
Willingham, AJ, 'What is eSports? A look at an explosive billion-dollar industry' *CNN* (27 August 2018) at https://edition.cnn.com/2018/08/27/us/esports-what-is-video-game-professional-league-madden-trnd/index.html (accessed 6 February 2020)

Online Resources

'33 Hollywood Actors Who Appear in Video Games' *GameSpot* (6 April 2020) at www.gamespot.com/gallery/33-hollywood-actors-who-appear-in-video-games/2900-31/#7 (accessed 13 December 2022)
'Adidas X Ivy Park Dreams of Ivytopia, A collection that inspires an escape to your personal nirvana this summer!' *Adidas* (8 July 2022) at https://news.adidas.com/originals/adidas-x-ivy-park-dreams-of-ivytopia--a-collection-that-inspires-an-escape-to-your-personal-nirvana-/s/72d05226-b86e-4e56-81e9-9b80ff3517df (accessed 26 January 2023)
'AEW Fight Forever' *ThQNordic* at https://aew.thqnordic.com (accessed 13 December 2022)
'AFC Richmond are in the Game' *FIFA23* at www.ea.com/en-gb/games/fifa/fifa-23/news/fifa-23-ted-lasso-afc-richmond? (accessed 13 December 2022)
'Agreement regarding the minimum requirements for standard player contracts in the professional football sector in the European Union and in the rest of the UEFA territory' *FIFPro* at www.uefa.com/MultimediaFiles/Download/uefaorg/EuropeanUnion/02/63/58/66/2635866_DOWNLOAD.pdf (accessed 1 November 2018)
'Apple launches "Ultimate Rivals" from Bit Fry Game Studios, an all-new sports games franchise available today exclusively on Apple Arcade' *Apple Newsroom* (12 December 2019) at www.apple.com/newsroom/2019/12/apple-launches-new-ultimate-rivals-sports-game-franchise-on-apple-arcade/ (accessed 13 December 2022)
'Crocs Collaborations' *Crocs* at www.crocs.com/collaborations.html (accessed 26 January 2023)
'Fyre Festival Failure and the Strength of Celebrity Endorsements' *Networks* (19 November 2019) at https://blogs.cornell.edu/info2040/2019/11/19/fyre-festival-failure-and-the-strength-of-celebrity-endorsements/#:~:text=The%20festival%20was%20endorsed%20by,being%20paid%20for%20their%20endorsements (accessed 24 January 2023)
'Gareth Southgate' *Monica Vinader* at www.monicavinader.com/style-me/gareth-southgate-world-cup-russia (accessed 24 January 2023)
'George Clooney becomes Nespresso global brand ambassador by extending his relationship with the brand in North America' *Nespresso* (3 November 2015) at www.nestle-nespresso.com/newsandfeatures/george-clooney-becomes-nespresso-global-brand-ambassador-by-extending-his-relationship-with-the-brand-in-north-america (accessed 4 April 2018)
'Glu Mobile Scaling Back on Celebrity Games' *Licensing International* (17 March 2017) at https://licensinginternational.org/news/glu-mobile-scaling-back-on-celebrity-games/ (accessed 13 December 2022)
'How EA quickly captures 3D scans of athletes' faces for its sports games' *Venture Beat* (20 January 2019) at https://venturebeat.com/business/how-ea-quickly-captures-3d-scans-of-athletes-faces-for-its-sports-games/ (accessed 26 January 2023)
'Lifetime Movie: A Case of Violated Privacy?' *The Authors Guild* (13 October 2020) at https://authorsguild.org/news/lifetime-movie-a-case-of-violated-privacy/ (accessed 2 December 2022)
'Madden NFL is one of the most successful video game series ever' *Madden Store* (1 November 2017) at www.madden-store.com/news/madden-nfl-is-one-of-the-most-successful-video-game-series-ever (accessed 3 October 2018)
'Morphe x Gabby Roberts' *Morphe* at https://eu.morphe.com/collections/morphe-x-abby-roberts-the-artcasts (accessed 26 January 2023)
'Print vs Digital: How to design mixed media marketing campaigns' *ProActive Marketing* at www.proactive.marketing/mixed-media-marketing/ (accessed 14 July 2019)
'Reebok x Cardi B' *Reebok* at www.reebok.com/us/cardi_b (accessed 26 January 2023)

'Serena Williams 2022: Net Worth, Salary and Endorsements' *Essentially Sports* (2022) at www.essentiallysports.com/tag/serena-williams/ (accessed 16 January 2023)
'Southgate's lucky £115 friendship bracelet to thank for World Cup success?' *BeSoccer* (2018) at www.besoccer.com/new/southgate-s-lucky-pound-115-friendship-bracelet-to-thank-for-world-cup-success-465160#:~:text=In%20the%20lead%2Dup%20to,item%20rose%20by%20350%20percent (accessed 23 January 2023)
'The 50 Top Video Game Design Companies' *GameDesigning* at www.gamedesigning.org/game-development-studios/ (accessed 1 November 2018)

Alvarado, J, 'Top five retail trends in celebrity merchandise: Kanye West Case Study' LinkedIn (12 December 2016) at www.linkedin.com/pulse/5-brand-merchandising-tips-from-marketing-genius-himself-alvarado/ (accessed 30 January 2023)
ASA, 'Recognising ads: Social media and influencers marketing' (29 December 2022) at www.asa.org.uk/advice-online/recognising-ads-social-media.html (accessed 26 January 2023)
——, 'Privacy: Implied endorsements' (5 May 2022) at www.asa.org.uk/advice-online/privacy-implied-endorsements.html (accessed 23 January 2023)
——, 'Online Affiliate Marketing' (17 August 2021) at www.asa.org.uk/advice-online/affiliate-marketing.html (accessed 23 January 2023)
——, 'Labelling of influencer advertising' (5 September 2019) at www.asa.org.uk/resource/labelling-of-influencer-advertising.html (accessed 25 January 2023)
——, 'Privacy: Permission' (11 June 2018) at www.asa.org.uk/advice-online/privacy-permission.html (accessed 23 January 2023)
——, 'Celebrities' (29 June 2017) at www.asa.org.uk/advice-online/celebrities.html (accessed 26 January 2023)
——, 'Codes and Rulings – Sanctions' at www.asa.org.uk/codes-and-rulings/sanctions.html (accessed 7 March 2017)
——, 'Privacy: Use of impersonators and caricatures, Advice Online' (8 April 2014) at www.asa.org.uk/advice-online/privacy-use-of-impersonators-and-caricatures.html (accessed 31 October 2022)
Badenhausen, K, 'The World's Highest-Paid Athletes 2022: LeBron scores $127 million' *Sportico* (11 May 2022) at www.sportico.com/personalities/athletes/2022/worlds-highest-paid-athletes-2022-lebron-1234674858/ (accessed 16 January 2023)
British Film Commission, 'Film Insurance' at http://dev.britishfilmcommission.org.uk/tv-production/entering-the-uk/film-insurance/ (accessed 1 October 2018)
Dayus, O, 'A game of two halves' *GameSpot* (19 September 2017) at www.gamespot.com/reviews/pes-2018-review/1900-6416757/ (accessed 9 April 2018)
Deleon, N, 'Conspiracy theory: Is EA setting up EA Sports MMA to flop in order to secure the UFC license later on?' *TechCrunch* (10 December 2009) at https://techcrunch.com/2009/12/10/conspiracy-theory-is-ea-setting-up-ea-sports-mma-to-flop-in-order-to-secure-the-ufc-license-later-on/ (accessed 13 December 2022)
Digital Media Law Project, 'False Light' (10 September 2022)at www.dmlp.org/legal-guide/false-light (accessed 8 October 2018)
EA Sports, 'FIFA23 Reveal Trailer| The World's Game' *YouTube* (20 July 2022) at www.youtube.com/watch?v=o3V-GvvzjE4 (accessed 13 December 2022)
——, 'FIFA 19 l Champions Rise l Official Launch Trailer' *YouTube* (18 September 2018) at www.youtube.com/watch?v=OumZxTdMq_c (accessed 8 October 2018)
——, 'Italian License Finally Here!' *FIFA Forums* (7 June 2018) at https://fifaforums.easports.com/en/discussion/396407/italian-licenses-finally-here (accessed 8 October 2018)
——, 'FIFA 17 – The Golden Controller – ft Reus, Hazard, Martial, James' *YouTube* (24 November 2016) at www.youtube.com/watch?v=y2njbeoClrw (accessed 10 April 2018)
——, 'Madden NFL 17 – Start Me ft. Von Miller' *YouTube* (18 August 2016) at www.youtube.com/watch?v=-pV7PFY_7n8 (accessed 10 April 2018)
F2 Freestylers – Ultimate Soccer Skills Channel, 'Incredible l Motion capture for FIFA 18 ft. Dele Alli & Akinfenwa', *YouTube* (3 October 2017) <https://www.youtube.com/watch?v=xb3H465Oil4> accessed 8 October 2018

Faber, J, 'Right of Publicity – Notable Cases' at http://rightofpublicity.com/notable-cases (accessed 10 January 2023)
Fair, L, 'FTC's Teami case: Spilling the tea about influencers and advertisers' *FTC* (6 March 2020) at www.ftc.gov/business-guidance/blog/2020/03/ftcs-teami-case-spilling-tea-about-influencers-and-advertisers (accessed 23 January 2023)
FIFA, 'FIFA eWorld Cup 2020' *FIFA* at www.fifa.com/fifaeworldcup/fifa-eclub-world-cup/ (accessed 6 February 2020)
FIFPRO, 'FIFPro Legal Department' *FIFPRO* at https://fifpro.org/en/players/legal/about-fifpro-legal-department (accessed 1 November 2018)
Film Emporium, 'Errors & Omissions (E&O) Insurance' *Film Emporium* at http://filmemporium.com/errors-omissions/ (accessed 1 October 2018)
Fish, M, 'Life Story Rights in the United Kingdom' (9 September 2013) *Fieldfisher* at www.fieldfisher.com/publications/2013/09/life-story-rights-in-the-united-kingdom (accessed 1 October 2018)
Floppy Deep Dive, 'One on One – Dr J vs Larry Bird' *YouTube* (21 November 2022) at www.youtube.com/watch?v=XXjIZIelTM8 (accessed 16 March 2023)
Fowler, B, '"Completely made up bullsh*t." Chrissy Teigen warns fans about fake endorsement scam' *Mama Mia* (14 January 2019) at www.mamamia.com.au/chrissy-teigen-twitter-scam/ (accessed 12 February 2019)
FTC, 'Disclosures 101 for Social Media Influences' (November 2019) at www.ftc.gov/business-guidance/resources/disclosures-101-social-media-influencers (accessed 26 January 2023)
——, 'Lord & Taylor Settles FTC Charges It Deceived Consumers Through Paid Article in an Online Fashion Magazine and Paid Instagram Posts by 50 "Fashion Influencers"' (15 March 2016) at www.ftc.gov/news-events/news/press-releases/2016/03/lord-taylor-settles-ftc-charges-it-deceived-consumers-through-paid-article-online-fashion-magazine (accessed 24 January 2023)
——, 'Guides Concerning the Use of Endorsements and Testimonials in Advertising: Federal Trade Commission 16 CFR Part 255' at www.ftc.gov/system/files/ftc_gov/pdf/P204500%20Guides%20Concerning%20Endors%20and%20Testimonials.pdf (accessed 24 January 2023)
——, 'CSGO Lotto Owners Settle FTC's First-Ever Complaint Against Individual Social Media Influencers' (7 September 2012) at www.ftc.gov/news-events/news/press-releases/2017/09/csgo-lotto-owners-settle-ftcs-first-ever-complaint-against-individual-social-media-influencers (accessed 21 January 2023)
Full Court, 'NBA 2k18–2 Best MyTeam Money Plays' *YouTube* (28 September 2017) at www.youtube.com/watch?v=Q2J0AX4wtTE (accessed 10 April 2018)
Golob, B, 'Brand alignment brings Sure and Southgate together for world cup semi-finals' *Communicate* (11 July 2018) at www.communicatemagazine.com/news/2018/brand-alignment-brings-sure-and-southgate-together-for-world-cup-semi-finals/ (accessed 25 January 2023)
Gottlieb, A, 'IDA Files Amicus Brief in FX Networks and Pacific 2.1 Entertainment vs Olivia de Havilland case' *Documentary.org* (26 January 2018) at www.documentary.org/advocacy/ida-files-amicus-brief-fx-networks-and-pacific-21-entertainment-vs-olivia-de-havilland-case (accessed 2 December 2022)
Guy, Z, 'Every Company That's Dropped Kanye West' *Vulture* (1 December 2022) at www.vulture.com/2022/12/kanye-west-dropped-brands-adidas-gap-what-did-ye-say.html (accessed 7 December 2022)
HMRC, 'Tax on payments for use of image rights' (16 August 2017) at www.gov.uk/guidance/tax-on-payments-for-use-of-image-rights (accessed 16 May 2018)
Hoskic, A, 'NCAA adopts interim name, image and likeness policy' *NCAA* (30 June 2021) at www.ncaa.org/news/2021/6/30/ncaa-adopts-interim-name-image-and-likeness-policy.aspx (accessed 27 January 2023)
IMS, 'Errors & Omissions Insurance' *IMS Film & Media Insurance* at https://filminsurance.co.uk/film-product-range/errors-omissions-insurance/ (accessed 1 October 2018)
Katz, M, 'FTC Staff reminds influencers and brands to clearly disclose relationship' (FTC, 1 April 2017) at www.ftc.gov/news-events/press-releases/2017/04/ftc-staff-reminds-influencers-brands-clearly-disclose (accessed 16 November 2017)

Kurnit, R, 'Right of Publicity' *Lexology* (22 October 2018) at https://gettingthedealthrough.com/area/45/jurisdiction/23/right-publicity-2018-united-states/ (accessed 4 November 2018)

La Playa, 'Errors and Omissions Insurance' *La Playa Insurance* at www.laplaya.co.uk/what-we-do/media-digitial-insurance/errors-and-omissions-insurance.htm (accessed 1 October 2018)

Lund, AH, 'What are sponsored photos and video on Instagram?' *Native Advertising Institute, Denmark* at https://nativeadvertisinginstitute.com/blog/what-are-sponsored-photos-and-videos-on-instagram/ (accessed 10 September 2018)

Mau, D, 'Justin Bieber Merch Boosts Sales and Social Engagement for Urban Outfits' *Fashionista* (23 November 2016) at https://fashionista.com/2016/11/justin-bieber-merch-urban-outfitters (accessed 13 September 2018)

Mooro, A, 'Why 2016 was the year we became obsessed with celeb merch' *Refinery29* (13 December 2016) at www.refinery29.uk/rise-of-celebrity-merchandise-2016 (accessed 12 September 2018)

Morson, J, 'The first celebrity fashion line was Amelia Earhart's' *Racked* (24 July 2017) at www.racked.com/2017/7/24/16000612/amelia-earhart-clothing-line (accessed 12 September 2018)

Murphy, R, 'FIFA 18 celebrations: How to do Pogba's dab, Dybala's mask & more on Xbox One and PS4' *Goal* (28 September 2017) at www.goal.com/en-gb/news/fifa-18-celebrations-how-to-do-pogbas-dab-dybalas-mask-more/4yn9zvszquin1mqhu9q25cafn (accessed 10 April 2018)

Natividad, A, 'How Charli D'Amelio become one of the biggest social media starts in the world' *The Richest* (08.07.22) at www.therichest.com/rich-powerful/how-charli-damelio-became-one-of-the-biggest-social-media-stars-in-the-world/ (accessed 16 January 2023)

Pinsent Masons, 'Football game banned over player's image rights' *Out-Law* (30 April 2003) at www.out-law.com/page-3520 (accessed 1 November 2018)

Presidio Sports Management, 'Exclusivity Clauses in Endorsement Contracts (Pro Contracts 101 Series) (26 February 2018) at www.presidiosportsmgmt.com/blog/exclusivityclauses (accessed 29 July 2019)

Pursey, J,'10 Great Unlicensed Sports Games' *GameRant* (20 December 2020) at https://gamerant.com/sports-games-best-unlicensed/#super-stickman-golf-3 (accessed 26 January 2023)

Reinckens, M and Ganas, M, 'The right of publicity in college sports' *Law in Sport* (18 September 2013) at www.lawinsport.com/blogs/dla-piper/item/the-right-of-publicity-in-college-sports (accessed 4 October 2018)

Ryan, F and Ganas, M, 'Athletes' Right of Publicity Claims Directed to Sports Video Games Not Pre-empted by Copyright Act' *Lexology* (23 January 2018) at www.lexology.com/library/detail.aspx?g=fcadf6f8-798a-43e7-84bd-414579eda2d8 (accessed 4 October 2018)

SEC, 'SEC Charges Kim Kardashian for Unlawfully Touting Crypto Security' (3 October 2022) at www.sec.gov/news/press-release/2022-183 (accessed 23 January 2023)

Stroud, J, 'FIFA 21: 300 players back Zlatan Ibrahimovic in image rights feud v EA Sports, says Mino Raiola' *GiveMeSport* (27 November 2020) at www.givemesport.com/1622309-fifa-21-300-players-back-zlatan-ibrahimovic-in-image-rights-feud-v-ea-sports-says-mino-raiola (accessed 26 January 2023)

Stubbsy, M, 'Konami's Adam Bhatti talks taking on EA and securing partnerships with Liverpool, Dortmund and more' *Red Bull* (5 September 2016) www.redbull.com/gb-en/how-pes-is-staking-a-claim-in-the-licensing-war (accessed 10 April 2018)

Swan, R, 'What Cristiano Ronaldo did to stun EA Sports staff during FIFA 18 motion capture shoot' *Give Me Sport* (11 June 2017) at www.givemesport.com/1075030-what-cristiano-ronaldo-did-to-stun-ea-sports-staff-during-fifa-18-motion-capture-shoot (accessed 10 April 2018)

Tarantino, B, 'You're getting sued for what? An E&O Odyssey (Pt 13)' *Entertainment & Media Law Signal* (29 July 2014) at www.entertainmentmedialawsignal.com/category/errors-and-omissions-insurance (accessed 12 April 2018)

Tiffany & Co, 'Tiffany Collections' at www.tiffany.com/collections/ (accessed 26 January 2023)

UK Intellectual Property Office, 'Manual of trade marks practice' (14 January 2019) at www.gov.uk/guidance/trade-marks-manual/the-examination-guide (accessed 31 October 2022)

Vandegrift, T, 'Why the New David Bowie Biopic "Stardust" Won't Feature His Music' *Showbiz CheatSheet* (29 August 2019) at www.cheatsheet.com/entertainment/why-the-new-david-bowie-biopic-stardust-wont-feature-his-music.html/ (accessed 6 February 2020)

Weber, C, 'Update on College Football' *EA* (26 September 2013) at www.ea.com/news/update-on-college-football (accessed 10 April 2018)

Xbox, 'Forza Motorsport 7: Built for Xbox One X' *YouTube* (7 November 2017) at www.youtube.com/watch?v=H38yNXIhV7I (10 April 2018)

——, 'Tony Hawk's Pro Skater 5 – Launch Trailer' *YouTube* (29 September 2015) at www.youtube.com/watch?v=05x2gGngJac (accessed 10 April 2018)

Yin-Poole, W, 'EA "closely monitoring" situation following "concerning" rape claim against FIFA 19 cover star Cristiano Ronaldo' *EuroGamer* (4 October 2018) at www.eurogamer.net/articles/2018-10-04-ea-closely-monitoring-situation-following-rape-allegations-against-fifa-19-cover-star-cristiano-ronaldo (accessed 8 October 2018)

Young, J and Elmeweihi, T, The Delicate Art of Making a Bio Pic w/o Getting Permission' *Front Row Insurance Brokers* (25 June 2015) at www.frontrowinsurance.com/articles/the-social-network-without-getting-permission-from-mark-zuckerberg-part-3 (accessed 1 October 2018)

Reports

Baker & McKenzie and FRAPA, *FRAPA Legal Report 2017: An overview of the legal status of formats* (FRAPA, 2017)

Deloitte, eSports Observer, *The rise of esports investments – A deep dive with Deloitte Corporate Finance LLC and The Esports Observer* (April 2019)

FTC, 'Federal Trade Commission 16 CFR Part 255: Guides Concerning the Use of Endorsements and Testimonials in Advertising' at www.ftc.gov/sites/default/files/attachments/press-releases/ftc-publishes-final-guides-governing-endorsements-testimonials/091005revisedendorsementguides.pdf (accessed 23 January 2023)

——, 'Federal Trade Commission Act Section 5: Unfair or Deception Acts or Practices' at www.federalreserve.gov/boarddocs/supmanual/cch/200806/ftca.pdf (accessed 24 January 2023)

International Bureau, *Character Merchandising* (WIPO 1994)

Khanom, R, *The evolution of celebrity endorsement in beauty* (Mintel Academic 2016)

Law Commission, *Patents, Trade Marks and Designs: Unjustified Threats Report* (Law Com 360, 12 October 2015)

——, 'Simplifying the law of groundless threats of patent, trade mark and design right infringement' (IA No: BISIPO010, 13 July 2015)

——, *Patents, Trade Marks and Design Rights: Groundless Threats Report* (Law Com 346, 5 March 2014)

Ledbury Research, *Counterfeiting Luxury: Exposing the Myths* (2nd edn, London, 2007)

Regulatory Policy Committee, *Simplifying the law of groundless threats of patent, trade mark and design right infringement* (Regulatory Policy Committee, RPC15-BIS-241213 July 2015)

Senate Judiciary Committee, *Report 515 – Trade Mark Law Revision Act of 1988*, 100th Congress, 2d Session

US Department of Commerce, 'Media and Entertainment Spotlight' *Select USA* at www.trade.gov/selectusa-media-and-entertainment-industry (accessed 16 January 2023)

——, *International Trade Association Top Markets Report – Media and Entertainment* (USA Department of Commerce 2016)

WIPO, *Mastering the Game: Business and Legal Issues for Video Game Developers* (Booklet No 8, 2014)

INDEX

www.ingramcontent.com/pod-product-compliance
Ingram Content Group UK Ltd.
Pitfield, Milton Keynes, MK11 3LW, UK
UKHW021908150926
475560UK00003B/242

9 781509 966097